Published by
James S. Kane
Portadown
Co. Armagh

With the financial assistance of Craigavon Borough Council

ISBN 978-0-9554987-0-1

Designed and Printed by

The Dargan Press Limited
15 Michelin Road
Newtownabbey
Co. Antrim
BT36 4PT

Contents

Welcome from the Mayor of Craigavon
Councillor Kenneth Twyble

I am both delighted and honoured to have the opportunity, personally and on behalf of Craigavon Borough Council, to wish James Kane every success with this publication.

It is always important to remember our local history and though this book, we will remember those from Portadown who have lost their lives during the Great War and during World War Two.

Mr Kane's research and attention to detail really does give us a taste of what life was like for those brave "Portadown Heroes", and their families, as they left Portadown for War and, in many cases, never to return.

Congratulations to James on this book. The Borough Council is pleased to be associated with it and I hope all who read it will be touched by its contents.

Councillor Kenneth Twyble
Mayor of Craigavon
2006-2007

Acknowledgements

First and foremost I would like to offer my sincere appreciation to the Mayor of Craigavon, Alderman Kenneth Twyble, and the Aldermen and Councillors of Craigavon Borough Council for their help and support in the publishing of this book. Without the council's considerable financial assistance, gratefully received, this book would not have been published.

Very special thanks to Alderman David Simpson, MP for Upper Bann, who, when he was Mayor of Craigavon, I initially approached with the idea of publishing Portadown Heroes.

My particular appreciation goes to Rosemary Mulholland, Paul Henry and Elaine Hill of Craigavon Borough Council Leisure and Museum Services who did diligent work behind the scenes in co-ordinating the entire project.

I wish to record my thanks to the following people who gave considerable help and assistance in the research for this book. In no particular order they are Albert Nicholl, Brian Courtney, David Armstrong, the Reverend David Chillingworth, Professor Keith Jeffery, Brian Horton, Amanda Moreno, curator of the Royal Irish Fusiliers Museum and the late Dan Murphy. A further list of those who rendered assistance is given in the bibliography and sources.

Thanks are due to Tom Irwin, Steven Thornberry and Trevor Bonis of the Friends of the Somme, Portadown Branch and to Rod Bedford who acted as an expert guide during two visits to the battlefields of the Somme and Ypres.

I would like to show my appreciation to R. E. Pike for kindly undertaking the important task of taking photographs of CWGC headstones and memorials in Belgium, France and Turkey. Unless otherwise stated all photographs of CWGC headstones and memorials appearing in the book are by courtesy of R. E. Pike.

Sincere thanks to all the staff, especially Alan McClean, of The Dargan Press Limited who made the publication of Portadown Heroes possible by their professional endeavours.

The names of the Portadown Heroes who are commemorated on Portadown War Memorial are arranged alphabetically by street name and townland for the Great War and in alphabetical order for World War Two. In my book I decided to arrange the names in chronological order of death by theatre of operations. The reason is to give the reader a better understanding of the campaigns and battles in which the men fought and a greater appreciation of the mounting casualties as both wars progressed. In each individual entry the number, which appears in brackets after Portadown War Memorial, is the order in which the name appears on the memorial.

Suffice to state that any errors or omissions are the sole responsibility of the author and will be rectified in any future edition. The author would be glad to receive further information or photographs on any serviceman commemorated on Portadown War Memorial.

Finally it only remains for me to dedicate Portadown Heroes to those who are nearest and dearest to me - my two beautiful daughters Emma and Helen; and to my wife, Diane, love as always.

James S. Kane
Portadown
2007

Foreword

In cities, towns and villages throughout Ireland - North and South - as well as across Great Britain, there are war memorials in urban centres, parks, at roadsides, and in many churches and other places, such as schools, banks, hospitals and so on. We may pass them everyday with scarcely a thought about their history, and the histories of those they commemorate. Portadown's impressive angel with a dying soldier is perhaps more difficult to miss than some, but few people these days will pause to contemplate what seems to be no more than a bald list of names. Yet each of these individuals has a story to tell; each of them had a family left behind to mourn, for whom that very monument may effectively be the only gravestone they have for a loved husband, father, brother or sweetheart. James Kane, in a marvellous work of research, has recovered the personal histories of the names on Portadown War Memorial - or nearly so, for some of their histories have eluded even his patient, painstaking endeavours.

Reading this book, one is struck by the variety of age, situation and experience to be found among the men (and one woman - a nurse) on this one memorial. Although the great majority of the three hundred-odd First World War dead fell on the Western Front in France and Belgium, and fully seventy men died in that terrible July of 1916 during the battle of the Somme, there are Portadown men who lie in Turkey, Greece, Serbia, Israel and (especially poignantly at this time of writing) Iraq. Men from both world wars died in Asia, so they also lie in India, Hong Kong and Singapore. There are heart-breaking stories of family tragedy: the two Abraham brothers killed together on 1 July, and another brother killed the following year; John Hayes, who also died on 1 July, and his two brothers who were killed later in the war; William Cooke, who left four children, and William Malcomson, a weaver, who left seven; Edward Jones, killed in Belgium whose widow named their yet-to-be-born son 'Edward Ypres Jones', after his dead father and place where he had died.

There are stories of high heroism, too, but not all the men on this memorial were heroes in the conventional sense. One man, serving in the Scottish Rifles, had

an extremely chequered military career, being charged with 'disorderly behaviour while drunk', 'not being shaved on parade', and even desertion, for which he got six months' detention in 1915. Another, serving with the Australian forces (and there are a fair number of Portadown men who emigrated to Australia and Canada who came back to serve), appears to have been murdered by a fellow-soldier. Two men died while prisoners-of-war in Germany, and are buried in Berlin. Another failed the medical for the British army and became an ambulance driver for the French Red Cross and lies forever in Serbia.

James Kane's book is a fine memorial in itself, and, when you have read it, you will no longer be able to pass the Portadown monument without remembering the real and precious lives behind the cold list of bronze names thereupon. It is, too, a memorial for the whole community. Those who, when they think of Portadown, only think of the Garvaghy Road or Obins Street (and folk from both these places are commemorated here) may be surprised to learn that among the wreaths laid on 13 November 1925, when the memorial was originally dedicated, was one from the Orange Order and also one from the Ancient Order of Hibernians. This memorial, and this book, belongs to us all.

Keith Jeffery
Professor of Modern History,
University of Ulster

Chapter 1
Portadown & District War Memorial

The first mention of a war memorial to commemorate the fallen of Portadown was at a meeting of the Comrades of the Great War held in Portadown Town Hall on 10 December 1918, one month after the Armistice. Lieutenant-Colonel Stewart Blacker DSO, former commander of the 9th Battalion Royal Irish Fusiliers, chaired the meeting and made the following resolution

That a suitable memorial be erected in Portadown to the memory of those from the town and district who have fallen in the Great War.

Portadown News
14 December1918

Soon the Urban District Council became involved and a public meeting was arranged for the Town Hall on 13 January 1919. Three proposals emerged and were voted upon - a new technical school, proposed by William Moffat Clow[1] JP, received 39 votes, a cottage hospital, proposed by Lieutenant-Colonel Stewart Blacker DSO received 10 votes, and an ornamental bridge over the River Bann, proposed by W.H. Atkinson, received four votes.

The meeting resolved that the best way forward was to erect and equip a building to be known as the "War Memorial Technical and Secondary Schools". Provision was to be made to record the names of the fallen on tablets with a memorial window and reading and recreation rooms for all returned servicemen. Mr Clow promised the sum of £1000 to the project. A Portadown War Memorial Committee was also formed from members of the Urban District Council with the power to co-opt interested individuals to oversee the memorial project.

The first meeting of the Portadown War Memorial Committee was held in Portadown Town Hall on 16 January 1919 under the chairmanship of William Moffat Clow, when 29 prominent town citizens were co-opted onto the committee. A week later the committee agreed that the amount needed for a memorial would be in the region of £10,000 made up from public subscriptions and donations from factory owners and businessmen. Events from this date onward moved rather slowly.

[1]Mr Clow's son, Malcolm Percy Clow, died on 11 July 1917 while on active service in Serbia.

A public meeting, under the chairmanship of W.J. Johnston JP, Chairman of the Urban Council, was held at Portadown Town Hall on March 1922 to once again consider the question of erecting a war memorial. William Moffat Clow explained that the economic situation over the past two years meant that donations from manufacturers were not forthcoming and this made it difficult to raise the necessary funds. He further explained that changes to the education system, brought about by the setting up of the Northern Ireland Parliament at Stormont, would mean that the technical school scheme could be funded from Government sources rather than public subscription and it would be inadvisable to carry on with the technical school scheme.

It has been decided that the Portadown War Memorial shall take the form of a Statue to be erected in a conspicuous position in one of the public streets of the town. It is estimated that the sum of £5,000 will be required to erect a statue symbolical of the contribution which Portadown made to His Majesty's Forces and of the homage that is due to the memory of the men who made the supreme sacrifice.

Portadown News
22 April 1922

A Representative Committee, which replaced the original War Memorial Committee, was formed to oversee the project. By November 1922 a model of the proposed memorial had been constructed and placed for public display in the window of Messrs. William Paul and Sons, drapery shop in High Street.

Another public meeting was held on 21 August 1923 to further discuss developments with Portadown War Memorial. This meeting was held at Portadown Town Hall under the chairmanship of W. H. Atkinson. On the proposal of Dr. George Dougan, seconded by John Gibson, it was agreed that

...the names of the men who died since the war from injuries received during the campaign should be inscribed on the memorial in the list of those that gave their lives.

After much discussion it was proposed by Mr. P.J. Sheil JP and seconded by Miss Jessie Collen

That the necessary funds be raised by public subscription, to be collected from the residents of the town and district; that the collectors be supplied with official receipts to be issued to the subscribers; and that each subscription of 5s and upwards be acknowledged in the local Press, in addition; that a list of the authorised collectors be sent to each householder by post, together with a subscription envelope, to be called

for within a few days after the publication of the list of collectors.

Portadown News
25 August 1923

Those present at the meeting unanimously agreed this and the formation of a War Memorial General Committee. This committee was made up from the three designated collecting districts - North Ward, South West Ward and South East Ward, each with its own sub-committee and known collectively as the Executive Committee, together with a number of prominent citizens and clergy from the town. From this date onwards the Portadown War Memorial project moved apace.

A list of all subscribers to Portadown War Memorial was published in the Portadown News dated 31 May 1924. Donations ranged from three pence to £50 and amounted to £1,965, 10 shillings and one penny. Most subscriptions came from individuals but there were also many from businesses, shops, factories and organisations. Although the vast majority were from the town of Portadown and district there were also a number from former town residents living in Belfast, England and the United States of America.

In January 1925 the contract for the Portadown War Memorial was awarded to the sculptor Henry Charles Fehr A.R.A., London at a cost of £2,000. The work was scheduled to take six months.

During this period the Urban District Council had been collating the names, unit details and addresses of those from Portadown and District who had been killed or had died during or as a result of service in the Great War. An alphabetical list of names with addresses of the fallen appeared in the Portadown News dated 7 January 1925. The Representative Committee also invited the next of kin, relatives and ex-servicemen to furnish further details of the fallen or to correct inaccuracies that may have appeared in the list.

A further more comprehensive list of the fallen, many with unit details and addresses, appeared in the Portadown News dated 25 April 1925. It was accompanied by a final appeal for further information especially in relation to rank and regimental details.

A number of names still appeared with a question mark as to their rank and unit - a situation the Representative Committee was anxious to address. If these details were for whatever reason not forthcoming or could not be ascertained it was decided that

'Private' would be entered as the person's rank and the 'Royal Irish Fusiliers' would be entered as their regiment. This decision led to a significant number of men being commemorated on Portadown War Memorial with incorrect regimental and rank details.

The dedication of Portadown War Memorial took place on 13 November 1925. Dignitaries present included the Right Honourable Sir James Craig, Prime Minister of Northern Ireland, Lieutenant-General Sir Travers Clarke, Lord Justice Best, the Most Reverend Charles F.M. D'Arcy DD, Church of Ireland Primate, the Very Reverend R.W. Hamilton, former Moderator of the General Assembly of the Presbyterian Church, the Reverend E. B. Cullen, President of the Methodist Church in Ireland and local parish priest the Very Reverend Canon T. McCormick, representing the Most Reverend Dr. O'Donnell the Roman Catholic Archbishop of Armagh who was unable to attend.

Senator H.B. Armstrong, His Majesty's Lieutenant for County Armagh, chaired the meeting. He related how the town of Portadown had had an impeccable war record second to none. Few towns in the British Empire had a nobler record of war service than Portadown a district famed throughout the land and abroad for its loyalty and patriotism. The men of Portadown, he went on, had seen service in all arms of the services at sea with the Royal and Merchant Navies; in the air with the Royal Flying Corps and the fledgling Royal Air Force; and on land with numerous regiments of the British Army as well as the armies of the Empire.

Lieutenant-General Travers Clarke KCB, KCMG, CB officially unveiled the memorial. He began his address by paying homage to the 14,000 Ulstermen who

Gave their lives so that the Empire might continue its work for mankind. Their bodies were scattered over two continents. In the lists of those whom the King delighted to honour appear constantly the names of Ulster heroes. No people of the Empire have a prouder record.

The Dead March was followed by the sounding of the Last Post with the Most Reverend Charles F. M. D'Arcy then leading the assembled crowd in a prayer of dedication after which the Reveille was sounded. The Very Reverend R.W. Hamilton, read the lesson, which was followed by a prayer led by, the Reverend E. B. Cullen.

Sir James Craig, proposed a vote of thanks to General Clarke for unveiling the memorial and paid tribute to the men of Portadown for

their sacrifice on the battlefield. Lord Justice Best seconded the motion

Dr. George Dougan, who had served with the Royal Army Medical Corps, officially handed over the Portadown War Memorial to W. J. Johnston, Chairman of the Urban District Council, who accepted the memorial on behalf of the council.

Major David Graham Shillington[2], formerly of the 9th Battalion, Royal Irish Fusiliers, proposed a vote of thanks to the chairman, which was seconded by R.M. Cullen, formerly an NCO with the Connaught Rangers.

The Very Reverend Canon T. McCormick, PP, pronounced the benediction and the ceremony ended with the playing of the National Anthem.

Unveiling of Portadown War Memorial 13 November 1925. (Billy England)

Six years after the end of World War Two and 26 years since the dedication of Portadown War Memorial the townsfolk assembled to pay tribute to the 66 service personnel[3] of the town who made the supreme sacrifice during World War Two. The ceremony took place on Armistice Day Sunday 11 November 1951. Three plaques containing the names of those who died together with a fourth plaque inscribed "Second World War" were positioned on the lower plinth of the war memorial below those from the Great War.

The Reverend Canon G.W. Millington, rector of St. Mark's Parish, conducted the ceremony and Dr. George Dougan[4] carried out the unveiling of the memorial plaques. The Reverend G.F. Whinnie, Honorary Chaplain to the Royal Air Force, lead the assembled in their dedication.

The Mayor of Portadown, Alderman Robert J. Magowan OBE, laid a wreath on behalf of Portadown Borough Council and then the British Legion and Territorial Army followed. District Inspector T.P.R. Kenny laid the Royal Ulster Constabulary wreath and his Great War comrade, R.M. Cullen, (both men had served in the Connaught Rangers) followed him. Then the various service and ex-service organisations paid their tributes - the Royal Naval Association, OCA Royal Artillery, Royal Air Force Association, Women's Royal Army Corps all laying wreaths in remembrance of fallen comrades.

The Reverend W.E. Marley Thompson, superintendent of Thomas Street Methodist Church, announced the final hymn *O God our Help in Ages Past* and this was followed by the benediction and National Anthem.

---

[2] Major Shillington's son, Thomas Shillington, died of wounds on 18 August 1917 in Belgium.

[3] A further name, James Whitla, was added in 2001.

[4] Dr. Dougan's son, Hampton Dougan, died on 20 October 1944 while on active service in India.

Chapter 2
The BEF in France and Belgium 1914

War began in August 1914 when the Germans put into operation the Schlieffen Plan - their strategy to defeat the French by a massive advance through Belgium and northern France. With the German advance the British Expeditionary Force moved to take up positions around the Belgian town of Mons. It was here on 23 August that the British first came face to face with the might of the advancing German army.

The German advance was halted on the River Marne when the British and French launched a counter-attack on 5/6 September. This battle, which saved Paris, became known as the 'Miracle of the Marne'. Then came the 'race to the sea' as the Allies and German armies tried to outflank each other - moves that brought the opposing forces ever closer to the English Channel.

With the winter setting in the Germans ceased their offensive and prepared to defend the territory they had occupied by 'digging in'. The Allies did likewise. The era of trench warfare had begun.

Total British casualties from the Battle of Mons on 23 August until the end of 1914 were in the region of 90,000 killed, wounded, missing or taken prisoner.

THE RETREAT FROM MONS (23 August- 5 September 1914)

The BEF met the full force of the German army at the Battle of Mons on 23 August. The British suffered 1,600 killed, wounded and missing and then began the epic retreat south. By 26 August II Corps had withdrawn to positions around the town of Le Cateau where eight German divisions attacked them. The British units held the line against vastly superior numbers until late in the day when the enemy succeeded in outflanking them. British losses were 8,000 killed, wounded and missing.

Robert McShane
Private 8751, 1st Battalion, Royal Irish Fusiliers

Born	Dungannon
Residence	West Street
Enlisted	Armagh
Died	Killed in action 27 August 1914, France
Buried	Esnes Communal Cemetery, Nord, France. Grave I.

Commemorated
Portadown War Memorial (238)
St. Mark's Parish Church War Memorial

Private R. McShane, R.I.F., has been killed in action at the front. He was for a long time a member of the Portadown Rechabites, who will learn of his death with sincere regret.

Portadown News
21 November 1914

Grave of Private Robert McShane.

George Neill
Private 10772, 1st Battalion, Royal Irish Fusiliers

Born	Portadown
Parents	Son of George and Mary Jane Neill of 6 Park Road, Portadown
Residence	Park Road
Enlisted	Portadown
Died	Killed in action 27 August 1914, France
Age	20
Buried	Honnechy British Cemetery, Nord, France. Grave I. C. 19.
Commemorated	Portadown War Memorial (197) St. Mark's Parish Church War Memorial

George's father George was employed as a weaver and his mother Mary Jane was from County Down. The couple had children Henry, Mary Ann, Rachel, George, James, Susanna and John. George was a member of Parkmount Temperance Flute Band.

Private George Neill, Portadown, has been reported by the War Office as missing. It is surmised that he is a prisoner in Germany, as he is officer's servant to Major Gray.

Portadown News
7 November 1914

The Neill family had a fine military tradition. George's father served in the Royal Irish Fusiliers during the South African or Boer War 1899-1902 and during the Great War. His brother John also served in the Royal Irish Fusiliers during the Great War and was wounded in the arm and leg. He rejoined his old unit during World War Two. Another brother James served with the 5th Battalion, Royal Irish Fusiliers in the Gallipoli campaign. After the war James emigrated to South Australia where he became a postmaster.

William John Magee
Private 3139, 1st Battalion, Irish Guards

Born	1885, Drumcree
Parents	Son of Thomas Magee of George Street, Portadown
Residence	George Street
Enlisted	6 October 1908, Liverpool
Died	Killed in action 4 September 1914, France
Age	29
Buried	Guards Grave, Villers-Cotterets Forest, Aisne, France. Grave 27.
Commemorated	Portadown War Memorial (111) St. Mark's Parish Church War Memorial

On enlistment in the 1st Battalion, Irish Guards his particulars were given as follows: occupation - carpenter, height - 5' 9", age - 23 years, marital status - single. Private Magee embarked for service in France at Southampton on 12 August 1914.

Mrs Magee, George's Street, Portadown, has received information from the War Office that her son, Private W. J. Magee, of the Irish Guards, who was reported missing some time ago, was killed in action early in September.

Portadown News
19 December 1914

Grave of Private William John Magee.

William James Cooke
Private 7720, 2nd Battalion,
South Lancashire Regiment

Born Portadown
Residence Mullentine
Enlisted Portadown
Died Died of wounds
28 September 1914,
France
Buried Villeneuve-
St.Georges Old
Communal
Cemetery,
Val de Marne,
France.
Grave I. 739.
Commemorated
Portadown War
Memorial (317)
St. Mark's Parish
Church War
Memorial

Mrs Cooke, Mullentine, has received intimation from the War Office that her son has been killed in action. Private Cooke leaves a wife and four children to mourn his loss.

Portadown News
14 November 1914

THE BATTLE OF ARMENTIERES (19 October - 2 November 1914)

The 1st Battalion, Royal Irish Fusiliers was engaged in heavy fighting against the German XIX Corps in the Armentieres area especially at Le Ruage (19 October) and Frelinghien (20 October) near the Belgian border. The battalion withdrew to the trenches around Houplines where it came under heavy shelling and infantry assaults from 21 October onwards.

Thomas John McCann
Private 11495, 1st Battalion,
Royal Irish Fusiliers

Born Portadown
Residence Wilson Street
Enlisted Portadown
Died Died of wounds
21 October 1914,
France
Buried Cite Bonjean
Military Cemetery,
Armentieres, Nord,
France.
Grave IX. A. 80.
Commemorated
Portadown War
Memorial (243)

Thomas Woodhouse
Private 8355, 1st Battalion, Royal Irish Fusiliers

Born	Portadown
Parents	Son of George and Elizabeth Woodhouse of Breagh (Drumcree Parish)
Residence	Breagh (Drumcree Parish)
Enlisted	Armagh
Died	Killed in action 21 October 1914, France
Age	30
Buried	Houplines Communal Cemetery Extension, Nord, France. Grave II. C. 20.
Commemorated	Portadown War Memorial (268) Drumcree Parish Church War Memorial

Thomas' father George was a farmer. He and his wife Elizabeth had children Martha, Thomas, Margaret, John, William, George, Samuel and Robert.

About 7 p.m. on October 21st the enemy attacked the right of the line with field guns, machine guns, rifle-fire and star shells. They had no success, and their discomfiture was announced by three cheers from the Faughs.
The 1st Battalion Faugh-A-Ballaghs in the Great War

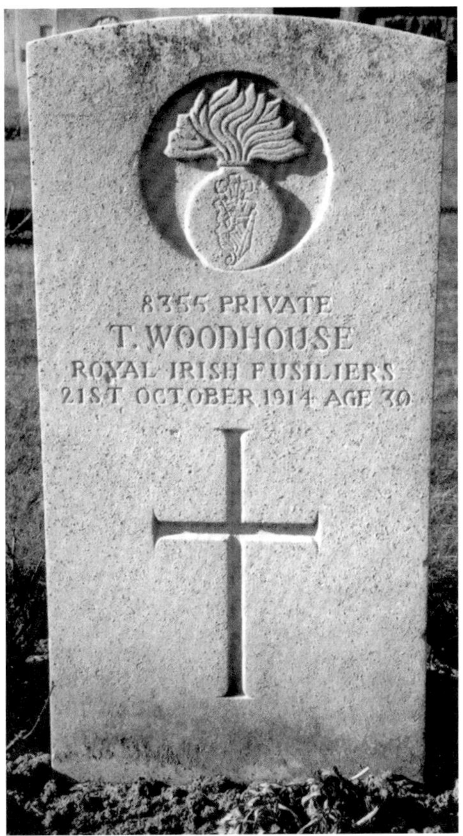

Grave of Private Thomas Woodhouse.

Francis William Todd
Private 7365, 1st Battalion, Royal Irish Fusiliers

Born	Shankill, Belfast
Parents	Son of William James and Harriet

	Todd of Belfast
Residence	Sandy Row
Enlisted	Portadown
Died	Killed in action 22 October 1914, France
Age	33
Buried	Houplines Communal Cemetery Extension, Nord, France. Grave II. C. 21.
Commemorated	Portadown War Memorial (210) First Presbyterian Church War Memorial, Edenderry,

Private Francis Todd had served in the South African or Boer War being awarded the Queen's South Africa Medal. Francis had also served in India and was a reservist. He was a member of the Ulster Volunteer Force.

News has reached Portadown announcing the death of Private Frank Todd, of the Royal Irish Fusiliers. The melancholy intelligence has come from his brother, Robert, who is also at the front, and who was beside the deceased when he was shot dead.

Portadown News
31 October 1914

Private Todd had a sister Florence. His brother Robert enlisted in the Royal Irish Fusiliers in 1898 and served during the South African War. He also served throughout the Great War.

Francis' nephew David Dawson Todd (**see entry WW2-55 Sergeant David Dawson Todd**) was lost on air operations in the Mediterranean on 30 August 1941.

Grave of Private Francis William Todd.

THE BATTLE OF LA BASSEE (16 October - 2 November 1914)

The Battle of La Bassee was one of a series of actions fought by the BEF between October and November 1914.

Johnston Chambers
Private 6621, 2nd Battalion,
South Lancashire Regiment

Born	Portadown
Residence	Queen Street
Enlisted	Armagh
Died	Killed in action 24 October 1914, France
Buried	No Known Grave
Commemorated	Le Touret Memorial, Pas de Calais, France. Panel 23. Portadown War Memorial (207) St. Mark's Parish Church War Memorial

Assurances have been received of the safety of Private Johnston Chambers, East Lancs. Regiment, (sic) who was reported to be absent from his regiment some time ago. He has three brothers with the Expeditionary Force.

Portadown Express
1 January 1915

Matthew Quinn
Private 7655, 2nd Battalion,
South Lancashire Regiment

Born	Drumcree
Parents	Son of Thomas and Mary Quinn of Castle Avenue, Portadown
Residence	Castle Avenue
Enlisted	Portadown

Le Touret Memorial.

Died Killed in action
24 October 1914,
France
Age 22
Buried No Known Grave
Commemorated
Le Touret Memorial,
Pas de Calais,
France. Panel 23.
Portadown War
Memorial (45)

Matthew's father Thomas was employed as a farm labourer. His mother Mary was a housekeeper. His parents had children John, George, James, Matthew and William. Matthew was employed as a weaver.

His brother William (see entry **46 Private William Quinn**) was killed in action on 14 March 1915 in Belgium. His brother John resided at 63 Jervis Street, Portadown.

THE FIRST BATTLE OF YPRES (18 October - 22 November 1914)

The First Battle of Ypres raged from 18 October-22 November and despite successive attacks the German Fourth and Sixth Armies were unable to affect a major breakthrough. In fact the Allies held the salient for the rest of the war although the town of Ypres was virtually destroyed by artillery fire.

British casualties were 55,000 killed, wounded and missing, Germany's totalled 130,000.

John Warnock
Private 2268,
4th (Queen's Own) Hussars

Born Dublin
Parents Son of John and
Margaret Warnock
Residence Park Road
Enlisted Lurgan
Died Died of wounds
31 October 1914,
Belgium
Buried No Known Grave
Commemorated
Ypres (Menin Gate)
Memorial, Ieper,
West Flaanderen,
Belgium.Panel 5
Portadown War
Memorial (202)

William John Jamison
Lance-Corporal 3105,
1st Battalion, Irish Guards

Born 1888, Drumcree
Residence Jervis Street
Enlisted 25 August 1908,
Portadown
Died Killed in action
6 November 1914,
Belgium
Age 26
Buried No Known Grave

Commemorated	Ypres (Menin Gate) Memorial, Ieper, West Flaanderen, Belgium. Panel 11. Portadown War Memorial (137)

William married Caroline McCann on 18 November 1911. They had two children, Violet born 29 August 1912 and Mary Catherine born 13 December 1913. Both children were born in Belfast.

On enlistment in the 1st Battalion, Irish Guards his particulars were given as follows: occupation - mill labourer, height - 5′ 9″.

Private Jamison embarked at Southampton on 12 August 1914 for service in France and Flanders. He was appointed unpaid Lance-Corporal in the field on 26 September 1914. Lance-Corporal Jamison was killed during German shelling and infantry attacks on the trenches near Zillebeke, south of Ypres.

Mrs Jameson of 13 Argyle Street, Belfast, has received official news that her husband, Lance-Corporal William J. Jameson, 1st Battalion Irish Guards, must be regarded as dead. Deceased has been missing since November 6, 1914 and is believed to have been killed about that time. He leaves a wife and two children. Lance-Corporal Jameson is a Portadown man, and his parents still reside in Jervis Street.

Portadown News
12 February 1916

There is a Private W. J. Jamison, 1st Battalion, Royal Irish Fusiliers commemorated on St. Mark's Parish Church War Memorial. However, it is unclear if this is the same person.

William Hanvey
Private 11158, 1st Battalion, Royal Irish Fusiliers

Born	Portadown
Parents	Son of William and Sarah Hanvey of Derryanville
Residence	Jervis Street
Enlisted	Armagh
Died	Died of wounds 8 November 1914, France
Age	21
Buried	Trois Arbes Cemetery Steenwerck, Nord, France. Grave II. I. 32.
Commemorated	Portadown War Memorial (136) Drumcree Parish Church War Memorial St. Mark's Parish Church War Memorial Thomas Street Methodist Church War Memorial

Grave of Private William Hanvey.

Private Hanvey had served for two years with the 1st Battalion, Royal Irish Fusiliers. He served in 'A' Company commanded by Major R. G. Shuter.

Private Hanvey was rescued and brought back to the trenches by a colleague (see entry **152 Private Thomas Cordner**). He died of wounds at No. 10 Field Ambulance.

Thomas Cordner
Private 11254, 1st Battalion, Royal Irish Fusiliers

Born	14 November 1895, Portadown
Parents	Son of Emily and stepson of Joseph McCrory of Foundry Street, Portadown
Residence	Joseph Street
Enlisted	Armagh
Died	Killed in action 9 November 1914, Belgium
Age	18
Buried	Strand Military Cemetery Ploegsteert, Comines-Warneton, Hainaut, Belgium. Grave IX. N. 4.
Commemorated	Portadown War Memorial (152) Seagoe Parish Church War Memorial

Thomas served in 'A' Company. Private Cordner had risked his life in helping one of his wounded colleagues (see entry **136 Private William Hanvey**). In a letter home, Private Edward Burns of Jackson's Row, Portadown, described the events

You ask me to let you know how poor Thomas Cordner met his death. Well it was trying to save W. Hanvey. After Hanvey got wounded Thomas went out to try and bring him into the trenches, when he also met the same fate. Both died shortly after. He was my best chum. He and I used to lie awake at night and talk how we would spend Christmas in Portadown. Little did we think he was so near the end.

Seagoe Parish Magazine
January 1915

Private Thomas Cordner. (Seagoe Parish Magazine)

Seagoe Parish Magazine also published extracts from letters Thomas had sent to his mother

Just a few lines in answer to your loving letter. Glad to hear you are not too bad. We came back to Shorncliffe this morning from Minster to mobilise. We expect to be in touch with the enemy on the 14th of this month, but, mother, I will go out with a good heart. We are in one of the divisions that go out first. I am sending you these photos and prayerbook. You can do what you wish with them, but if ever I have the luck to come home I would like to get some of them. I send the children my best love. I would like to hear from you before I go out. From your loving son, to mother, til death.

Seagoe Parish Magazine
August 1915

William John Woods
Private 7445, 1st Battalion,
Royal Irish Fusiliers

Born	Portadown
Parents	Son of John Woods of Portadown
Residence	Charles Street
Enlisted	Portadown
Died	Killed in action 14 November 1914, France
Age	33
Buried	Houplines Communal Cemetery Extension, Nord, France. Grave II. D. 11.
Commemorated	Portadown War Memorial (60) St. Mark's Parish Church War Memorial Thomas Street Methodist Church War Memorial

William was the husband of Minnie Dowling (formerly Woods) of 10 Carleton Street, Portadown.

Private Woods, Portadown, has been killed in action at the front. He was in the reserve when the war broke out, and his wife is now residing in Scotland.

Portadown Express
4 December 1914

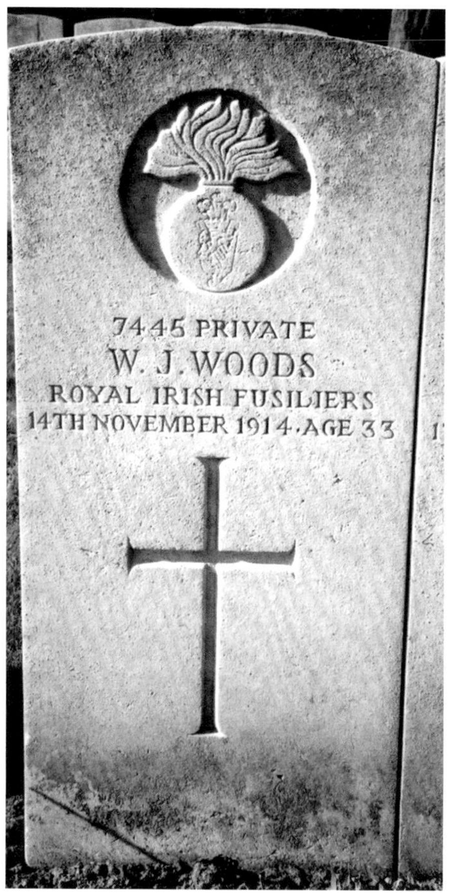

Grave of Private William John Woods.

James Beattie
Private 6461, 2nd Battalion, Sherwood Foresters (Notts & Derby Regiment)

Born	Drumcree
Residence	Montague Street
Enlisted	Lurgan
Died	Killed in action 24 November 1914, Belgium
Age	50
Buried	No Known Grave
Commemorated	Ploegsteert Memorial Comines-Warneton, Hainaut, Belgium. Panel 7. Portadown War Memorial (169)

James was the husband of Margaret Beattie and the couple had five children.

In a letter to his former workmates at the Parkside weaving factory Sergeant Samuel McCullough wrote

Our regiment has lost a large number of men since I came out, amongst them J. Beattie, that I came away with from Portadown; he was killed first time he was in the trenches. The snipers are at it all day and night; you don't be long in stopping one if you happen to let your head get too far out of the earth, the Germans being only 300 yards away.

Portadown Express
19 February 1915

Ploegsteert Memorial. (Author's Collection)

Chapter 3
Trench Warfare 1915-1916

After the ebb and flow of the early months of the Great War both sides settled into a pattern of static warfare. The rival armies constructed elaborate trench systems containing dugouts, fire steps, lookout and listening posts, machine gun positions and mortar pits. In No Man's Land coils of barbed were laid to restrict movement. These trench systems would eventually stretch from the Belgian coast to the borders of Switzerland, 450 miles away and would come to characterise warfare on the Western Front for the next four years.

The first major British offensive of 1915 took place at the French town of Neuve Chapelle on 10-12 March. During the opening barrage more shells were fired than during the four years of the South African War 1899-1902.

On 22 April the Germans launched a major offensive at Ypres. These battles, which raged until 25 May, are collectively known as the Second Battle of Ypres. British casualties in defence of the Ypres salient were 60,000 killed, wounded or missing. Germany suffered 35,000 casualties.

The British mounted further offensives at Aubers Ridge on 9 May, Festubert on 15 May and Loos on 25 September. Although some gains were made there were no decisive breakthroughs.

On 21 February 1916 the Germans launched a massive assault directed at the French town of Verdun. The battle lasted for six months and cost the French 500,000 casualties. The Germans who suffered 400,000 casualties called off the attack in the wake of the British offensive on the Somme, which began on 1 July 1916.

John Quinn
Private 9891, 2nd Battalion,
Royal Irish Fusiliers

Born	Portadown
Residence	West Street
Enlisted	Portadown
Died	Killed in action 19 January 1915, Belgium
Buried	No Known Grave
Commemorated	Ypres (Menin Gate) Memorial, Ieper, West Flaanderen, Belgium. Panel 42.

Portadown War Memorial (242)
St. Mark's Parish Church War Memorial.

John was a member of the Ulster Volunteer Force. Private Quinn had previous military service in India.

...he was being relieved from the trench when a German bullet struck him.

Portadown News
13 February 1915

David H. Cranston
Private 10997, 2nd Battalion, Royal Irish Fusiliers

Born	Portadown
Parents	Son of Joseph and Martha Cranston of 115 Parkmount, Portadown
Residence	Garvaghy Road
Enlisted	Portadown
Died	Died of wounds 13 February 1915, Belgium

The Menin Gate, Ypres.

Age 21
Buried Dickebusch Old Military Cemetery, Dikkebus, Belgium. Grave A. 9.
Commemorated
Portadown War Memorial (105)
St. Mark's Parish Church War Memorial

Alfred Doherty
Lance-Corporal 10674, 2nd Battalion, Royal Irish Fusiliers

Born Portadown
Parents Son of Annie Anderson of Battlehill
Residence Battlehill
Enlisted Portadown
Died Killed in action 24 February 1915, Belgium
Buried No Known Grave
Commemorated
Ypres (Menin Gate) Memorial, Ieper, West Flaanderen, Belgium. Panel 42.
Portadown War Memorial (265)
LOL 371 War Memorial, Drumnahuncheon Orange Hall

Alfred was the son of Annie Anderson by her first marriage. He had served for about six years in the army and had been stationed in India. He was a member of the Ulster Volunteer Force and Drumnahuncheon LOL 371.

Alfred's comrades wrote to his mother

I am sorry to let you know that 10674 Lance-Corporal Alfred Doherty was killed in action on the 24th February about 1030 by a bullet. He only lived a short while after being hit, but had no pain. In his pockets we found his "Princess Mary Gift" which was given to the Colour Sergeant to be sent home. I am very sorry about Alf as he was getting on very well. He was promoted full Corporal a few days before he was killed.

Private Robert Dawson,
Portadown Express
5 March 1915

...just a line to let you know that your son is dead, and I am glad I was not far from him when he passed away. You will feel proud at having a son who died fighting for his home and country. I am very sorry at his death, but the best of friends must part.

Private D. Grimley,
Portadown News
6 March 1915

BATTLE OF NEUVE CHAPELLE (10-12 March 1915)

The British IV Corps and Indian Corps of General Alexander Haig's First Army took part in the attack,

which was preceded by a one-hour artillery bombardment by 300 guns. The village was captured after heavy fighting. British casualties were 13,000 killed, wounded or missing.

Thomas F. Mighton
Rifleman 5556, 1st Battalion, Royal Irish Rifles

Born Shankill, Belfast
Residence Foundry Street
Enlisted Belfast
Died Killed in action 10 March 1915, France
Buried No Known Grave
Commemorated
Le Touret Memorial, Pas-de-Calais, France.
Panel 42 & 43.
Portadown War Memorial (95)
St. Mark's Parish Church War Memorial
Seagoe Parish Church War Memorial

Thomas was a member of the Ulster Volunteer Force.

Private Thomas Mighton, Royal Irish Fusiliers, (sic) late of Portadown, has been killed in action at the front.

Portadown News
15 May 1915

William Henry Armstrong DCM
Lance-Corporal 7599, 1st Battalion, Royal Irish Fusiliers

Born Portadown
Parents Son of Henry and stepson of Mary Ann Armstrong of 19 Irwin Street, Portadown
Residence Irwin Street
Enlisted Portadown
Died Killed in action 11 March 1915, Belgium
Age 29
Buried No Known Grave
Commemorated
Ploegsteert Memorial, Belgium.
Panel 9.
Portadown War Memorial (128)
St. Mark's Parish Church War Memorial
Seagoe Parish Church War Memorial

William Henry had served for seven years in India and was employed at the Post Office when he was recalled to the colours. He arrived in France in August 1914 and took part in the Retreat from Mons.

In January 1915 William Henry wrote home giving his account of how he had captured two German officers

How did you get to know about the two German officers I captured? Of course, it's true. I did surprise two in a wood and captured them, although they were both well armed. I didn't give them time to draw their revolvers till I covered them with my rifle, and rather than let me pass the death sentence on them they handed me over their arms and came along with me.

Seagoe Parish Magazine
December 1916

In a letter home Private John Girvan wrote

Harry Armstrong was killed in the trench on Friday by a sniper. He had his head out above the trench and the sniper had seen him. All here that belonged to Portadown were sorry to hear it. The snipers are all good shots, so you see we have not much of a chance when one of them sees you. Harry has died for His King and Country. He was a very goodhearted fellow.

Seagoe Parish Magazine
June 1915

BATTLE OF ST. ELOI (14/15 March 1915)

The battle began at 5pm on 14 March 1915 with a German attack, which was preceded by the explosion of two underground mines tunnelled beneath the British lines. During the evening the Germans captured the village but by nightfall in was in British hands once more.

William Quinn
Private 10348, 2nd Battalion, Royal Irish Fusiliers

Born	Portadown
Parents	Son of Thomas and Mary Quinn of Castle Avenue, Portadown
Residence	Castle Avenue
Enlisted	Portadown
Died	Killed in action 14 March 1915, Belgium
Age	20
Buried	No Known Grave
Commemorated	Ypres (Menin Gate) Memorial, Ieper, West Flaanderen, Belgium. Panel 42. Portadown War Memorial (46)

The death is reported of Private William Quinn, son of Thomas Quinn, Castle Avenue, Portadown. He was serving with the Royal Irish Fusiliers, and took part in very severe fighting at the front.

Portadown News
10 April 1915

Private Quinn's younger brother Matthew (see entry **45 Private Matthew Quinn**) was killed in action on 24 October 1914 in France.

James Gracey
Rifleman 9969, 2nd Battalion, Royal Irish Rifles

Born	Seagoe
Parents	Son of W. J. and Isabella Gracey of 1 Florence Court, Portadown
Residence	Florence Court
Enlisted	Waringstown
Died	Died of wounds 15 April 1915, Belgium
Age	19
Buried	Voormezele Enclosure No. 3, Belgium. Grave XIV. G. 2.
Commemorated	Portadown War Memorial (92) Seagoe Parish Church War Memorial

James' father W. J. Gracey had seen service with Lord Roberts in the Afghanistan War of 1881 and had taken part in the 300-mile march from Kabul to Kandahar. James was the husband of Margaret Gracey.

Rifleman Gracey was wounded in action on 13 April 1915 and was evacuated to No. 10 Casualty Clearing Station at Hazebrouck, where he succumbed to his injuries.

The wife of Private (sic) James Gracey, R.I.R., has received official notification that her husband has died from wounds received on the battlefield. Private Gracey, whose mother resides in Florence Court, is the son of a soldier who served with Lord Roberts in Afghanistan.

Portadown Express
30 April 1915

His brother Joseph Gracey served as a Private with the 1st Battalion, Royal Irish Fusiliers during the Great War.

There is a Private James Gracey, 2nd Battalion, Royal Irish Fusiliers commemorated on St. Mark's Parish Church War Memorial. However, it is unclear if this is the same person.

Grave of Rifleman James Gracey.

BATTLE OF ST. JULIEN (2ND YPRES)

(22-25 April 1915)

On 22 April the Germans tried to break the stalemate north of the Ypres salient by an attack preceded by the first use of poison gas.

On 24/25 April British, Empire and French troops attacked the German lines under heavy machine gun and sustained shellfire and more use of poison gas. These battles, which raged until 25 May, are collectively known as the Second Battle of Ypres.

George Hospital Adamson
Private 8105, 1st Battalion, Royal Irish Fusiliers

Born	Portadown
Parents	Son of Robert and Melissa Adamson of 1 Century Street, Portadown
Residence	Garvaghy Road
Enlisted	Portadown
Died	Killed in action 25 April 1915, Belgium
Age	18
Buried	No Known Grave
Commemorated	Ypres (Menin Gate) Memorial, Ieper, West Flaanderen, Belgium. Panel 42. Portadown War Memorial (104) First Presbyterian Church War Memorial, Edenderry

George's mother Melissa was employed as a linen weaver and had children Robert, William and George Hospital. His grandmother was Mary Hospital who in 1901 resided in Seagoe Upper with her two daughters and five grandchildren.

George was a member of Parkmount Temperance Flute Band.

News is to hand that Private George Adamson, 1st Batt. Royal Irish Fusiliers, was killed in action at Ypres on April 25. Prior to being called up on the reserve deceased resided with his mother at 5 George's Street, Portadown, and now resides at 37 Parker Street, Belfast. Private Adamson had not attained his eighteenth birthday.

Portadown News
29 May 1915

William Malcomson
Private 4142, 1st Battalion, Royal Irish Fusiliers

Born	9 February 1879, Seagoe Upper
Parents	Son of John and Elizabeth Malcomson of Portadown
Residence	Watson Street

Enlisted	Finner Camp, Co. Donegal
Died	Killed in action 25 April 1915, Belgium
Age	36
Buried	No Known Grave
Commemorated	Ypres (Menin Gate) Memorial, Ieper, West Flaanderen, Belgium. Panel 42. Portadown War Memorial (230) Seagoe Parish Church War Memorial

William married Hannah Jane Hara, daughter of Robert Hara, a mechanic of Edenderry on 31 December 1898 at Seagoe Parish Church. The couple resided at 4 Watson's Lane, Portadown. Both were employed as weavers.

They had seven children Marion born 6 April 1899 and who died in infancy aged two months, William Elliot born 3 March 1901 and who died in infancy aged three months, John born 10 August 1902, May born 16 May 1905, Ethel Florence born 6 October 1907, Norman born 13 July 1909 and Myrtle Violet born 24 November 1912.

Private James Wells of Carrickblacker Road, Portadown was standing beside Private Malcomson when he was killed and Wells narrowly escaped being killed himself when three bullets pierced his uniform. In a letter home he wrote

In a recent advance we gained two miles of ground but we lost a great many men. My chum W. Malcolmson was killed. If you are talking to his wife tell her that he died happy and suffered no pain.

Armagh Guardian
4 June 1915

William had two brothers who served during the Great War. Robert who served in the 1st Battalion, Royal Irish Rifles and Joseph (see entry **150 Rifleman Joseph Malcomson**) who was killed in action on 16 June 1915.

John Mills
Private 8527, 1st Battalion, Royal Irish Fusiliers

Born	Portadown
Parents	Son of John and Martha Mills of 7 Cree Street, Shettleston, Glasgow
Residence	Mourneview Street
Enlisted	Lurgan
Died	Killed in action 25 April 1915, Belgium
Age	28
Buried	No Known Grave

Commemorated
Ypres (Menin Gate) Memorial, Ieper, West Flaanderen, Belgium.
Panel 42.
Portadown War Memorial (183)

Charles Tedford
Private 7354, 1st Battalion, Royal Irish Fusiliers

Born — Portadown
Parents — Son of Nicholas and Marguerite Tedford of 15 Irwin Street, Portadown
Residence — Derrycaw
Enlisted — Portadown
Died — Killed in action 25 April 1915, Belgium
Age — 29
Buried — No Known Grave
Commemorated
Ypres (Menin Gate) Memorial, Ieper, West Flaanderen, Belgium.
Panel 42.
Portadown War Memorial (289)

Charles father Nicholas was employed as an agricultural labourer. His parents had children Susan, Maria, Maggie and Charles. Charles was the husband of Susan S. McCormick (formerly Tedford).

Lance-Corporal (sic) Charles Tedford 1st Battalion, Royal Irish Fusiliers, son of Nicholas Tedford, Irwin Street, Portadown, was killed in action on the 25 April, near Ypres. He was a reservist and was called up at the outbreak of war. Deceased resided at Bank Lane, Coatbridge, Scotland. He leaves a wife and three children.

Portadown News
5 June 1915

Francis Greenaway
Private 6119, 1st Battalion, Royal Irish Fusiliers

Born — Portadown
Residence — John Street
Enlisted — Armagh
Died — Died of wounds 28 April 1915, France
Buried — Boulogne Eastern Cemetery, Pas de Calais, France. Grave VIII. B. IV.
Commemorated
Portadown War Memorial (145)
St. Mark's Parish Church War Memorial

Francis was the husband of Emily Greenaway (nee Brownlee). They had a daughter Sarah Hanna Evelyn. He was a reservist and was called up on the outbreak of war.

Private Frank Greenaway, R.I. Fusiliers, has been wounded in the side by a rifle bullet, and is now in hospital. Before the mobilisation Private Greenaway was an active member of the U.V.F.

Portadown Express
14 May 1915

Private Greenaway died of wounds received at the Battle of St. Julien (2nd Ypres), Belgium.

His wife died shortly afterwards. Their Aunt McCracken in King Street, Portadown, raised their daughter, Sarah.

Francis' brother John (see entry **146 Corporal John Greenaway**) died of wounds on 16 February 1917 in Mesopotamia.

Private Francis Greenaway. (Doris McMullen)

Sarah Greenaway, left, at the grave of her father. (Doris McMullen)

BATTLE OF FREZENBURG (2ND YPRES) (8-13 May 1915)

Frezenburg was a village situated about four miles west of Ypres and two miles south of St. Julien. On 4 May British units made a withdrawal from positions around Frezenburg and Zonnebeke to the west of Ypres. On 8 May the Germans exploited the situation by attacking in great strength and occupying a series of important positions in the heights around Ypres.

James Dalzell
Sergeant 5505, 1st Battalion, Royal Irish Fusiliers

Born	Drumcree
Parents	Son of James and Sarah Dalzell of 15 Fowler's Entry, Portadown
Residence	Fowler's Entry
Enlisted	Portadown
Died	Died of wounds 12 May 1915, France
Age	23
Buried	Bailleul Communal Cemetery Extension, Nord, France. Grave I. A. 138.
Commemorated	Portadown War Memorial (96) St. Mark's Parish Church War Memorial

James was employed at Tavanagh weaving factory and was a drill instructor in the Ulster Volunteer Force.

Mrs Dalzell, Fowler's Entry, Portadown, has received official intimation that her son, Sergeant James Dalzell, has been killed in action. Deceased was on the reserve when called up, and was a very popular soldier...

Portadown News
5 June 1915

Sergeant Dalzell died at No. 3 Casualty Clearing Station from wounds received in action either at the Battle of St. Julien or Frezenburg (2nd Ypres), Belgium.

John Grimason
Private 6234, 2nd Battalion, Royal Irish Fusiliers

Born	Portadown
Parents	Son of John and Mary Grimason of 14 Carleton Street, Portadown
Residence	Carleton Street
Enlisted	7 October 1914, Portadown
Died	Killed in action 13 May 1915, Belgium
Age	17
Buried	No Known Grave
Commemorated	Ypres (Menin Gate) Memorial, Ieper, West Flaanderen, Belgium. Panel 42. Portadown War Memorial (38) St. Mark's Parish Church War Memorial

John's father John was a tailor by trade and his mother Mary was from County Down. The couple had children Mary, Sarah, Rebecca - all employed as winders in the linen industry; and George, Martha and John. John was employed at the

building firm of Mr. Lutton in Carleton Street.

Private Grimason was in a group assembling in a wood preparing to go into the trenches when shrapnel hit them. Private Grimason was killed and six of his comrades were wounded. The conditions at the front were graphically described by members of 'A' Company 2nd Battalion, Royal Irish Fusiliers in a letter to the editor of the Portadown Express.

Our first real "scrap" was at St. Eloi on 14th February, and again at the same place on 14th March. The latter engagement was a set-off against Neuve Chapelle; we gave them a real good "hiding"on each occasion and showed them how Irishmen could fight. The battalion received the highest praise from General French...Our next hot place was Ypres; it was like hell here; we were at the firing line for five days and had to put up with a lot of hardship...The worst experience we had was here; it was our last 48 hours; just before we were relieved we were taken from our own part of the line to strengthen a point where the Germans were making very determined efforts to break through.... Our company had 57 casualties here; it was on the way to the trench that poor Grimason was killed.

Portadown Express
11 June 1915

John's brother George (see entry **37 Able Seaman George Grimason**) died on 9 October 1915 whilst serving with the Royal Navy.

William Liggett
Private 6757, 1st Battalion, Canadian Infantry (Western Ontario Regiment)

Born	11 May 1887, Portadown
Parents	Son of Alexander and Mary Jane Liggett of 227 Three Rivers Massachussetts, USA
Residence	Obins Street
Enlisted	22 September 1914, Valcartier, Canada
Died	Died of wounds 15 May 1915, France
Age	28
Buried	St. Sever Cemetery, Rouen Seine, Maritime, France. Grave A. 9. 23.
Commemorated	Portadown War Memorial (188) Drumcree Parish Church War Memorial St. Mark's Parish Church War Memorial

William's father Alexander was employed as a general labourer. He and his wife Mary Jane had children Joshua, Susanna, William, Alexander and Francis. In 1901 the family resided at 58 Obins Street,

Portadown. Joshua and Susanna were employed as weavers.

William had served for seven years in the Royal Irish Fusiliers and had then emigrated to the United States. On the outbreak of war he crossed the border into Canada to re-enlist.

On enlistment his particulars were given as follows: occupation - gardener, height - 5'9", complexion - fair, eyes - blue, hair - brown and distinguishing marks - a tattoo of a woman on right forearm.

On 22 April 1915 Private Liggett received a gunshot wound to his left side, which quickly paralysed his left leg. He was rushed to the Regimental Dressing Station and then moved to No. 10 General Hospital at Rouen where he underwent surgery to remove a bullet lodged in his spine. Despite treatment Private Liggett's condition deteriorated and he died on 15 May 1915. Sister Dogherty, a nurse who had been tending William, wrote to Mrs Liggett

I am deeply grieved to tell you of your son's death. He died very peacefully, and asked me a few hours previously to send you his last love. He was quite conscious to the last and very happy and resigned to die. Poor boy, had he lived he would have been a cripple for life, so God in His mercy saw fit to take him to Himself. He died from a bullet wound in the spine. After he was operated upon, and the bullet removed, he suffered much less pain, but he gradually grew weaker and passed away on the morning of 15th May. He is buried in a lovely little cemetery, which is always kept covered in beautiful flowers.

Portadown News
5 June 1915

His widowed mother Mary Jane moved to the United States after the end of the Great War.

Grave of Private William Liggett.

Thomas Thompson
Private 6615, 1st Battalion, Canadian Infantry (Western Ontario Regiment)

Born	12 December 1894, Mullavilly
Parents	Son of David Thompson of Ballyworkan
Residence	Ballyworkan
Enlisted	20 September 1914, Valcartier, Canada
Died	Killed in action 15 June 1915, France
Age	20
Buried	No Known Grave
Commemorated	Vimy Memorial Pas de Calais Portadown War Memorial (262)

Thomas was a member of the Ulster Volunteer Force and had been a staff sergeant in the Mullavilly Company of the Church Lads' Brigade.

On enlistment his particulars were given as follows: occupation - labourer, height - 5'5", complexion - fair, eyes - blue, hair - light brown. He sailed with his unit on the SS *Laurentic* on 3 October 1914. Thomas received a gunshot wound in the arm on 24 April 1915. After treatment he rejoined his unit and was killed in action on 15 June 1915.

Private Thomas Thompson of the Canadian Expeditionary Force was killed in action on 15th June. He was a native of Mullavilly, Tandragee, where his parents reside, and went to Canada only a few months before returning with the first contingent...

Portadown News
17 July 1915

Vimy Memorial.

Joseph Malcomson
Rifleman 4894, 2nd Battalion, Royal Irish Rifles

Born	1 July 1885, Seagoe
Parents	Son of John and Elizabeth Malcomson of Portadown
Residence	Joseph Street
Enlisted	Waringstown
Died	Killed in action 16 June 1915, Belgium
Age	29
Buried	No Known Grave
Commemorated	Ypres (Menin Gate) Memorial, Ieper, West Flaanderen, Belgium. Panel 40 Portadown War Memorial (150) Seagoe Parish Church War Memorial

Joseph was in the reserve and was called up on the outbreak of war. Mrs Malcomson wrote a letter enquiring into the circumstances surrounding her second son's death. The reply was from Lieutenant T. H. Ivey

Having only recently joined this Company I did not know your son Joseph, but on receipt of your letter I caused enquiries to be made, and found that he was killed near Hooge on June 16th. A shell burst in the midst of a party killing nine of them outright. I deeply sympathise with you in your sad loss; everyone spoke so highly of your boy; they all lost a brave and cheerful comrade.

Seagoe Parish Magazine
September 1915

Joseph's brother William (see entry **230 Private William Malcomson**) was killed in action on 25 April 1915.

As a consequence of these two brothers being killed in action within two months of each other the military authorities, under the command of General Sir John French, informed Mrs Malcomson that her remaining son Robert serving with the 1st Battalion, Royal Irish Rifles would be transferred from the firing line to a transport unit. In early 1918 Robert was discharged from further service.

Henry Sinnamon
Private 18535, 2nd Battalion, Royal Irish Fusiliers

Born	Portadown
Parents	Son of Henry and Elizabeth Sinnamon of 5 Florence Court, Portadown
Residence	Florence Court
Enlisted	Portadown
Died	Killed in action 1 July 1915, France

Grave of Private Henry Sinnamon.

Age	43
Buried	Houplines Communal Cemetery Extension-Nord, France. Grave III. A. 11.
Commemorated	Portadown War Memorial (93) Seagoe Parish Church War Memorial

Henry had previous service in the army and volunteered on the outbreak of war. A widower, Henry remarried 37-year-old spinster Sarah Pickering on 2 October 1914 at Seagoe Parish Church. Both were employed as weavers. His daughter Sarah was born on 12 December 1915. He also had children from his previous marriage.

Mrs Sinnamon, Florence Court, has now received official intimation that her husband, Private Henry Sinnamon, was killed in action in France on the 1st inst. He was attached to the 3rd Battalion, R. I. F., (sic) and was only a short time at the front...

Portadown News
24 July 1915

Robert Lynn
Driver 45206, 87th Battery, Royal Field Artillery

Born	County Tyrone
Parents	Son of James and Elizabeth Lynn of Mousetown, Coalisland, County Tyrone
Residence	Cecil Street
Enlisted	Belfast
Died	Killed in action 6 August 1915, Belgium
Age	30
Buried	Hop Store Cemetery, Ieper, West-Vlaanderen, Belgium. Grave I. E. 9.

Commemorated	Portadown War Memorial (54) St. Mark's Parish Church War Memorial

Robert had previously served in the King's Own Regiment with the serial number 8858.

The family was from Mousetown, Coalisland. Robert was one of four brothers who made the supreme sacrifice during the Great War. Sergeant William Edward Lynn 1st Battalion, Royal Irish Fusiliers, was killed in action 17 July 1916 in France. Private John Lynn, 1st Battalion, Royal Inniskilling Fusiliers died of wounds on 9 August 1916 in Belgium. Sergeant James Lynn, 906th Company, Royal Army Service Corps died on 7 August 1920 in Palestine.

George Rodgers Gunner 32466, 59th Siege Battery, Royal Garrison Artillery

Born	Knocknamuckley
Parents	Son of Joseph H. and Mary Ann Rodgers of Ballygargan
Residence	Ballygargan
Enlisted	Portadown
Died	Killed in action 19 September 1915, France
Age	25
Buried	Vermelles British Cemetery, Pas de Calais, France. Grave I. F. 30.
Commemorated	Portadown War Memorial (259)

The 1901 Census Return lists the following children of Joseph H., a farmer, and Mary Ann Rodgers - James William, Isaac, John, Jane, Joseph H, George, David and Thomas. The family headstone in Knocknamuckley Church of Ireland Churchyard, Portadown refers to children Joseph, John H. and Mary who died in infancy; David who died on 12 December 1890 aged three; George who was killed in action on 19 September 1915 aged 25; John who died on 8 November 1930 aged 47 and Rachel who died on 29 December 1931 aged 40.

George had served six years in the army, four of them in India. When his unit was transferred from India to the Western Front George was able to spend a few days home on leave over Christmas 1914.

Mr. J. H. Rodgers, Ballygargan, Portadown, has received official notification that his son, Gunner Geo. Rodgers, R.G.A. was killed in action on September 19th...

Portadown News
30 October 1915

Grave of Gunner George Rodgers.

THE BATTLE OF LOOS (25 September - 16 October 1915)

The Battle of Loos began following a four-day bombardment, which included the use of poison gas, by the British for the first time. Overall British casualties from 25 September to 16 October were 15,800 killed or missing and 34,500 wounded.

Thomas Conway
Private 16498, 15th Battalion, Durham Light Infantry

Born	Dublin
Parents	Adopted son of Jane Nugent of 21 Marley Street, Portadown
Residence	Marley Street
Enlisted	Gateshead, England
Died	Killed in action 25 September 1915, France
Age	24
Buried	No Known Grave
Commemorated	Loos Memorial, Pas de Calais, France. Panel 106 & 107. Portadown War Memorial (157)

During the Battle of Loos the 15th Battalion, Durham Light Infantry lost 12 officers and 450 men killed, wounded or missing.

Joseph Henry McCardle
Private S/1925, 10th Battalion, Gordon Highlanders

Born	County Armagh
Parents	Son of Thomas and Margaret McCardle of Killycomain
Residence	Clounagh
Enlisted	Clydebank, Scotland

Loos Memorial.

Died — Killed in action 25 September 1915, France
Buried — No Known Grave
Commemorated — Loos Memorial, Pas de Calais, France. Panel 115 to 117
Portadown War Memorial (280)
Seagoe Parish Church War Memorial

Joseph's father Thomas was a labourer. He and his wife Margaret had children William John, Joseph Henry, Thomas, Maggie and Mary Jane who was born in 1897.

Joseph Henry and his brother William John both married sisters Hannah Jane and Margaret Parks of Edenderry. The double wedding took place in Seagoe Parish Church on 10 October 1908. Joseph, a labourer, was 24 years old and his bride Hannah Jane, a weaver, was 18 years old.

As no news has yet been heard of Private J. McCardle, Gordon Highlanders, it is feared that he has been killed. His wife lives at Clounagh.

Portadown News
27 November 1915

His brother William (see entry **281 Rifleman William John McCardle**) was killed in action on 5 March 1917.

Herbert Watson
Lance-Corporal 19897, 11th Battalion, Highland Light Infantry

Born	Portadown
Parents	Son of Thomas H. Watson of 146 Park Road, Portadown
Residence	Park Road
Enlisted	Hamilton, Lanarkshire, Scotland
Died	Killed in action 25 September 1915, France
Age	19
Buried	No Known Grave
Commemorated	Loos Memorial, Pas de Calais, France. Panel 108 to 112. Portadown War Memorial (203) Thomas Street Methodist Church War Memorial

Lance-Corporal Herbert Watson, son of Mr. Thomas Watson, Park Road who has been missing since September 25th 1915, is now officially reported as having been killed on that date. Lance-Corporal Watson was attached to the 11th Highland Light Infantry. Mr. D. Lloyd has conveyed to Mr. And Mrs. Watson the King and Queen's sympathy in their sorrow.

Portadown News
7 October 1916

WATSON—In loving memory of (No. 19897), Corporal Herbert Watson, H.L.I., aged 19 years, killed in action at the Battle of Loos, 25th September, 1915, third and dearly-beloved son of T. H. Watson.
Sadly missed by his loving father, mother, sisters and brothers.
146, Park Road, Portadown.

The Portadown News
SATURDAY, SEPTEMBER 27, 1919.

Obituary notice for Lance-Corporal Herbert Watson. (Portadown News)

Joshua Moore
Private 5868, 1st Battalion, Royal Irish Fusiliers

Born	Portadown
Parents	Son of Sarah Moore of 7 Henry Street, Portadown
Residence	Henry Street
Enlisted	Portadown
Died	Killed in action 8 December 1915, France
Buried	Sucrerie Military Cemetery Colincamps,Somme, France. Grave I. C. 21.

Commemorated
Portadown
War Memorial (123)

Joshua had sisters and four brothers Thomas, John, William Henry, who lived in the United States and Alexander who served as a Driver with the 15th Field Ambulance, Army Service Corps during the Great War.

Private Moore was shot in the head by a German sniper and lived only a few hours. Previously on New Year's Day 1915 he had survived shrapnel wounds and spent a short time at home. His mother received a letter from her son's platoon commander, T. Palmer

I am very sorry to have the painful duty of informing you that No. 5868 Private J. Moore was killed on 8 December. He was one of the best men in my platoon, and you have the satisfaction of knowing that he was a brave soldier. Officers, non-commissioned officers and men were very sorry at losing their comrade. Personally, I am much grieved at having to send you the sad news.

Portadown News
25 December 1915

Thomas Nicholson
Private 16425, 9th Battalion, Royal Irish Fusiliers

Born	Portadown
Parents	Son of Robert G. and Letitia Nicholson of Drumcree, Portadown
Residence	West Street
Enlisted	Belfast
Died	Died of wounds 13 February 1916, France
Age	40
Buried	Forceville Communal Cemetery and Extension, Somme, France. Grave I. D. 11.
Commemorated	Portadown War Memorial (240) St. Mark's Parish Church War Memorial

Thomas was a member of the Ulster Volunteer Force and, like many of his colleagues, joined the 9th Battalion when it was reformed as part of the 36th (Ulster) Division. Private Nicholson along with another soldier was engaged in carrying provisions to the forward trenches when shell fragments struck them. Thomas was bought to hospital but died of his injuries.

Lieutenant-Colonel Stewart Blacker wrote a letter every day of the war to his wife Eva

12 February 1916
This morning they put some 4.2 shells into the village, and killed 1 man and wounded 1,

I'm grieved to say...In addition to the morning strafe, when they put in about 30 H.E.s - 4.2 I think - they kept putting in an odd one at intervals through the day.

13 February 1916
The wounded man of yesterday has died - Nicholson, 'B' Coy.

Seagoe Parish
Magazine 1923

His death is a sad blow to his young wife, with whom there will be heartfelt sympathy in her bereavement.

Portadown Express
18 February 1916

A brother formerly of the 5th Royal Irish Fusiliers was stationed in India but was invalided home a year before the outbreak of war. He was employed as a caretaker in Portadown Town Hall.

George McFadden
Private 419113, 42nd Battalion, Canadian Infantry, (Quebec Regiment)

Born	16 May 1886, Castle Island House, Portadown
Parents	Son of William J. and Elizabeth McFadden of Castle Island House, Garvaghy Road, Portadown
Residence	Garvaghy Road
Enlisted	23 June 1915, Niagara, Ontario, Canada
Died	Died of wounds 27 March 1916, Belgium
Age	29
Buried	Lijssenthoek Military Cemetery, Poperinge, West Vlaanderen, Belgium. Grave V. B. 26.
Commemorated	Portadown War Memorial (109) St. Mark's Parish Church War Memorial

George was a member of Portadown Football Club and his brother William played as a goalkeeper for the club.

George was living in Hamilton, Ontario when war was declared. On enlistment his particulars were given as follows: occupation labourer, height - 5' 7½", complexion - ruddy, eyes - blue, hair - dark.

George arrived in England on 26 August 1915 and the next day, at Shorncliffe, was taken on strength of the 17th Battalion, Canadian Infantry. On 26 September George was transferred to the 42nd Battalion, Canadian Infantry and

just over a week later the unit sailed for France arriving at Boulogne on 9 October.

Private McFadden was part of a section from 'B' Company, which was sent out on patrol on the night of 22/23 March 1916. He received a gunshot wound to his upper right arm, suffering a compound fracture as a result. George, although suffering from pain and the initial stages of shock, remained conscious and was able to talk to pals. His comrades took him to No. 1 Canadian Field Ambulance where his wounds were dressed. Despite treatment his condition worsened through loss of blood and severe shock and Private McFadden succumbed to his injuries on 27 March 1916.

Sister M. Hopton, sister in charge of the ward, wrote to George's father on 28 March 1916

Dear Mr. McFadden I am very sorry to tell you that your son, Pte McFadden, 419113, 42nd B. W. Can. passed away yesterday afternoon. He was so plucky and brave all through his illness. Everything was tried to save his life, but it was not possible. I should like to tell you of my deep sympathy with you in your great loss.

Portadown Express
31 March 1916

Robert Henry Brown
Private 6133, 1st Battalion, Royal Irish Fusiliers

Born	11 April 1889, Lurgan
Parents	Son of William and Ellen Brown
Residence	Union Street
Enlisted	Armagh
Died	Died of wounds 4 April 1916, France
Age	26
Buried	Berles-Au-Bois Churchyard Extension, Pas de Calais, France. Grave C. 9.
Commemorated	Portadown War Memorial (223) St. Mark's Parish Church War Memorial Seagoe Parish Church War Memorial

Robert was employed as a weaver before the war. He married Mary Elizabeth Hewitt, daughter of Robery Henry Hewitt, a ploughman from Edenderry on 20 November 1909 in Seagoe Parish Church. Mary was 22 years old and employed as a winder. They had four children, three of who are listed in Seagoe Parish Church

Records - Mary Ellen born 28 November 1909, Robert Henry born 28 March 1911, and William born 27 November 1913.

Robert had seen much action at the front and had sustained injuries when an exploding shell buried him. He had been sent on home leave to recuperate from his ordeal.

During a subsequent engagement Private Brown was wounded in the leg. He had just taken shelter in a nearby house when seconds later a shell came through the roof killing four men, wounding him and some other men who had also taken refuge in the building. Private Brown died soon after from his wounds. In a letter home to his wife Private Joshua Liggett DCM wrote

Grave of Robert Henry Brown.

We have made Private Brown's grave the most beautiful one in France. Nearly every Portadown man sent a flower of some kind, as he was well liked by the whole battalion.

Portadown News
22 April 1916

Two of Robert's brothers also served during the Great War; John in the 2nd Battalion, Royal Irish Fusiliers and William James in the Royal Field Artillery both being discharged on medical grounds due to wounds received at the front.

John Vennard
Private 19750, 9th Battalion, Royal Irish Fusiliers

Born	Portadown
Residence	Church Street
Enlisted	Portadown
Died	Died of wounds 9 April 1916, France
Buried	Beauval Communal Cemetery, Somme, France. Grave D. 30.

Commemorated
Portadown War Memorial (68)
St. Mark's Parish Church War Memorial

John was the husband of Sarah Vennard and the couple had two children Minnie and Mabel.

Private Vennard enlisted in the 10th Battalion, Royal Irish Fusiliers and was subsequently drafted into the 9th Battalion two months before he died.

Private J. Vennard, Portadown, has died of wounds and was buried last Sunday. Much sympathy is expressed for his young wife.

Portadown News
15 April 1916

By 1917 his widow and two children were residing in Widmer Street, Toronto, Canada.

William Ernest Albert Clayton
Second-Lieutenant,
9th Battalion,
Cheshire Regiment

Parents — Son of Reverend William John Clayton of Downpatrick
Residence — Portmore Street
Died — Died of wounds 22 April 1916, France
Age — 27
Buried — Merville Communal Cemetery, Nord, France. Grave VII. A. 12.
Commemorated
Portadown War Memorial (204)
Thomas Street Methodist Church War Memorial

William Ernest's father William John was a Methodist Minister in Downpatrick and formerly of Ballyclare and his brother, the Reverend C. M. Clayton, was a minister in Dolphin's Barn, Dublin.

The Bank of Ireland employed William firstly at the Donegall Place Branch in Belfast and latterly at the Portadown Branch. He was a member of the Officers Training Corps at Queen's University and a member of Portadown Rowing Club. He received a commission in the Cheshire Regiment in December 1914.

Second-Lieutenant Clayton was wounded on 13 April 1916 when a shell exploded above his trench. He was hit in the side by shrapnel and succumbed to his injuries on 22 April. A few weeks previously William had been appointed battalion grenadier officer and had passed a special course in bombing.

...The news of Lieutenant Clayton's death was received with sincere regret by his numerous friends in Portadown.

Portadown News
29 April 1916

Grave of Second-Lieutenant William Ernest Albert Clayton.

Joseph Henry Hughes
Private 18568, 1st Battalion, Royal Irish Fusiliers

Born Drumcree
Parents Son of Robert and Frances Eliza Hughes of Portadown.
Residence Union Street
Enlisted Portadown
Died Died of wounds 2 May 1916, France
Age 26
Buried Doullens Communal cemetery Extension No. 1, Somme, France Grave I. D. 9.
Commemorated Portadown War Memorial (224) St. Mark's Parish Church War Memorial

Private W. Hayes wrote to Joseph's mother

We all thought that your son Joe would recover from the wounds he received, but to the sorrow of every man in the platoon he passed away. On behalf of the men of his platoon I beg to convey to you their deepest sympathy in the loss you have sustained. We mourn his loss. We miss him greatly as he was a good soldier. We know that you will miss him, but he died a soldier's death for his God, King and country, and you may be proud of him.

Portadown News
17 June 1916

Joseph had a brother Thomas and sister-in-law Grace who resided at 96 West Street, Portadown.

George Tollerton
Rifleman 6050, 14th Battalion, Royal Irish Rifles

Born	Magheragall, Lisburn
Parents	Son of Thomas Tollerton
Residence	Mary Street
Enlisted	Belfast
Died	Killed in action 6 May 1916, France
Buried	Authvile Military Cemetery, Somme, France. Grave D. 48
Commemorated	Portadown War Memorial (162) St. Mark's Parish Church War Memorial

George was married with two children. He was employed as a fireman for the Great Northern Railway Company, Portadown Railway Station.

He enlisted in the 14th Battalion, Royal Irish Rifles that was formed from the Young Citizen Volunteers unit of the Ulster Volunteer Force.

Rifleman Tollerton was on duty in the trenches as part of a machine gun team when it came under heavy bombardment from the enemy. A trench mortar shell exploded in the trench killing him instantly. In a letter to George's widow Lieutenant R. Renwick, Machine Gun Officer, 14th Battalion, Royal Irish Rifles wrote

During the bombardment he stood by his gun with great courage and his name has since appeared in battalion orders for gallantry.

Portadown News
20 May 1916

George had two brothers serving with the colours during the Great War and his father Thomas served as a Rifleman in the 11th Battalion, Royal Irish Rifles.

Thomas George Sloane
Rifleman 18780, 14th Battalion, Royal Irish Rifles

Born	Portadown
Parents	Son of Benjamin and Eliza Harriet Sloane of 9 Elswick Street, Belfast
Residence	Bridge Street
Enlisted	Belfast
Died	Killed in action 6 May 1916, France
Age	26
Buried	Authvile Military Cemetery, Somme, France. Grave D. 50.

Commemorated
Portadown War Memorial (19)

Thomas was the nephew of Miss McDowell of the Albert Hotel, Portadown and was employed by Messrs Young and Hyde Ltd. of Bedford Street, Belfast.

He enlisted after war was declared and underwent training at Finner Camp, County Donegal and at Randalstown. The circumstances of his death were explained in a letter to his mother

The platoon to which he belonged had the honour of holding the most difficult and dangerous portion of our line, and your boy was on sentry duty during the whole of the bombardment. How he held to his post under a positive shower of high explosive shell and shrapnel will never be understood. The place where he was stationed was comparable only to an inferno, and the finger of death was pointed at every man in that platoon. Knowing this as they did they never flinched and refused to retire, thus proving themselves as brave as any heroes whose names and deeds we have been taught to glorify. Your son was one of these, and the post which he held was blown to pieces by a shell containing 200lbs of explosives.

Portadown News
20 May 1916

Family grave of Rifleman Thomas George Sloane. (Author's Collection)

Joseph McCourt
Lance-Corporal 18220,
8th Battalion,
Royal Irish Fusiliers

Born	Portadown
Parents	Son of Patrick and Elizabeth McCourt of 40 Obins Street, Portadown
Residence	Obins Street
Enlisted	Portadown
Died	Died of wounds 27 May 1916, France
Age	38
Buried	Bethune Town Cemetery, France. Grave V. D. 42.

Commemorated
Portadown War Memorial (190)

Mrs McCourt received a letter from Captain George Craven, Military Chaplain

Your husband was brought into my hospital severely wounded in the leg. I saw him at once and gave him the last sacrament, as I did not think he would recover. He himself thought he would but he gradually sank and

died on 27th May. ...I warmly sympathise in your loss. I hope the thought of his happy death in our Lord's grace will console you and help you to bear your heavy cross. I shall pray for him in my Mass. May God bless you and strengthen you in your trial.

Portadown News
6 July 1916

Alexander Porter
Private 7825, 1st Canadian Mounted Rifles (Saskatchewan Regiment)

Born	26 March 1891, Portadown
Parents	Son of Elizabeth Porter of 188 Leopold Street, Belfast
Residence	Union Street
Enlisted	5 February 1915, Toronto, Canada
Died	Killed in action 2 June 1916, France & Flanders
Age	25
Buried	No Known Grave
Commemorated	Ypres (Menin Gate) Memorial, Ieper, West Flaanderen, Belgium. Panel 30 & 32 Portadown War Memorial (225) St. Mark's Parish Church War Memorial

The family moved to Belfast with Alexander going to Canada. His mother resided in Leopold Street before moving to 9 Geoffrey Street, Belfast.

On enlistment in 'C' Squad, 7th Canadian Mounted Rifles Alexander's particulars were given as follows: occupation - riveter, height - 5'8", complexion - sandy, eyes - blue, hair - sandy. He had previously served in the Territorials.

On 27 April 1915 he was taken on strength of the Canadian Cavalry Depot at Canterbury. The next day he was admitted to the Military Hospital, Canterbury with a contusion and spent four days in hospital. On 10 September he was transferred to the 3rd Canadian Mounted Rifles. Private Porter embarked for France on 22 September. He transferred to the 1st Canadian Mounted Rifles on 2 January 1916 due to a reorganisation in the field. Private Alexander was posted "missing believed killed 2-5 June 1916".

Private Alexander Porter is also announced killed. He enlisted in Belfast (sic), but resided for several years in Union Street, Portadown.

Portadown News
24 June 1916

Edward Marshall
Private A/4151, 3rd Battalion, Canadian Infantry (Central Ontario Regiment)

Born	9 August 1890, Portadown
Parents	Son of Martha Jane Marshall of 52 Portmore Street, Portadown
Residence	Meadow Lane
Enlisted	12 April 1915, Toronto, Canada
Died	Killed in action 13 June 1916, France
Age	25
Buried	No Known Grave
Commemorated	Ypres (Menin Gate) Memorial, Ieper, West Flaanderen, Belgium. Panel 18-24-26-30. Portadown War Memorial (166) St. Mark's Parish Church War Memorial Seagoe Parish Church War Memorial

Edward, formerly of Killicomaine, emigrated to Canada around 1910. He enlisted in the 35th Battalion, Canadian Expeditionary Force. On enlistment his particulars were given as follows: height - 5'8", complexion - dark, eyes - blue, hair - black.

Edward embarked for France on 16 July 1915 and on 17 July was taken on strength of the 3rd Battalion. On 13 June 1916 Private Marshall and four of his colleagues were killed instantly when a dugout they were in received a direct hit from a high explosive shell.

His widowed mother and sister resided at 18 Meadow Lane, Portadown at the time.

John Matthews
Private 3973, 26th Battalion, Australian Imperial Force

Born	Ballintaggart, Portadown
Parents	Son of James and Ann Matthews of 21 James Street, Portadown
Residence	James Street
Died	Died of wounds 21 June 1916, France
Age	23
Buried	Wimereux Communal Cemetery, Pas de Calais, France. Grave I. N. 10A.
Commemorated	Portadown War Memorial (129)

Seagoe Parish Church War Memorial

John was educated at Edenderry National School. He was employed as a labourer and also served for three years in the Armagh Militia. Both John and his brother Moses emigrated to Brisbane, Queensland, Australia when John was aged 20.

Moses resided at Mountain View Farm, Brandon Townsville, Queensland. He also served with the 26th Battalion, Australian Imperial Force.

According to a report in the Portadown News dated 16 September 1916 Moses helped to carry his injured brother to a place of safety under heavy shellfire. Private John Matthews was brought to the Australian Base Hospital in Wimereux where he died of his injuries. His mother received a letter from Sister Shoolbridge.

Grave of Private John Matthews.

It is with heartfelt sorrow I write to tell you of the last days of your son John.... Of course from his wounds there was always the chance of haemorrhage, but we hoped for nothing excessive, and he seemed to be tiding over the time very well and all were pleased with his progress, when alas! Early Wednesday morning there came an excessive haemorrhage, and although the doctors operated and stopped the haemorrhage, he was too weak to rally and so quietly sank. His last words were "Oh! Sister I am so tired; so tired." Weak as he had been for some hours, he lived on until midday, and he always managed a smile in answer to me, said which flowers he liked best beside him, and so when he died I laid some of them on his breast. Thursday he was buried at 2p.m. on a bright sunny day, on the slope of a hill beside many other brave lads.

Portadown News
1 July 1916

John McKee
Private 7953, 2nd Battalion, Royal Munster Fusiliers

Born	Drumcree
Parents	Son of Henry McKee of 8 William Street, Portadown
Residence	Curran Street
Enlisted	Portadown
Died	Killed in action 25 June 1916, France
Age	29
Buried	No Known Grave
Commemorated	Arras Memorial, France. Bay 9. Portadown War Memorial (82)

John was the husband of Sarah McKee and they resided at 37 Curran Street, Portadown.

Arras Memorial.

Chapter 4
The Somme 1-15 July 1916

A total of 17 infantry divisions were earmarked for the Somme offensive, which was to take place over a broad front stretching from Gommecourt in the north to Montauban in the south.

Owing to heavy rain the offensive was postponed for two days with the new date being set for the morning of 1 July. Despite all the intensive planning, training, the massive artillery bombardment and high morale of the troops the battle of the Somme was a disaster of monumental proportions. By the end of the first day of the Battle of the Somme the British losses were in the region of 19,000 killed, 2,000 missing, 35,000 wounded and 600 prisoners of war. Total casualties of 57,500 in a single day - by far the worst losses suffered by the British Army in its entire history.

Ulster Tower, Thiepval. (Author's Collection)

The 36th (Ulster) Division suffered over 5,000 casualties of which 2,000 lay dead or dying on the battlefield. From 1 July-17 July 1916 a total of 70 soldiers from Portadown were killed or died of wounds received in action during the Battle of the Somme.

1st Battalion, Royal Irish Fusiliers

The 1st Battalion formed part of the 10th Infantry Brigade of the 4th Division. On 1 July the battalion assembled in trenches at Sunken Road, half a mile north west of Auchonvillers. Casualties were three officers wounded, other ranks suffered 10 killed, 90 wounded and seven missing.

Francis McCann
Private 6135, 1st Battalion, Royal Irish Fusiliers

Born Portadown
Residence Obins Street
Enlisted Armagh
Died Killed in action
1 July 1916, France
Buried No Known Grave
Commemorated
Thiepval Memorial, Somme,France. Pier and face 15A.
Portadown War Memorial (189)

Intimation has been received that Private Frank McCann, has been wounded and missing. His mother resides in Obin Street.

Portadown News
19 August 1916

Ephraim Sherman
Private 4777, 1st Battalion, Royal Irish Fusiliers

Born Portadown
Parents Son of Mary Sherman of 43 Montague Street, Portadown
Residence Montague Street
Enlisted Finner Camp, Co. Donegal
Died Killed in action
6 July 1916, France
Age 29
Buried Auchonvillers Military Cemetery, Somme, France. Grave II. E. 34.
Commemorated
Portadown War Memorial (176)
Thomas Street Methodist Church War Memorial

On July 6th the Battalion suffered from shellfire, one starry shell falling amongst a fatigue party and another wrecking the orderlies' dugout at Battalion headquarters.

The 1st Battalion Faugh-A-Ballaghs in the Great War

Private Sherman's mother received a letter from Sergeant J. Hughes, 1st Battalion, and Royal Irish Fusiliers

It is with feelings of deep emotion that I convey to you the news of the death of your son Ephraim in action. I feel no words of mine can console you in the loss you have sustained in this, the common cause. You will find some consolation in the fact that in death he found no pain, and that it was during the progress of the Allies' offensive that he passed to the great beyond.

Portadown News
5 August 1916

Clounagh LOL 9 unfurled a banner on 8 July 1921 featuring portraits of Privates Ephraim Sherman and James Gordon (see **29 Private**

James Gordon) two members of the lodge who had been killed in action at the Battle of the Somme.

A handsome new banner for L.O.L. No. 9 Portadown District, was unfurled on Friday evening by Mrs. D. G. Shillington. On the front of the banner is a painting of King William crossing the Boyne, and on the reverse side a very realistic representation of the Battle of the Somme, with the portraits of Pte. Ephraim Sherman and Pte. Jas. Gordon, Royal Irish Fusiliers, two members of the Lodge who fell in the Great War on 1st July 1916.

Portadown News
9 July 1921

Orange Memorial, Thiepval. (Author's Collection)

Ephraim had a brother William who resided at Highland Park, Detroit, Michigan, USA.

His cousin Richard (see entry **177 Corporal Richard Sherman**) died of wounds on 1 April 1918 at Rouen in France.

John Martin
Sergeant 10261, 1st Battalion, Royal Irish Fusiliers

Born	Shankill, Lurgan
Residence	Water Street
Enlisted	Lurgan
Died	Died of wounds 15 July 1916, Battle of the Somme, France
Buried	Auchonvillers Military Cemetery, Somme France. Grave II. D. 2.
Commemorated	Portadown War Memorial (229) St. Mark's Parish Church War Memorial

John served in France from 19 December 1914 first as a Lance-Corporal and later earning promotion to Acting Sergeant. He died of wounds, received at the Battle of the Somme, at No. 10 Field Ambulance.

Sergeant T. J. Steenson, Parkmount, and Pte. (sic) John Martin, Water Street, are announced killed. The former was serving with the Australians, and the latter with the R.I.F.

Portadown News
14 July 1917

9th Battalion, Royal Irish Fusiliers

The 9th Battalion, commanded by Lieutenant-Colonel Stewart Blacker, was formed from the Armagh, Monaghan and Cavan Volunteers of the Ulster Volunteer Force. It formed part of the 108th Infantry Brigade of the 36th (Ulster) Division.

On 1 July it attacked north of the River Ancre, one of the objectives being Beaucourt Railway Station.

William James Cordy Private 14048, 9th Battalion, Royal Irish Fusiliers

Born	2 June 1878, Seagoe
Parents	Son of Robert and Jane Cordy (nee Craig) of Lower Seagoe
Residence	Sandy Row
Enlisted	Portadown
Died	Killed in action 26 June 1916, France
Age	38
Buried	Hamel Military Cemetery, Beaumont-Hamel. Grave I. C. 9.
Commemorated	Portadown War Memorial (209) St. Mark's Parish Church War Memorial Seagoe Parish Church War Memorial

William was employed as a weaver before the war. He was the husband of Margaret Young, daughter of Brown Young, of Sandy Row, Portadown. The couple had three children William Browne born 23 May 1911, Eveline born 11 April 1913 and Robert David born 27 February 1915 and who died in infancy on 7 March 1915. They resided at 5 Sandy Row, Meadow Lane, Portadown.

William was a regular worshipper at church services and a member of the men's Bible class. He was also a member of the Bann Lily Lodge of the British Order of Ancient Free Gardeners. William was a member of the Ulster Volunteer Force.

Private Cordy served in 'B' Company. For seven days prior to the start of the Battle of the Somme the British artillery shelled the German lines and the enemy returned fire on a number of occasions. On 24 June two men

were killed and 11 wounded. On 25 June there were three more casualties and on 26 June the 9th Battalion suffered three men killed and 17 wounded. One of these soldiers was Private William Cordy.

...He was carrying rations to the men across ground exposed to shell-fire, a high explosive shell burst quite close to him and a fragment of it penetrated his side. He only lived a few minutes, but had time to send a loving message to his wife and little ones.

Seagoe Parish Magazine 1916

Grave of Private William James Cordy. (Author's Collection)

Absolom Abraham
Private 13974, 9th Battalion, Royal Irish Fusiliers

Born — Portadown
Parents — Son of George and Mary Ann Abraham of 36 Henry Street, Portadown
Residence — Charles Street
Enlisted — Portadown
Died — Killed in action 1 July 1916, France
Age — 19
Buried — No Known Grave
Commemorated — Thiepval Memorial, Somme, France. Pier and face 15A. Portadown War Memorial (55) St. Mark's Parish Church War

Absolom was one of three brothers killed during the Great War.

Mrs Abraham, Ballinteggart, has received official intimation that her son Absalom, (sic) has been killed in action.

Portadown News 22 July1916

His brothers James William (see entry **56 Private James William Abraham**) was killed in action on 1 July 1916 at the Battle of the Somme and Thomas Robert (see entry **57 Private Thomas Robert

Abraham) died of wounds on 17 April 1917 in France. Another brother Charles John resided in Richhill.

Amongst the large number of beautiful private wreaths was one from Mrs. M. A. Abraham, 34 Henry Street, in memory of her three sons, James Wm., Thomas Robert and Absolom.

Portadown News
18 November 1933

James William Abraham
Private 20292, 9th Battalion, Royal Irish Fusiliers

Parents	Son of George and Mary Ann Abraham of 36 Henry Street, Portadown
Residence	Charles Street
Enlisted	Glasgow, Scotland
Died	Killed in action 1 July 1916, France
Buried	No Known Grave
Commemorated	Thiepval Memorial, Somme, France. Pier and face 15A. Portadown War Memorial (56) St. Mark's Parish Church War Memorial

James was living in Clydebank at the time of his enlistment. He previously served in the Royal Inniskilling Fusiliers with the serial number 22376. He served in 'C' Company.

James was one of three brothers killed during the Great War. His brothers Absolom (see entry **55 Private Absolom Abraham**) was also killed in action on 1 July 1916 at the Battle of the Somme and Thomas Robert (see entry **57 Private Thomas Robert Abraham**) died of wounds on 17 April 1917 in France.

William James Allen
Private 20531, 9th Battalion, Royal Irish Fusiliers

Born	19 June 1887, Portadown
Parents	Son of James and Susanna Allen of 40 Bridge Street, Portadown
Residence	Joseph Street
Enlisted	Portadown
Died	Killed in action 1 July 1916, France
Age	29
Buried	No Known Grave
Commemorated	Thiepval Memorial, Somme, France. Pier and face 15A. Portadown War Memorial (151)

Seagoe Parish Church War Memorial

William James' father James was employed as a tenter. He and his wife Susanna had eleven children William James born 1887, Susanna born 1888, Margaret Jane born 1890, Jemima born 1892, Mary Anne born 1894, Joseph born 1896, Arthur born 1899, Charlotte born 1901, Elizabeth born 1903, Georgina born 1904, and Florence born 1906.

William James came home from the United States to enlist in the 9th Battalion, Royal Irish Fusiliers. He served in 'B' Company. His mother received a letter from Sergeant James Sheppard

I am sorry to say that your son William James has passed the "border-line". I have made enquiries from the boys of his company, and they state that Wm. James was lying out in "No Man's Land" - dead. Of course one doesn't know whether to take this statement as correct or otherwise. However, seeing that you have not had any word of his being alive or a prisoner, I am afraid that there is little hope. When your son was alive I saw him almost daily, and he was always the same, a happy, bright, and cheery soldier. No doubt the news of his death has brought sadness to many of his chums....

Portadown News
2 September 1916

In 1919 his widow Sarah, and their three boys emigrated to Three Rivers, Massachusetts, USA. The Government granted Mrs Allen a free passage on account of her husband's sacrifice during the Great War. She remarried a Mr. Proctor.

Family grave of Private William James Allen. (Author's Collection)

Thomas Joyce Atkinson
Major, 9th Battalion, Royal Irish Fusiliers

Born	30 January 1878, Portadown
Parents	Son of Wolsey Richard and Alice Joyce Atkinson of Eden Villa, Bachelor's Walk, Portadown
Residence	Edenderry
Enlisted	Portadown
Died	Killed in action 1 July 1916, France
Age	38
Buried	Ancre British Cemetery, Beaumont Hamel, Somme, France. Grave VIII. A. 5.
Commemorated	Portadown War Memorial (91) Seagoe Parish Church War Memorial Family Memorial Seagoe Parish Church Royal Courts of Justice War Memorial, Belfast

Thomas Joyce was a member of the well-known Atkinson family of Eden Villa, Bachelor's Walk, Portadown. His father Wolsey Richard had been a bank manager with 40 years service who had become a gentleman farmer. He was instrumental in the formation of Portadown Agricultural Society and inaugurated Portadown Show. Wolsey Richard was treasurer of the Ulster Fruit Growers Association and an office bearer in Portadown Rowing Club.

Major Thomas Joyce Atkinson. (Seagoe Parish Magazine)

Wolsey Richard was closely associated with Seagoe Parish Church and had held a number of positions in the church such as churchwarden, treasurer and secretary of the Select Vestry and representative at the General Synod.

Wolsey Richard and his wife Alice Joyce had five children Wolsey Arthur born 20 December 1876 died 22 July 1899 as a result of an accident, Thomas Joyce Atkinson born 1878, Charlotte Elizabeth Buckby born 11 May 1880 died 15 April 1906, Alice Mary Isobel born 1883 and Georgina Eleanor born 1885.

Thomas graduated from Trinity College, Dublin in 1898 and subsequently took an MA. He was called to the bar and then became a partner in the firm of Messrs Carleton, Atkinson and Sloan, Solicitors, Church Place, Portadown.

He was a prominent member of Seagoe Parish Church and was churchwarden and also represented the Parish at the Diocesan Synod. He was on the committee of Portadown Unionist Club and a member of Portadown Rowing Club.

Thomas organised the signing of the Ulster Covenant in Seagoe Parish Church on Ulster Day 28 September 1912. He also played a prominent role in the Ulster Volunteer Force and was second in command to Major Stewart Blacker, commanding officer, of the Portadown Battalion, UVF.

On the outbreak of war he gained a commission in the 9th Battalion, Royal Irish Fusiliers rising to the rank of Major. He was Adjutant to Lieutenant-Colonel Stewart Blacker.

In the attack of the 36th (Ulster) Division on 1 July 1916 Major Thomas Joyce Atkinson was in command of 'B' Company, 9th Battalion, Royal Irish Fusiliers, which was positioned on the right centre of the battalion advance. Major Atkinson's company penetrated three German lines and a small body of men reached Beaucourt Station but were unable to hold the position due to a lack of support.

Grave of Thomas Joyce Atkinson. (Author's Collection)

Of the many brave men who have gone forth from this Parish at Duty's call to fight for King and Country none were more highly esteemed than Major Atkinson....On the formation of the Ulster Volunteer Force he threw himself heart and soul into that great movement against the Home Rule menace. His energy and diligence went far towards making the Portadown Battalion one of the most efficient in Ulster.

Seagoe Parish Magazine
September 1916

William Henry Best
Private 13977, 9th Battalion, Royal Irish Fusiliers

Born Armagh
Residence Clounagh
Enlisted Portadown
Died Killed in action 1 July 1916, France
Buried No Known Grave
Commemorated
Thiepval Memorial, Somme, France. Pier and face 15A.
Portadown War Memorial (278)
Tartaraghan Parish Church War Memorial

William was the husband of Maggie Best.

Private Harry Best, 9th R.I.F., Ormond St., is reported killed in action on the 1st inst. He was formerly in the employment of Portadown Co-operative Society and leaves a widow but no children.

Portadown News
21 July 1916

William Bowles
Private 13976, 9th Battalion, Royal Irish Fusiliers

Born Portadown
Parents Son of Ellen Bowles of 3 Montague Street, Portadown
Residence Montague Street
Enlisted Portadown
Died Killed in action 1 July 1916, France
Buried No Known Grave
Commemorated
Thiepval Memorial, Somme, France. Pier and face 15A.
Portadown War Memorial (171)
Armagh Road Presbyterian Church War Memorial

William's mother Ellen was employed as a washerwoman. She had children James, Ellen, Robert, Minnie, William and Henry.

William was a member of the Ulster Volunteer Force. His brother Henry saw active service during the Great War.

David John Burrows
Private 14028, 9th Battalion, Royal Irish Fusiliers

Born Loughgall
Parents Son of John and Helena Burrows of 90 Thomas Street, Portadown
Residence Thomas Street
Enlisted Portadown
Died Killed in action 1 July 1916, France
Age 22
Buried Ancre British Cemetery, Beaumont Hamel, Somme, France. Grave II. D. 2.
Commemorated Portadown War Memorial (219) Thomas Street Methodist Church War Memorial

David's mother Helena was from England. She had boys David John, William and Lynn. David was employed by Mr. James Walsh, High Street, Portadown before he enlisted. One of his brothers served at Salonika during the Great War.

John Campbell
Private 20024, 9th Battalion, Royal Irish Fusiliers

Born Portadown
Residence Foybeg
Enlisted Belfast
Died Killed in action 1 July 1916, France
Buried Ancre British Cemetery, Beaumont Hamel, Somme, France. Grave VIII. A. 10.
Commemorated Portadown War Memorial (303) St. Mark's Parish Church War Memorial

Private J. Campbell, West Street, is also reported killed.

Portadown News
16 September 1916

James Fulton
Private 14170, 9th Battalion, Royal Irish Fusiliers

Born Portadown
Parents Son of William John and Eliza Fulton of 22 Mary Street, Portadown
Residence Mary Street
Enlisted Portadown
Died Killed in action 1 July 1916, France
Age 19
Buried No Known Grave

Commemorated
Thiepval Memorial, Somme, France. Pier and face 15A.
Portadown War Memorial (160)
St. Mark's Parish Church War Memorial

James' father William John was employed as a weaver and his mother Eliza was a housekeeper. The couple had boys James and George.

James served in 'B' Company. His brother George also served during the Great War.

James Gordon
Private 14217, 9th Battalion, Royal Irish Fusiliers

Born	Portadown
Residence	Carrickblacker Road
Enlisted	Belfast
Died	Killed in action 1 July 1916, France
Buried	No Known Grave
Commemorated	Thiepval Memorial, Somme, France. Pier and face 15A. Portadown War Memorial (29) Seagoe Parish Church War Memorial

In Affectionate and Loving Remembrance

OF MY DEAR HUSBAND,

Private JAMES GORDON,

9th Battalion R.I.F.,

Who was Killed in Action at the Battle of the Somme, July 1st. 1916.

INTERRED SOMEWHERE IN FRANCE.

Memorial card for Private James Gordon. (Ross Raymond)

Thomas Street
Methodist Church
War Memorial

James was a member of the Ulster Volunteer Force.

Private Gordon served in 'C' Company and was designated as a Verey Light carrier for the attack on 1st July 1916.

Clounagh LOL 9 unfurled a banner on 8 July 1921 featuring portraits of Privates James Gordon and Ephraim Sherman (see **176 Private Ephraim Sherman**).

William Gordon
Sergeant 14221, 9th Battalion, Royal Irish Fusiliers

Born	Portadown
Parents	Son of Robert and Mary Gordon of 8 Cecil Street, Portadown
Residence	Castle Avenue
Enlisted	Portadown
Died	Killed in action 1 July 1916, France
Age	27
	Buried Hamel Military Cemetery, Beaumont Hamel, France. Grave I. B. 7.
Commemorated	Portadown War Memorial (44) Armagh Road Presbyterian Church War Memorial

William was the husband of Elizabeth Gordon and the couple had three children. The family resided at 19 Castle Avenue, Portadown, later moving to 5 Castle Avenue.

William was a member of the Ulster Volunteer Force and of Parkmount Temperance Flute Band.

Grave of Sergeant William Gordon. (Author's Collection)

Sergeant Gordon served in 'D' Company. Mrs Gordon received a letter from Lieutenant T. F. Gillin

I am writing to you to sympathise with you in your sad bereavement. We, who are left of D Co., greatly regret the loss you have sustained by the death of your husband. He was one of our best sergeants, and a most willing worker. He was severely wounded while leading his men but managed to get back to the trench, where I regret to say he died shortly afterwards.

Portadown News
29 July 1916

William's brother Lance-Corporal Robert Gordon was wounded in action on 8 November 1915 at the Battle of St. Eloi. He had a sister Phoebe and brother-in-law John Cooke who served during the Great War. His sister Jane married Henry Jones and was the sister-in-law of Edward Jones (see entry **217 Private Edward Jones**) who was killed in action at the Battle of Langemarck on 16 August 1916.

James Gregg
Private 17556, 9th Battalion, Royal Irish Fusiliers

Born Portadown
Residence John Street
Enlisted Belfast
Died Killed in action 1 July 1916, France
Buried No Known Grave
Commemorated
Thiepval Memorial, Somme, France. Pier and face 15A. Portadown War Memorial (144)

Private Gregg served in 'C' Company.

Joseph Hall
Private 17386, 9th Battalion, Royal Irish Fusiliers

Born St. Saviour's, Armagh
Residence Battlehill
Enlisted Portadown
Died Killed in action 1 July 1916, France
Buried No Known Grave
Commemorated
Thiepval Memorial, Somme, France. Pier and face 15A. Portadown War Memorial (266)

It is reported that the body of Private Joseph Hall who was recently reported missing has been recovered.

Portadown News
16 September 1916

William Harper
Private 14247, 9th Battalion, Royal Irish Fusiliers

Born	Glasgow
Parents	Son of William and Matilda Harper of 35 Montague Street, Portadown
Residence	Montague Street
Enlisted	Portadown
Died	Killed in action 1 July 1916, France
Age	28
Buried	No Known Grave
Commemorated	Thiepval Memorial, Somme, France. Pier and face 15A. Portadown War Memorial (173) St. Mark's Parish Church War Memorial

William's father William was a carpenter by trade and his mother Matilda was a cook. The couple had children William and Maggie.

William had three children Tillie, Maggie and William and resided at 35 Montague Street, Portadown. He was a member of the Ulster Volunteer Force.

On enlistment he served in 'C' Company. Private Harper's widow received a letter from Lieutenant R. S. Flood

I am writing to sympathise with you in the very serious loss you have sustained by the death of your husband on July 1st. I would have written before now but we were on the move and it was impossible. I know that words are very little consolation to you in your deep sorrow, but your husband died fighting for a great cause, which we are all engaged in defending. The services he, and many of his townsmen and comrades rendered shall never be forgotten.

Portadown News
5 August 1916

William's widow died on 1 July 1917 exactly one year after the death of her husband. His son William emigrated to Toronto, Canada.

John Hayes
Private 14303, 9th Battalion, Royal Irish Fusiliers

Born	Portadown
Parents	Son of Thomas Hayes of Sarah Street, Portadown
Residence	Sarah Street
Enlisted	Belfast
Died	Killed in action 1 July 1916, France
Age	37
Buried	Ancre British Cemetery, Beaumont Hamel, Somme, France. Grave VIII. A. 20.

Commemorated	Portadown War Memorial (212) St. Mark's Parish Church War Memorial

John's father Thomas was employed as a general labourer. He had children John, Minnie, Bella, Sarah, Alexander, Annie, Lillie and William. The family resided at Junction Row in 1901.

Grave of Private John Hayes. (Author's Collection)

John was the husband of Elizabeth Hayes and the couple had four children. The family resided at 12, 21 and later at 28 Sarah Street, Portadown. John was a sawyer by trade and was employed by Messrs T. A. Shillington & Son, Castle Street, Portadown.

Private Hayes served in 'B' Company.

John was one of three brothers killed during the Great War. William (see entry **213 Private William Hayes**) was killed in action on 12 October 1916 at the Battle of Le Transloy and Alexander (see entry **211 Private Alexander Hayes**) died on 31 July 1918 while serving in France.

Wesley Hayes
Private 18558, 9th Battalion, Royal Irish Fusiliers

Born	Portadown
Parents	Son of James and Martha J. Hayes of Clonroot
Residence	Clonroot
Enlisted	Newtownards
Died	Killed in action 1 July 1916, France
Buried	Ancre British Cemetery, Beaumont Hamel, Somme, France. Grave VIII. A. 14.

Commemorated
Portadown War Memorial (276)

Wesley's father James was employed as a labourer and his mother Martha was a housekeeper. The couple had children Mary, Martha, John, James and Wesley.

Wesley was a member of the Ulster Volunteer Force.

Grave of Private Wesley Hayes. (Author's Collection)

William George Henry
Lance-Corporal 14276, 9th Battalion, Royal Irish Fusiliers

Born	Portadown
Residence	Charles Street
Enlisted	Portadown
Died	Killed in action 1 July 1916, France
Buried	Ancre British Cemetery, Beaumont Hamel, Somme, France. Grave VIII. A. 11.
Commemorated	Portadown War Memorial (59) St. Mark's Parish Church War Memorial Drumcree Parish Church War Memorial

William was the husband of Martha Henry and the couple had four children. The family resided at 89 Charles Street, Portadown. William was a member of the Ulster Volunteer Force. His parents, brothers and sisters resided at 25 Mary Street, Portadown.

Lance-Corporal W. G. Henry, Corcrain, who was wounded at the battle of the Somme, is reported missing. Since July 1st every effort has been made to trace him but in vain, and

Grave of Lance-Corporal William George Henry. (Author's Collection)

his wife and children still hope that he may yet turn up.

Portadown News
9 September 1916

His brother Joseph served in the North Irish Horse during the Great War.

James Hewitt
Private 14309 9th Battalion, Royal Irish Fusiliers

Born	Portadown
Parents	Son of William John and Annie Jane Hewitt of Ballinteggart
Residence	Kilmoriarty
Enlisted	Belfast
Died	Killed in action 1 July 1916, France
Buried	No Known Grave
Commemorated	Thiepval Memorial, Somme, France. Pier and face 15A. Portadown War Memorial (306) St. Mark's Parish Church War Memorial

James father William John was a farmer and had children Alice, James, Thomas, George, Joseph, Sarah and Ann. James was the husband of Lucy Hewitt and the couple had four children. The family resided at 13 James Street, Portadown.

James' brother Thomas (see entry **256 Private Thomas Hewitt**) was also killed in action on 1 July 1916 at the Battle of the Somme.

James Hewitt
Lance-Corporal 16423,
9th Battalion,
Royal Irish Fusiliers

Born	Portadown
Parents	Son of Robert and Agnes Hewitt of Clounagh
Residence	Clounagh
Enlisted	Belfast
Died	Killed in action 1 July 1916, France
Age	18
Buried	No Known Grave
Commemorated	Thiepval Memorial, Somme, France. Pier and face 15A. Portadown War Memorial (279) St. Mark's Parish Church War Memorial

Lance-Corporal Hewitt served in 'B' Company.

Thomas Hewitt
Private 14315, 9th Battalion,
Royal Irish Fusiliers

Born	Portadown
Residence	Bridge Street
Enlisted	Belfast
Died	Killed in action 1 July 1916, France
Age	19
Buried	No Known Grave
Commemorated	Thiepval Memorial, Somme, France. Pier and face 15A. Portadown War Memorial (15) Drumcree Parish Church War Memorial

Thomas was a member of the Ulster Volunteer Force.

Thomas Hewitt
Private 22755, 9th Battalion,
Royal Irish Fusiliers

Born	Portadown
Parents	Son of William John and Annie Jane Hewitt of Ballinteggart
Residence	Ballinteggart
Enlisted	Belfast
Died	Killed in action 1 July 1916, France
Age	24
Buried	No Known Grave
Commemorated	Thiepval Memorial, Somme, France. Pier and face 15A. Portadown War Memorial (256)

Thomas' brother James (see entry **306 Private James Hewitt**) was also killed in action on 1 July 1916 at the Battle of the Somme.

Thomas Henry Holmes
Private 14250, 9th Battalion, Royal Irish Fusiliers

Born	13 April 1888, Portadown
Parents	Son of David and Sarah Jane Holmes of Killycomain
Residence	Killycomain
Enlisted	Portadown
Died	Killed in action 1 July 1916, France
Age	28
Buried	No Known Grave
Commemorated	Thiepval Memorial, Somme, France. Pier and face 15A. Portadown War Memorial (305) Seagoe Parish Church War Memorial

Thomas Henry's father David was employed as a land steward and later as a quarry foreman. He was the husband of Sarah Jane Holmes (aka Martha Jane). They had a large family some are listed in Seagoe Church Records and some are recorded on the family headstone.

The eldest son Wilson was born in 1885 and died 1909, Thomas Henry born 1888 and died 1916, Myrtle Sylvia born 1897, James born 1890 and died 1914 in South Africa, Miriam born 1892 and died 1915,

Family grave of Private Thomas Henry Holmes. (Author's Collection)

Norman Sydney born 1894 and died 1918. Other children were Margaret, Maria, Evelyn and Dorcas.

Thomas Henry was employed as a tenter before the outbreak of war. He was the husband of Frances Jane Hanna Holmes of 4 Marr Street, Govan. The couple had two children Wilson born 3 June 1911 and Thomas James born 23 April 1913. Both children were born in Portadown.

Thomas was a member of the Ulster Volunteer Force and after enlistment in the army served in 'B' Company.

His brother Norman Sydney (see entry **305 Driver Norman Sydney Holmes**) was killed in action on 31 March 1918 in France.

William Hull
Corporal 14268, 9th Battalion, Royal Irish Fusiliers

Born Portadown
Parents Son of William John and Sarah Hull of 7 Victoria Terrace, Portadown
Residence Garvaghy Road
Enlisted Portadown
Died Killed in action 1 July 1916, France
Age 25
Buried No Known Grave
Commemorated Thiepval Memorial, Somme, France. Pier and face 15A. Portadown War Memorial (107) St. Mark's Parish Church War Memorial

William's father William John was employed as a weaver and his mother Sarah was a linen yarn reeler. The couple had children Lily, May Jane, William, Sarah, George and David.

William was a member of the Bann Lily Lodge of the British Order of Free Gardeners and Parkmount Temperance Flute Band.

He had two brothers who served during the Great War. David and George (see entry **106 Rifleman George Hull**) who died on 4 July 1916 from wounds received at the Battle of the Somme.

Andrew Johnston
Private 14349, 9th Battalion, Royal Irish Fusiliers

Born Newtownards
Parents Son of Ann Johnston of 149 West Street, Portadown
Residence West Street
Enlisted Portadown
Died Killed in action 1 July 1916, France
Buried No Known Grave
Commemorated Thiepval Memorial, Somme, France. Pier and face 15A. Portadown War Memorial (233) St. Mark's Parish Church War Memorial

Andrew was a member of the Ulster Volunteer Force.

Charles Moore Johnston Captain, 9th Battalion, Royal Irish Fusiliers

Born	1886, Portadown
Parents	Son of Charles and Marian Johnston of Beechcote, Portadown
Residence	Carrickblacker Avenue
Enlisted	Portadown
Died	Killed in action 1 July 1916, France
Age	30
Buried	Mesnil Communal Cemetery Extension, Somme, France. Grave III. B. 17.
Commemorated	Portadown War Memorial (25) Lurgan College War Memorial St. Mark's Parish Church War Memorial

Charles Moore's father Charles was Chairman of Messrs Thompson, Kelly & Co. Ltd., linen manufacturers of Belfast. He was chairman of Portadown Unionist Club, and a member of North Armagh Unionist Association and the Ulster Unionist Council. Charles was a member of the Town Commissioners Board and the Urban Council from 1893 and Chairman of Portadown and Banbridge Joint Water Board from 1902. He served on the County Armagh Grand Jury from 1904 and became High Sheriff in 1905.

Charles and his wife Marian, who was born in England, had five children John Courtney, William, Annie, Marian Elizabeth and Charles Moore.

Charles Moore was educated at Lurgan College from 1897-1900 and afterwards at Campbell College, Belfast and the Royal School of Mines, London. This school, founded in 1851, specialised in geology and earth sciences.

Charles Moore was the husband of Muriel Florence Johnston. They had two children. He played a leading role in the formation of the Portadown Battalion of the Ulster Volunteer Force.

He was a member of Portadown Rowing Club, and captain of Portadown Rugby Club and like his father was a member of Portadown Unionist Club.

Charles Moore gained a commission in the 9th Battalion, Royal Irish Fusiliers and rose to the rank of Captain. Captain Johnston was in command of 'C' Company, which was positioned on the left of centre for the attack on 1 July.

Lieutenant-Colonel Blacker to his wife Eva:

4 July 1916
Poor C.(harles) J.(ohnston). We found him last night, at last, but he must have been killed almost at once. Oh! How I feel for his poor wife and mother.

Seagoe Parish Magazine
1923

James Joyce
Private 14355, 9th Battalion, Royal Irish Fusiliers

Born	Portadown
Parents	Son of William J. Joyce of Drumnakelly
Residence	West Street
Enlisted	Portadown
Died	Killed in action 1 July 1916, France
Age	18
Buried	Ancre British Cemetery, Beaumont Hamel, Somme, France. Grave IV. D. 17.
Commemorated	Portadown War Memorial (235) Armagh Road Presbyterian Church War Memorial

James was a member of the Ulster Volunteer Force. His father also served with the Royal Irish Fusiliers. He had a brother William.

Mr. James Joyce, West Street, Portadown, would be grateful for any information concerning the fate of his son Private James Joyce, who fought at the battle of the Somme with the R.I.F. and has since been posted as missing.

Portadown News
6 July 1918

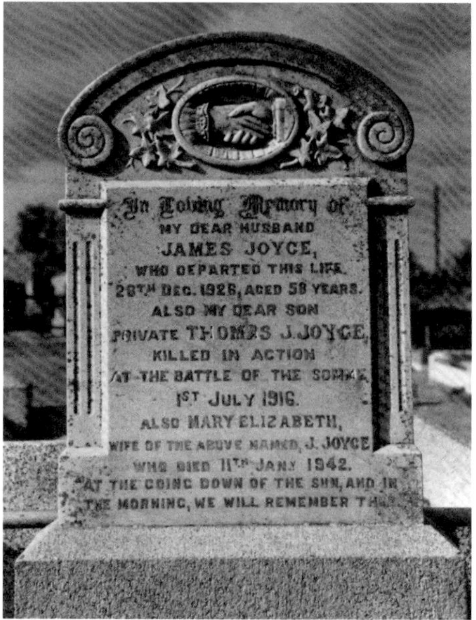

Family grave of Private James Joyce. (Author's Collection)

Thomas J. Joyce
Private 16114, 9th Battalion, Royal Irish Fusiliers

Born	Portadown
Parents	Son of James and Mary Elizabeth Joyce of Portadown
Residence	Portmore Street
Enlisted	Monaghan

Died Killed in action 1 July 1916, France
Buried No Known Grave
Commemorated Thiepval Memorial, Somme, France. Pier and face 15A. Portadown War Memorial (205)

Private Thomas Joyce, Portmore Street, missing.

Portadown News
15 July 1916

Charles Kelly
Private 18398, 9th Battalion, Royal Irish Fusiliers

Born Dobbin
Parents Son of John and Alice Kelly of Battlehill
Residence Battlehill
Enlisted Portadown
Died Killed in action 1 July 1916, France
Age 27
Buried Hamel British Cemetery, Beaumont Hamel, Somme, France. Grave II. C. 33.
Commemorated Portadown War Memorial (267)

Private Kelly served in 'B' Company.

The body of Private Charles Kelly, Battlehill, Portadown has been recovered.

Portadown News
9 September 1916

He had brothers John and Joseph and a sister Annie.

Grave of Private Charles Kelly. (Author's Collection)

John Lyttle
Private 19948, 9th Battalion, Royal Irish Fusiliers

Born Portadown
Parents Son of William and Mary E. Lyttle of Church Street, Tandragee
Residence Ballyworkan

Enlisted	Portadown
Died	Killed in action 1 July 1916, France
Age	21
Buried	Ancre British Cemetery, Beaumont Hamel, Somme, France. Grave VIII. A. 88.
Commemorated	Portadown War Memorial (261) Armagh Road Presbyterian Church War Memorial St. Mark's Parish Church War Memorial

A soldier at the front in a letter to a Portadown friend states that Private John Lyttle, R.I.F., Ballyworkan, who has been missing since the 1st July, was killed on that date.

Portadown News
21 October 1916

James Magee
Private 14460, 9th Battalion, Royal Irish Fusiliers

Born	Portadown
Parents	Son of William John and Elizabeth Magee of 6 Henry Street, Portadown
Residence	Kilmoriarty
Enlisted	Portadown
Died	Killed in action 1 July 1916, France
Age	27
Buried	No Known Grave
Commemorated	Thiepval Memorial, Somme, France. Pier and face 15A. Portadown War Memorial (307) St. Mark's Parish Church War Memorial

James' father William John died on 22 October 1916 and was buried in Drumcree Church of Ireland Churchyard, Portadown. James was the husband of Emily Magee (nee Whalley). He was a member of the Ulster Volunteer Force and Kilmoriarty LOL 31.

James brother-in-law Thomas Francis Whalley (see entry **308 Lance-Corporal Thomas Francis Whalley**) served with the Royal Irish Fusiliers during the Great War and died on 24 February 1920.

Robert Magee
Sergeant 14466, 9th Battalion, Royal Irish Fusiliers

Born	Portadown
Residence	Coronation Street
Enlisted	Portadown
Died	Killed in action 1 July 1916, France
Age	38

Buried Ancre British Cemetery, Beaumont Hamel, Somme, France. Grave VIII. A. 36.
Commemorated Portadown War Memorial (69)

Alexander McCabe
Private 14573, 9th Battalion, Royal Irish Fusiliers

Born 5 April 1896, Portadown
Parents Son of Joseph and Dinah McCabe of Seagoe
Residence Seagoe
Enlisted Portadown
Died Killed in action 1 July 1916, France
Age 20
Buried No Known Grave
Commemorated Thiepval Memorial, Somme, France. Pier and face 15A. Portadown War Memorial (320) Seagoe Parish Church War Memorial

Alexander's father Joseph was caretaker of Seagoe Parish Church Churchyard from 1905 until his death in 1924. In 1887 he married Dinah Brown (aka Diana), daughter of Joseph Brown, a weaver from Ballinacor.

They had nine children Samuel born 1888, Thomas born 1890, Joseph born 1892, James born 1894, Alexander born 1896, David William, born 1898, George born 1900 and who died in 1905, Albert Edward born 1904 and who died in 1907, and an unnamed son who died in infancy.

Alexander was a member of the Ulster Volunteer Force.

Private McCabe took part with the R.I.F. in the battle of the Somme, where he fell for his country's honour. He has two more brothers serving, one in France and the other in the Balkans.

Portadown News
2 September 1916

His brother Thomas saw service as a Sergeant in the Army Service Corps during the Great War.

Robert Taylor Montgomery
Second-Lieutenant, 9th Battalion, Royal Irish Fusiliers

Parents Son of Thomas James and Sarah Montgomery of 9 High Street, Portadown
Residence High Street
Died Killed in action 1 July 1916, France

Buried No Known Grave
Commemorated
Thiepval Memorial, Somme, France. Pier and face 15A.
Portadown War Memorial (127)
Seagoe Parish Church War Memorial

Thomas James and Sarah Montgomery had five daughters Marian, Nora Kathleen, Nellie, Gertie and Louisa who was born 9 January 1895 and three sons Robert, Charles who was born 9 February 1892 and John who died on 17 February 1906 aged 23 years.

He was the proprietor of T. J. Montgomery, Grocers, Provision and Tea Merchants. He was an expert in tea blending and won many prizes and diplomas in competitions. His youngest son Charles took over the running of the family business.

Thomas James was a member of Seagoe Parish Church Select Vestry and had also been churchwarden.

Robert Taylor was a member of Seagoe Church Lads' Brigade and was a diligent attender at Sunday school and later went on to teach at the morning and afternoon classes.

He was an instructor in ambulance field drill for the members of the Medical Corps of the Portadown Battalion of the Ulster Volunteer Force. Shortly before enlisting Robert was presented with a compact dressing case by Dr. Dougan at a ceremony held on 1 October 1914 in the Anchor Café, Edenderry.

Second-Lieutenant Robert Taylor Montgomery. (Seagoe Parish Magazine)

He enlisted in the 9th Battalion, Royal Irish Fusiliers as a Private but was quickly promoted to Sergeant and just before the 36th (Ulster) Division set off for France he gained his commission.

An officer wrote to Robert's brother Charles

As he was always, he died - a brave man. He was hit in the foot in the attack, and got into a shell hole. Soon afterwards a wounded man was crying out for water, and your brother got out with a water bottle to give him some. He was hit in the head and killed at once. We miss him greatly in the company, as an officer, and as a friend....

Portadown Express
4 August 1916

Robert's mother Sarah died on 19 April 1917.

Joseph Parks
Private 14599, 9th Battalion, Royal Irish Fusiliers

Born: Portadown
Parents: Son of David and Hannah Parks of Clounagh Cottages, Portadown
Residence: Clounagh
Enlisted: Portadown
Died: Killed in action 1 July 1916, France
Age: 23
Buried: Ancre British Cemetery, Beaumont Hamel, Somme, France. Grave VIII. A. 90/93.
Commemorated: Portadown War Memorial (282)
St. Mark's Parish Church War Memorial
Seagoe Parish Church War Memorial

Joseph was a member of the Ulster Volunteer Force. He was a sprinter and on one occasion won the Portadown News challenge cup for flat racing.

Private Parks served in 'B' Company.

Mystery still surrounds the fate of Private Joseph Parkes, (sic) Clounagh. He has been reported missing, and a notification from the War Office led his mother to believe that he was a prisoner, but the words 'prisoner of war' were partly obliterated. His anxious mother still awaits definite news.

Portadown News
2 September 1916

William Patterson
Private 18610, 9th Battalion, Royal Irish Fusiliers

Born: Hillsborough
Residence: Park Road
Enlisted: Belfast
Died: Killed in action 1 July 1916, France
Buried: No Known Grave
Commemorated: Thiepval Memorial, Somme, France. Pier and face 15A.

Portadown War Memorial (198)
St. Mark's Parish Church War Memorial

William was a member of Parkmount Temperance Flute Band.

His mother resided at 13 Water Street, Portadown and his sister and brother-in-law S. and E. Wright resided at 20 Park Road, Portadown.

Mrs Patterson, Water Street, fears that the worst has happened to her son, William. He has not been heard of since July 1st, and a soldier serving in another regiment has sent home some documents which he says he found on Private Patterson, who was lying dead on the field. He was attached to the 9th Battalion, and before enlisting was a member of Corcrain flute band (sic).

Portadown News
26 August 1916

George Patton
Private 14618, 9th Battalion, Royal Irish Fusiliers

Born Portadown
Parents Son of George and Eliza Patton of Portadown
Residence West Street
Enlisted Belfast
Died Killed in action 1 July 1916, France
Age 42
Buried No Known Grave
Commemorated
Thiepval Memorial, Somme, France. Pier and face 15A.
Portadown War Memorial (241)
St. Mark's Parish Church War Memorial

George was the husband of Eliza Jane Patton and the couple had a son and daughter. The family resided at 121 West Street, Portadown.

George was a member of the Bann Lily Lodge of the British Order of Ancient Free Gardeners.

William Henry Pentland
Private 17842, 9th Battalion, Royal Irish Fusiliers

Born Aldershot
Residence Mary Street
Enlisted Lurgan
Died Killed in action 1 July 1916, France
Buried Ancre British Cemetery, Beaumont Hamel, Somme, France. Grave VIII. A. 7.
Commemorated
Portadown War Memorial (161)

St. Mark's Parish Church War Memorial

William was the husband of Mary Anne Pentland.

Private Pentland served in 'C' Company and was designated as a Lewis Gun ammunition carrier for the attack on 1st July 1916. His widow received a letter from a comrade of her son

Words fail to express how sorry I am at the loss of William. He was like a father to us out here, and the good advice he gave us was the means of keeping a lot of us out of danger. There was not a braver soldier in the ranks, and he was loved by all his comrades. We who are left of his platoon tender you our deepest sympathy, and pray that God may comfort you in your trouble.

Portadown News
26 August 1916

John Phillips
Private 18246, 9th Battalion, Royal Irish Fusiliers

Born	Portadown
Residence	Park Road
Enlisted	Belfast
Died	Killed in action 1 July 1916, France
Buried	No Known Grave
Commemorated	Thiepval Memorial, Somme, France. Pier and face 15A. Portadown War Memorial (199) St. Mark's Parish Church War Memorial

John was employed as a hairdresser before the outbreak of war.

Private Phillips served in 'C' Company.

Since July 1st no definite news has been heard of Private John Phillips. It was said that he was wounded and may be a prisoner, but his mother who resides in Park Road, has received no communication from him.

Portadown News
26 August 1916

William Robb
Corporal 14626, 9th Battalion, Royal Irish Fusiliers

Born	Portadown
Parents	Son of Seth and Elizabeth Robb of 69 Garvaghy Road, Portadown
Residence	Garvaghy Road
Enlisted	Portadown
Died	Killed in action 1 July 1916, France
Buried	Hamel Military Cemetery, Beaumont Hamel, France. Grave I. B. 7.

Commemorated
Portadown War Memorial (110)
Thomas Street Methodist Church War Memorial

William's father Seth was a laundry house proprietor. His mother Elizabeth was born in County Down. The couple had children Lily, May, William and Cecil. In 1901 William was learning the trade of carpentry. William was a member of the Ulster Volunteer Force. He took an interest in athletics and was a member of Portadown Rowing Club as well as Portadown Football Club.

Grave of Corporal William Robb. (Author's Collection)

Corporal Robb served in 'C' Company.

Andrew Rowan
Private 14655, 9th Battalion, Royal Irish Fusiliers

Born	Loughgilly
Parents	Son of John and Margaret Rowan of 29 Coronation Street, Portadown
Residence	Coronation Street
Enlisted	Belfast
Died	Killed in action 1 July 1916, France
Age	35
Buried	Ancre British Cemetery, Beaumont Hamel, Somme, France. Grave VIII. A. 8.

Commemorated
Portadown War Memorial (73)
Armagh Road Presbyterian Church War Memorial
St. Mark's Parish Church War Memorial

Andrew was the husband of Hannah J. Rowan and they resided at 14 Coronation Street, Portadown. They had one son, D. J. Rowan.

Private Rowan served in 'B' Company.

Thomas J. Russell
Lance-Corporal 14630, 9th Battalion, Royal Irish Fusiliers

Born	Portadown
Parents	Son of Robert Russell of 68 Park Road, Portadown
Residence	Park Road
Enlisted	Portadown
Died	Killed in action 1 July 1916, France
Buried	No Known Grave
Commemorated	Thiepval Memorial, Somme, France. Pier and face 15A. Portadown War Memorial (200) Thomas Street Methodist Church War Memorial

Thomas' father Robert was originally from the Drumgor area and was employed as a power loom operative by Messrs. Spence Bryson and Co. Ltd.

Thomas was the husband of Sarah Jane Russell and they resided at 140 Park Road, Portadown. He was a member of the Ulster Volunteer Force.

Thomas had four brothers Joseph, Robert who resided in Belfast, John who emigrated to Niagara Falls, USA and William George. He also had a sister Jennie who resided in Hamiliton, Ontario, Canada.

His brother William George served during the Great War with the Irish Guards and was awarded the Distinguished Conduct Medal for bravery in the field. Another of Thomas' brothers served in the 9th Battalion, Royal Irish Fusiliers and was wounded on 1 July 1916 at the Battle of the Somme.

Joseph Stothers
Private 14683, 9th Battalion, Royal Irish Fusiliers

Born	Portadown
Parents	Son of Ellen Stothers of 12 Bright Street, Portadown
Residence	Bright Street
Enlisted	Belfast
Died	Killed in action 1 July 1916, France
Buried	No Known Grave
Commemorated	Thiepval Memorial, Somme, France. Pier and face 15A. Portadown War Memorial (21) Seagoe Parish Church War Memorial

Joseph was a member of the Ulster Volunteer Force.

The four Stothers brothers Maxwell, Jackson, Joseph and William James all joined the Royal Irish Fusiliers on the outbreak of

war. Maxwell (see entry **22 Private Maxwell Stothers**) died on as a result on an accident on 7 October 1916. Jackson (see entry **20 Private Jackson Stothers**) died on 7 January 1917 in Dublin.

William James was wounded on 1 July at the Battle of the Somme whilst serving in the 9th Battalion, Royal Irish Fusiliers. He was the only brother to survive the war.

Their mother Ellen died on 17 August 1933.

Mrs Stothers lost three sons in the Great War. (Seagoe Parish Magazine)

An old and esteemed resident of Portadown passed away on Thursday last, 17th inst., in the person of Mrs Ellen Stothers, 12 Bright Street.

Mrs. Stothers, who was over eighty years of age, possessed a kindly and sympathetic disposition, and won the esteem and regard of all with whom she came into contact. She had a retentive memory, and even in advanced years displayed a keen interest in passing events. The eventide of her life was somewhat clouded by sorrow at the loss of her three sons - Maxwell, Joseph and Jackson Stothers, who made the supreme sacrifice in the Great War, serving with the 9th Royal Irish Fusiliers. A surviving son, Wm. James Stothers, was also a member of the 9th Royal Irish Fusiliers, and was wounded in the Battle of the Somme. Mrs. Stothers, who was predeceased some eight years ago by her husband, had not recently enjoyed good health, and her passing has evoked sincere sympathy.

Portadown News
26 August 1933

Moses Teggart
Private 14712, 9th Battalion, Royal Irish Fusiliers

Born	Portadown
Parents	Son of Annie Teggart of Derrycorr, Annaghmore
Residence	Union Street
Enlisted	Portadown
Died	Killed in action 1 July 1916, France
Age	19
Buried	No Known Grave

Commemorated
Thiepval Memorial, Somme, France. Pier and face 15A.
Portadown War Memorial (227)
St. Mark's Parish Church War Memorial
Thomas Street Methodist Church War Memorial

Moses was a member of the Ulster Volunteer Force.

It is reported that Private Moses Taggart (sic), 10 Henry Street, died on the battle-field from heart failure, brought on by the excitement of the charge.

The family resided at 10 Henry Street, Portadown. He had a sister Rachel and brother-in-law William Stevenson who served during the Great War.

Thiepval Memorial.

Robert Totten
Private 17554, 9th Battalion, Royal Irish Fusiliers

Born Portadown
Residence Henry Street
Enlisted Belfast
Died Killed in action 1 July 1916, France
Buried Ancre British Cemetery, Beaumont Hamel, Somme, France. Grave VIII. A. 4.
Commemorated Portadown War Memorial (125) St. Mark's Parish Church War Memorial

Private Robert Totten, Sarah Street, missing, is now announced killed.

Portadown News
11 September 1916

Thomas George Troughton
Private 14196, 9th Battalion, Royal Irish Fusiliers

Born Richhill
Parents Son of William and Annie Troughton of Mulladry, Richhill
Residence Mulladry
Enlisted Armagh
Died Killed in action 1 July 1916, France
Age 22
Buried No Known Grave
Commemorated Thiepval Memorial, Somme, France. Pier and face 15A. Portadown War Memorial (316) Richhill War Memorial LOL 371 War Memorial, Drumnahuncheon Orange Hall

Thomas' father William was employed as an agricultural labourer and his mother Annie was a linen weaver. The couple had children Frank, Thomas George and John. Thomas was a member of Drumnahuncheon LOL 371.

John Vallely
Private 16428, 9th Battalion, Royal Irish Fusiliers

Born Shankill, Belfast
Residence John Street
Enlisted Portadown
Died Killed in action 1 July 1916, France
Buried No Known Grave
Commemorated Thiepval Memorial, Somme, France. Pier and face 15A. Portadown War Memorial (149)

St. Mark's Parish
Church War
Memorial

John was a member of the Ulster Volunteer Force.

Mrs. Vallely, John Street, has received unofficial word that her son L. Vallely (sic) R.I.F., has been killed in action.

Portadown Express
11 August 1916

William James Wilson
Corporal 14767, 9th Battalion, Royal Irish Fusiliers

Born — Portadown
Parents — Son of John and Louisa Wilson of Richhill
Residence — Baltylum
Enlisted — Belfast
Died — Killed in action 1 July 1916, France
Age — 20
Buried — No Known Grave
Commemorated — Thiepval Memorial, Somme, France. Pier and face 15A. Portadown War Memorial (264)

Frederick James Woods
Private 14796, 9th Battalion, Royal Irish Fusiliers

Born — Portadown
Parents — Son of John and Christina Woods of Derrybroughas
Residence — Derrybroughas
Enlisted — Portadown
Died — Killed in action 1 July 1916, France
Age — 24
Buried — No Known Grave
Commemorated — Thiepval Memorial, Somme, France. Pier and face 15A. Portadown War Memorial (287) Drumcree Parish Church War Memorial

Frederick's father John was a farmer and had children Loftus, Stewart, Mary, John, Anne and Frederick James.

Frederick was employed as a clerk at the Parkside weaving factory. He was a member of the Ulster Volunteer Force.

News is anxiously awaited by Mrs. Woods, Derrybroughas House, Portadown, regarding the fate of her son, Lance-Corporal (sic) Fred J. Woods (14796) D Company Armagh Volunteers, who is reported missing.

Portadown News
19 August 1916

William Samuel Wylie
Private 18104, 9th Battalion, Royal Irish Fusiliers

Born — Portadown
Residence — Derrymacfall

Enlisted	Portadown
Died	Killed in action 1 July 1916, Battle of the Somme, France
Buried	No Known Grave
Commemorated	Thiepval Memorial, Somme, France. Pier and face 15A. Portadown War Memorial (294) Drumcree Parish Church War Memorial

Private Wylie served in 'C' Company and was designated as a member of the Bombing Team for the attack on 1st July 1916.

William Hughes
Sergeant 14321, 9th Battalion, Royal Irish Fusiliers

Born	Portadown
Parents	Son of William Hughes of Mandeville Street, Portadown
Residence	Mandeville Street
Enlisted	Belfast
Died	Died of wounds 11 July 1916, France
Buried	Boulogne Eastern Cemetery, Pas de Calais, France. Grave VIII. D. 104.
Commemorated	Portadown War Memorial (155) St. Mark's Parish Church War Memorial

Grave of Sergeant William Hughes.

Sergeant Hughes died of wounds received at the Battle of the Somme.

Lieutenant - Colonel Stewart Blacker to his wife Eva

17 July 1916
I'm so grieved for Willie Hughes. He was one of the best in the Battalion. He had written to the S. Maj. He was all right. Cheery to the end, a gallant fellow.

Seagoe Parish Magazine
1923

He had a brother Thomas and sister-in-law Sadie who resided at 16 Ridgeway Street, Stranmillis, Belfast.

Thomas Kilpatrick
Private 14379, 9th Battalion, Royal Irish Fusiliers

Born	Portadown
Parents	Son of William John Kilpatrick of Mountpleasant, Seagoe
Residence	Seagoe
Enlisted	Portadown
Died	Died of wounds 11 July 1916, France
Age	20
Buried	Abbeville Communal Cemetery, Somme, France. Grave V. E. 13.
Commemorated	Portadown War Memorial (319)

Thomas was a member of the Ulster Volunteer Force.

For seven days prior to the start of the Battle of the Somme the British artillery shelled the German lines and the enemy returned fire on a number of occasions. On 24 June two men were killed and 11 wounded. On 25 June there were three more casualties and on 26 June the 9th Battalion suffered three men killed and 17 wounded. Private Kilpatrick was one of these casualties being wounded 25-27 June and succumbing to his injuries on 11 July at No. 2 Stationary Hospital.

His mother received many condolence letters, including six from hospital chaplains and many from nurses who tended her son. She also received letters from Major Thomas J. Atkinson, 'B' Company Commander, who was killed in action on 1 July and Lieutenant Geoffrey St. George Shillington Cather who was awarded a posthumous Victoria Cross.

One letter was from the Reverend E. Milner-White

Dear Madam By now you will have heard of your son's death in this hospital. I was often with him and we had prayers together. He remembered in them all he loved at home. After he quietly and painlessly lost consciousness I commended a gallant spirit into the hands of God.

Seagoe Parish Magazine
1916

Thomas had two brothers who also served during the Great War.

108th Company, Machine Gun Corps

In October 1915 the Machine Gun Corps was formed at Brigade level with a Machine Gun Company comprising 16 machine guns and crews. With the advent of this new unit servicemen ceased to belong to their parent regiment and became members of the Machine Gun Corps.

William John Brown
Sergeant-Major 17775, 108th Company, Machine Gun Corps

Born	Seagoe
Residence	Jervis Street
Enlisted	Belfast
Died	Killed in action 1 July 1916, France
Buried	No Known Grave
Commemorated	Thiepval Memorial, Somme, France. Pier and face 15A & 15B. Portadown War Memorial (132) First Presbyterian Church War Memorial, Edenderry

William was the husband of Maggie Brown and the couple had three children Orby, Maud and Bertha. The family resided at 10 Jervis Street, Portadown.

William previously served in the Royal Irish Fusiliers with the serial number 9/15859. He visited home on leave in March 1916.

Mrs Brown received a letter from Second-Lieutenant W. Wesley Ashcroft, Machine Gun Officer

Your husband died a noble death, and although this is but small consolation to you I fear, I am happy to be able to tell you that he was held in the very highest respect by all ranks in this company. Always at his duty and always ready to help wherever he could, it will be difficult to fill his place, and all those left behind feel we have lost a ready, worthy friend and soldier.

He was awaiting orders with a reserve gun in his dugout when a German shell made a direct hit. I fear all were killed, at any rate your husband was recovered, but I regret to say only lived about five minutes. This was on the night of the day the attack was launched.

Portadown News
5 August 1916

William had a sister Annie and brother-in-law J. J. Dougan who resided in Lisburn.

John Courtney
Private 17783,
108th Company,
Machine Gun Corps

Born	Armagh
Parents	Son of William and Mary Jane Courtney
Residence	Mulladry
Enlisted	Armagh
Died	Killed in action 1 July 1916, France
Age	32
Buried	No Known Grave
Commemorated	Thiepval Memorial, Somme, France. Pier and face 5C &12C. Portadown War Memorial (315) LOL 371 War Memorial, Drumnahuncheon Orange Hall

John was the husband of Annie Courtney. He was a member of Drumnahuncheon LOL 371.

John had previously served in the Royal Irish Fusiliers with the serial number 14123.

Private John Courtney, R.I.F. Richhill, has been dangerously wounded.

Portadown News
22 July 1916

David Orr
Corporal 17778,
108th Company,
Machine Gun Corps

Born	Portadown
Parents	Son of Mary Orr of 15 Bridge Street, Portadown
Residence	Bridge Street
Enlisted	Portadown
Died	Killed in action 1 July 1916, France
Age	22
Buried	No Known Grave
Commemorated	Thiepval Memorial, Somme, France. Pier and face 5AC & 12C. Portadown War Memorial (17) First Presbyterian Church War Memorial, Edenderry

David was employed as an apprentice mechanic in Messrs Hamilton Robbs' factory before the outbreak of war. He was a member of the Ulster Volunteer Force.

David had previously served in the Royal Irish Fusiliers with the serial number 14592. His mother received a letter from Gunner Joseph Murphy

...David had been with us since the earlier part of the war, when we were stationed in England. Amongst a splendid lot of fellows, he was one of the best. He was a real soldier in every sense, and I don't think he really knew what fear was. It was only a week from today when we got the order to charge the German trenches, and you can take it from me that he did his part in it. He was wounded in the arm at first, but his bravery was so great he could not stop at that, and on his way up with the gun he got hit, the fatal shot just catching him on the stomach. I can assure you he died without any pain as from the time he got it he only lasted about two minutes. He was brought in at night and buried in a soldier's graveyard just behind the firing line along with a few more of his comrades from Portadown.

Portadown News
29 July 1916

William James Rountree
Private 18697, 108th Company, Machine Gun Corps

Parents	Son of Thomas and Annie Rountree of Clonroot
Residence	Clonroot
Enlisted	Belfast
Died	Killed in action 1 July 1916, France
Age	24
Buried	Connaught Cemetery, Somme, France. Grave II. B. 5.
Commemorated	Portadown War Memorial (277)

James' father Thomas and mother Annie were both employed as linen weavers. The couple had children William James, Thomas, Anna Jane and Mary Frances.

James had previously served in the Royal Inniskilling Fusiliers with the serial number 14925.

Private J. Rowantree (sic), Portadown, who was previously reported missing, is now officially announced killed. He was attached to a machine gun corps.

Portadown News
14 April 1917

Grave of Private William James Rountree.

Thomas also served during the Great War and it is believed that he was stationed in Dublin during the Easter Rising of 1916.

2nd Battalion, Royal Inniskilling Fusiliers

The 2nd Battalion formed part of the 96th Infantry Brigade of the 32nd Division. The division was positioned on the right flank of the 36th (Ulster) Division. The 2nd Battalion occupied positions in Caterpillar Wood in front of the village of Thiepval.

Joseph Doak
Sergeant 6935, 2nd Battalion, Royal Inniskilling Fusiliers

Born	Lurgan
Parents	Son of John and Susan Doak
Residence	Mourneview Street
Enlisted	Portadown
Died	Died of wounds 15 July 1916, France
Age	32
Buried	Warloy-Baillon Cemetery Extension, Somme, France. Grave III. E. 25.
Commemorated	Portadown War Memorial (182) St.. Mark's Parish Church War Memorial

Joseph was the husband of Alice Jane Doak (nee Patton) and the couple had six children. The family resided at 25 Mourneview Street, Portadown. His mother resided at 14 Castle Avenue, Portadown.

He was a member of Prince of Wales LOL 56 and Parkmount Temperance Flute Band. A footballer he played for the Commercials.

Joseph had served throughout the South African War 1899-1902 and on account of his military experience was appointed as an instructor in the Ulster Volunteer Force.

Sergeant Doak was in the Special Reserve and was called up on the outbreak of war. When in action on 21 September 1914 he, together with nine other men, helped capture 42 German prisoners. His unit lost all its officers during the engagement. On another occasion he had a fortunate escape when a German sniper's bullet struck his cap and was deflected away from his head by the wire in the rim.

In February 1915 Sergeant Doak was evacuated to No. 13 Southern Hospital in France suffering from wounds to the legs, boils and severe strain. He was later transferred to a hospital in England.

His wife received a letter from Sergeant Hugh Lavery

I regret having to inform you of the death of your husband 6935 Sergeant J. Doak, who was wounded on the night of the 13th July 1916. He was taken to hospital at once, but when we came out of the trenches I was informed that he was dead. I went up to see, and found it was too true. He was wounded in two places - arm and leg... I may tell you that he died a soldier's death, and we all mourn his loss. We all share the sorrow for you and your family. He was one of the finest fighting soldiers we had, and fought with his men - taking the lead of his Platoon when he got wounded.

Portadown Express
15 December 1916

Grave of Sergeant J. Doak

Sergeant Doak was taken out of the line by Private B. Scanlon and evacuated to hospital where he died on 15 July 1916.

11th Battalion, Royal Inniskilling Fusiliers

The 11th Battalion was formed from the Donegal and Fermanagh Volunteers of the Ulster Volunteer Force. It formed part of the 109th Infantry Brigade of the 36th (Ulster) Division. Their objective was a well-defended area known as the 'Crucifix'.

The battalion was caught in the flank by heavy machine gun fire and suffered heavy casualties amounting to 12 officers and 577 other ranks killed, wounded or missing.

Thomas Green
Private 14871, 11th Battalion, Royal Inniskilling Fusiliers

Born	Glasgow
Parents	Son of William John and Sarah Jane Green
Residence	Ormond Street
Enlisted	Glasgow, Scotland
Died	Killed in action 1 July 1916, France
Age	34
Buried	No Known Grave

Commemorated
Thiepval Memorial, Somme, France. Pier and face 4D & 5B.
Portadown War Memorial (195)
St. Mark's Parish Church War Memorial

Thomas was the husband of Margaret Green and the couple resided for a time in Glasgow. They had four children. One daughter named Annie, died on 9 May 1916 and was interred in Lambhill Cemetery, Glasgow. Their Portadown address was 21 Ormond Street.

8th Battalion, Royal Irish Rifles

The 8th Battalion was formed from the East Belfast Volunteers of the Ulster Volunteer Force. It formed part of the 107th Infantry Brigade of the 36th (Ulster) Division.

The 107th Brigade was held in reserve ready to support the 108th and 109th Brigades in their advance towards the Schwaben Redoubt. By 1100am the battalion had broken through and had advanced on the 'Hansa Line' north of Stuff Redoubt.

Robert Hutchinson
Rifleman 1031, 8th Battalion, Royal Irish Rifles

Born — Magherafelt
Residence — South Street
Enlisted — Belfast
Died — Killed in action 2 July 1916, France
Buried — No Known Grave
Commemorated
Thiepval Memorial, Somme, France. Pier and face 15A & 15B.
Portadown War Memorial (216)
Thomas Street Methodist Church War Memorial

Mystery surrounds the fate of (1031) Rifleman Robert Hutchinson, who has been missing since July 2nd. Any information concerning him would be thankfully received by his anxious wife, Mrs. Hutchinson, 21 South Street, Portadown.

Portadown News
16 September 1916

David McKinley
Rifleman 317, 8th Battalion, Royal Irish Rifles

Born — Portadown
Residence — Carleton Street
Enlisted — Belfast
Died — Killed in action 2 July 1916, France

Buried No Known Grave
Commemorated
Thiepval Memorial, Somme, France. Pier and face 15A & 15B. Portadown War Memorial (41)

David was married and his wife was employed as manageress of the Co-operative Society drapery establishment in Mandeville Street, Portadown.

10th Battalion, Royal Irish Rifles

The 10th Battalion, commanded by Lieutenant-Colonel H. C. Bernard, was formed from the South Belfast Volunteers of the Ulster Volunteer Force. It formed part of the 107th Infantry Brigade of the 36th (Ulster) Division.

The 107th Brigade was held in reserve ready to support the 108th and 109th Brigades in their advance on the Schwaben Redoubt.

William Osmond Green Second-Lieutenant, 10th Battalion, Royal Irish Rifles

Parents Son of William John and Elsbeth Green of Bridge Street, Portadown
Residence Bridge Street
Died Killed in action 1 July 1916, France
Age 20
Buried No Known Grave
Commemorated
Thiepval Memorial, Somme, France. Pier and face 15A & 15B Portadown War Memorial (13) St. Mark's Parish Church War Memorial

William Osmond's father William John was from County Down and was employed as a commercial traveller. His mother Elspeth was from County Cork. The couple had children William Osmond and Reginald Stuart.

William Osmond was educated at Wesley College, Dublin. He was a keen athlete, swimmer and cricketer and also played left wing on the Wesley rugby team. William represented his school in rowing and was in the winning team in the Schools' Rowing Cup at the 1912 Drogheda Regatta. He later became a member of Portadown Rowing Club.

William entered Trinity College to continue his studies with a view to taking holy orders in the Church of Ireland. At Trinity he joined the Officers Training Corps and gained a

commission in February 1915. He was attached to the 17th Battalion, Royal Irish Rifles and was sent to the Officers School of Instruction at Queen's University, Belfast for six weeks training.

William was appointed as Second-Lieutenant in the 10th Battalion, Royal Irish Rifles and undertook three months further training at Ballykinlar before being posted to England and then France. Three days after arriving in France he was in the trenches and remained in and out of the front line until March 1916. At the end of April he was granted a few days home leave.

On 1 July 1916 Second-Lieutenant Green, together with his platoon, was entrusted with the very important task of cutting the wire, which would have hindered the battalion's advance. Captain Fullerton, RAMC wrote to William's father

He very gallantly led his men through an awful fire. He did what you should feel proud of, and was a credit to Ulster and his parents.

Portadown News
15 July 1916

On 2 October 1921 a silver alms dish was presented to St. Mark's Parish Church by William's parents in memory of their son. The inscription read

To the glory of God and in proud and loving memory of Lieutenant William Osmond Green, T.C.D. 10th Batt., Royal Irish Rifles, who fell at Thiepval, 1st July 1916, doing his duty to his king and country in the Great War. Aged 20 years. Presented to Portadown Parish Church by his parents, William John and Elsbeth Green.

Portadown News
15 October 1920

11th Battalion, Royal Irish Rifles

The 11th Battalion was formed from the South Antrim Volunteers of the Ulster Volunteer Force. It formed part of the 108th Infantry Brigade of the 36th (Ulster) Division.

The battalion was positioned on the right centre of the advance south of the River Ancre and attacked German positions between St. Pierre Divion and the Schwaben Redoubt. By 1100am the battalion was occupying positions north of Stuff Redoubt.

William James Boyd Rifleman 1069, 11th Battalion, Royal Irish Rifles

Born	Portadown
Residence	Derrymacfall
Enlisted	Belfast
Died	Killed in action 1 July 1916, France
Age	35
Buried	No Known Grave

Commemorated
Thiepval Memorial, Somme, France. Pier and face 15A & 15B.
Portadown War Memorial (292)

According to the 1901 Census Return William James resided with his brother John. John was a butcher by trade and was married to Ellen and had children Dinah Jane and Hannah Bella.

14th Battalion, Royal Irish Rifles

The 14th Battalion was formed from the Young Citizen Volunteers of the Ulster Volunteer Force. It formed part of the 109th Infantry Brigade of the 36th (Ulster) Division. The battalion crossed Thiepval Road to attack the Schwaben Redoubt - undoubtedly the strongest fortified position in the German lines.

Joseph A. Gregg
Rifleman 17773, 14th Battalion, Royal Irish Rifles

Born	Gilford, Co. Down
Parents	Son of S. Wilson of 11 Legmore Terrace, Portadown
Residence	Atkinson's Avenue
Enlisted	Belfast
Died	Killed in action 1 July 1916, France
Buried	No Known Grave

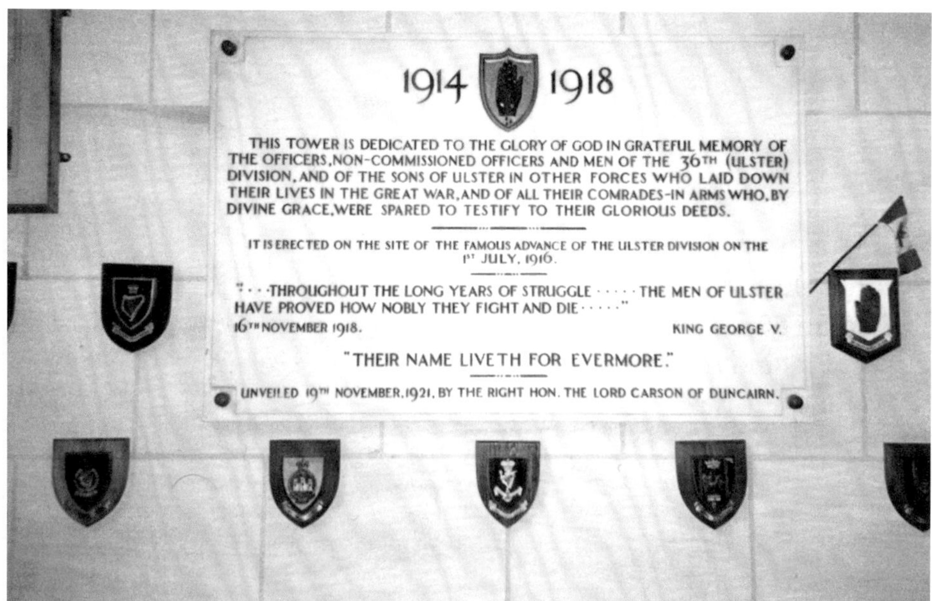

Interior of the Ulster Tower, Thiepval. (Author's Collection)

Commemorated
Thiepval Memorial, Somme, France. Pier and face 15A & 15B.
Portadown War Memorial (3)
St. Mark's Parish Church War Memorial

Rifleman Joseph Gregg (17773), Royal Irish Rifles, has been officially reported missing since July 1. Information regarding him would be thankfully received by his anxious mother, Mrs. S. Wilson, 11 Legmore Terrace, Portadown.

Portadown News
16 September 1916

16th (Pioneer) Battalion, Royal Irish Rifles

The 16th Battalion was formed from the Second County Down Volunteers of the Ulster Volunteer Force.

George Hull
Rifleman 6957,
16th (Pioneer) Battalion, Royal Irish Rifles

Born	Portadown
Parents	Son of William John and Sarah Hull of 7 Victoria Terrace, Portadown
Residence	Garvaghy Road
Enlisted	Belfast
Died	Died of Wounds 4 July 1916, France
Buried	Puchevillers British Cemetery, Somme, France. Grave I. C. 3.

Commemorated
Portadown War Memorial (106)
St. Mark's Parish Church War Memorial

George was the husband of Ethel Hull. She later resided at 40 Montrose Street, Belfast.

At a meeting held in Park Road School members of Parkmount Temperance Flute Band passed a resolution in memory of fallen colleagues.

We, the members of the committee of Parkmount Temperance Flute Band, having heard with deep regret the death of three esteemed members of our band, viz. Sergeant William Gordon, Castle Avenue, Corporal William Hule and Rifleman George Hule (sic), Victoria Terrace, offer our sincere and heartfelt sympathy with their parents, wives and families in their sorrow and bereavement, in the death of these three gallant soldiers, who laid down their lives for King and country in that glorious advance of the Ulster Division on that memorable and never-to-be-forgotten 1st of July 1916, in the Battle of the Somme.

Portadown News
22 July 1916

George's brother William (see entry **107 Corporal William Hull**) was killed in action on 1 July 1916 at the Battle of the Somme.

William James McGrattan Rifleman 249, 16th (Pioneer) Battalion, Royal Irish Rifles

Born Knocknamuckley
Residence Knocknamuckley
Enlisted Lurgan
Died Killed in action 7 July 1916, Battle of the Somme, France
Buried No Known Grave
Commemorated Thiepval Memorial, Somme, France. Pier and face 15A &15B. Portadown War Memorial (310)

Rifleman W. J. McGrattan, Hacknahay, Portadown, is officially reported, "missing believed killed".

Portadown News
9 September 1916

2nd Battalion, Royal Berkshire Regiment

The 2nd Battalion was a regular army battalion commanded by Lieutenant-Colonel A. M. Holdsworth. It formed part of the 25th Brigade of the 8th Division and was positioned on the right flank of 32nd Division.

On 1 July the battalion was in positions facing the village of Ollivers.

Samuel James Winter Private 27471, 2nd Battalion, Royal Berkshire Regiment

Born Drumcree
Residence Sarah Street
Enlisted Lisburn
Died Killed in action 1 July 1916, Battle of the Somme, France
Buried No Known Grave
Commemorated Thiepval Memorial, Somme, France. Pier and face 11D. Portadown War Memorial (215) St. Mark's Parish Church War Memorial

Private Winter had previously served in the Army Cyclist Battalion with the serial number 963.

Chapter 5
The Western Front July-December 1916

The Battle of the Somme continued through July, August and September with the British slowly advancing their lines forward at great cost.

The forces of the Empire were to the forefront of many battles with the South Africans, the Australians of the 1st Anzac Corps, the Canadians and New Zealanders all being involved. In September came the battles of Guillemont and Ginchy. The village of Thiepval, an objective on 1 July, finally fell on 27 September. On 12 October came the Battle of Le Transloy.

The Somme offensive finally came to an end on 18 November 1916. British and Empire losses were around 400,000 killed, wounded and missing; French casualties were nearly 200,000; with Germany suffering losses of over 400,000.

James Benson
Private 55571, 19th Battalion, Canadian Infantry, (Central Ontario Regiment)

Born	8 February 1891, Portadown
Parents	Son of John and Jane Benson of Canagolamore, Derrykeevin Post Office
Residence	Canagola
Enlisted	11 November 1914, Toronto, Canada
Died	Killed in action 25 July 1916, Belgium
Age	25
Buried	Bedford House Cemetery, Ieper, West-Vlaanderen, Belgium. Enclosure No. 4I. Grave G. 2.
Commemorated	Portadown War Memorial (272) Drumcree Parish Church War Memorial

The family headstone in Drumcree Churchyard records the following children of John, a farmer, and Jane Benson of Canagolamore two unnamed daughters who died in infancy, a daughter Elizabeth and sons James, Thomas William and John George. There was also a daughter Mary it is unclear if she was one of the daughters who died in infancy. Their father John died on 19 October 1913.

On enlistment James' particulars

were given as follows: occupation - machine hand, height - 5'8", complexion - dark, eyes - brown, hair - dark. He sailed with his unit from Montreal on the SS *Scandinavian* on 13 May 1915, arriving in England on 22 May. The next day he reported at Shorncliffe Barracks.

On 14 September 1915 James sailed from Folkstone and disembarked at Boulogne the next day. In May 1916 James enjoyed eight days leave in England before returning to the front. His mother received a letter from Lieutenant-Colonel W. R. Turnbull

Dear Mrs Benson - It is with profound regret that I have to inform you of the death of your son No. 55571 Private J. Benson of the Battalion under my command, which occurred on the night of the 25th July.

He was on duty with the Machine-Gun Section of the Battalion, in the front line trenches, when the enemy exploded a mine in the vicinity of the trench, which your son was assisting to hold. The explosion caused the dugout in which he was located to collapse, and when the debris could be cleared away his body was found crushed with the weight of the fallen timbers and earth...

Portadown Express
11 August 1916

James' brother Private 13014845 John George Benson, Pioneer Corps died on 13 March 1944 at a military hospital in Glasgow and lies buried in Drumcree Churchyard. He is not commemorated on Portadown War Memorial.

James Redmond
Private 5007, 1/6th Battalion, Argyll and Sutherland Highlanders

Born	Portadown
Residence	Curran Street
Enlisted	Paisley, Renfrewshire, Scotland
Died	Killed in action 29 July 1916, France
Buried	No Known Grave
Commemorated	Thiepval Memorial, Somme, France. Pier and face 15A & 16C. Portadown War Memorial (83)

James was employed as a plater's helper before enlisting.

He embarked for France on 16 June 1916. Private Redmond was killed when the Germans shelled his company at Longueval.

Samuel Fleming
Private 3663, 6th Battalion, Cameronians (Scottish Rifles)

Born	Drumcree
Residence	Roughan

Enlisted	Hamilton, Scotland
Died	Died of wounds 3 August 1916, France
Buried	Warloy-Baillon Communal Cemetery Extension, Somme, France. Grave VII. E. 8.
Commemorated	Portadown War Memorial (318) Drumcree Parish Church War Memorial St. Mark's Parish Church War Memorial

Private S. Fleming, a former Portadown man has died in hospital from wounds received in action. He was serving in the Scottish Rifles.
Portadown News
16 September 1916

Millar Cole
Sergeant 7422, 1st Battalion, Royal Inniskilling Fusiliers

Born	Milltown
Parents	Son of James Cole
Residence	Castle Avenue
Enlisted	Portadown
Died	Killed in action 8 August 1916, Belgium
Age	31
Buried	Potijze Chateau Wood Cemetery, Belgium. Grave F. 1.
Commemorated	Portadown War Memorial (42) St. Mark's Parish Church War Memorial

Millar was the husband of Mary Ann Cole of Ann Street, Gilford.

A report in the Portadown News dated 9 September 1916 states that Sergeant Cole died from the effects of gas poisoning.

Grave of Sergeant Millar Cole.

William G. Forker MM Sergeant-Major S/5025, 11th Battalion, Argyll and Sutherland Highlanders

Born	Orhmorah, East Indies
Residence	Church Street
Enlisted	Dunfermline, Scotland
Died	Killed in action 13 August 1916, France
Age	36
Buried	Adanac Military Cemetery, Somme, France. Grave V. A. 15.
Commemorated	Portadown War Memorial (65) St. Mark's Parish Church War Memorial

William was the husband of Georgina Forker of 17 Ormonde Street, Portadown. The couple had two children Willie and Annie.

Sergeant-Major Forker took part in the Battle of Loos 25 September 1915 and was later awarded the Military Medal for taking part in a raid on German trenches under shell and machine gun fire. He was killed in a subsequent raid on enemy trenches. His widow received a letter from Lieutenant W. D. Fyfe

Grave of Sergeant-Major William G. Forker MM.

...I hope you will let me express my deep sympathy with you. The loss is a heavy one; he was such a good soldier - far above the average - and at the same time he had such consideration for the men under him that he would never ask anyone to do anything or go anywhere he would not do or go himself. He was brave and courageous. I felt this at once last October when I was attached to his platoon, and I will long remember how he encouraged everyman, and inspired them with some of his own courage, when we were having a pretty unhappy time. Ever

since then, though I had to go to another platoon, Sergeant Forker and I were great friends, and we often "talked things over" together. He frequently spoke of his home, of you, and the children. What greater praise can a man have, than that those who know, say of him, that he was a great soldier, and these words can be truly said of Sergeant Forker.

Portadown News
23 September 1916

Sergeant-Major Forker's widow Georgina received the Military Medal on her late husband's behalf.

Patrick Joseph Monaghan Private 20541, 7th Battalion, Royal Irish Fusiliers

Residence Marley Street
Enlisted Portadown
Died Killed in action 22 August 1916, France
Buried Bois-Carre Military Cemetery Haisnes, Pas de Calais, France. Special Memorial 22.
Commemorated Portadown War Memorial (158)

Intimation has been received that Private Patrick Monaghan, Marley Street, Portadown has been killed at the front. He was employed as a lighter man, and was well known. It is stated that he was in the act of writing a letter home when a shell exploded nearby killing him instantaneously.

Portadown News
2 September 1916

Grave of Private Patrick Joseph Monaghan.

Robert Harper Cooper
Private 3549, 1st Battalion, Australian Imperial Force

Born	Drumcree
Parents	Son of Thomas Sproule Cooper of 28 Malt Street, Grosvenor Road, Belfast
Residence	Atkinson's Avenue
Enlisted	27 July 1915, Liverpool, New South Wales, Australia
Died	Feloniously killed (manslaughter) 28 August 1916, Etaples, France
Age	31
Buried	Etaples Military Cemetery, France. Grave X. A. 12A.
Commemorated	Portadown War Memorial (1) Thomas Street Methodist Church War Memorial

Robert was a carpenter by trade but was also employed as a life insurance agent before emigrating around 1908. He first travelled to Ontario, Canada and then Toronto, Alberta and Vancouver before finally venturing to Newcastle, New South Wales, Australia.

On enlistment in the 11th Reinforcements of 1st Battalion, Australian Imperial Force Robert's particulars were given as follows: occupation - carpenter ($2^1/_2$ years Harland and Wolff) height - 5'$6^1/_2$", complexion - dark freckles, eyes - brown, hair - brown, age - 29 years 11 months. He was unmarried.

He embarked for the Middle East on 5 October 1915 and was hospitalised at No. 1 Auxiliary Hospital at Heliopolis. On 8 February 1916 he was admitted to hospital at Abassia and in March was admitted to the No. 1 Australian Dermatology Hospital.

On 18 March 1916 Private Cooper was taken on strength of 1st Battalion, Australian Imperial Force. He embarked at Alexandria on 22 March on HMT *Ivernia* and arrived at Marseilles on 28 March from where he proceeded to the front.

On 23 July he took part in the fighting around Delville or 'Devil's' Wood and was wounded in action on 26 July. On 29 July Private Cooper was admitted to No. 6 Field Ambulance with a sprained ankle and three days later was transferred to No. 3 Casualty Clearing Station. On 29 July he was conveyed to No. 20 General Hospital at Camiers by ambulance train.

There is considerable mystery surrounding the death of Private

Robert Harper Cooper. He was initially reported accidentally "killed on 31 August 1916" and then this report was subsequently amended to "killed in action on 28 August 1916".

Grave of Private Robert Harper Cooper.

On 31 March 1917 after an Adjutant General Court of Inquiry it was deemed that Private Robert Harper Cooper had been "feloniously killed (manslaughter) at Etaples on 28 August 1918" and this cause and date of death was entered in his service records. No further details were given on the circumstances surrounding his death.

In Private Cooper's service records there are copies of correspondence between the Australian military authorities and his relatives. The early correspondence mentions Robert being killed in action, and discussions on his personal belongings and will. After the Court of Inquiry the authorities informed Thomas that his brother "was feloniously killed (manslaughter)". No other details were given in the letter dated 24 July 1917.

28 Malt Street
Grosvenor Road, Belfast
30 December 1917

Having waited for three months for more details of my brother's death, I again write to you for fuller information. When my brother left his situation in Australia to enlist, it was to fight the Germans, and if he had been killed by the Germans I would have said that was what he expected, but to be informed that he was feloniously killed and to get no more word is not justice...

Letter from Thomas Cooper to Australian Base Records Office London

Robert had sisters Elizabeth, Sarah and Kate.

Denis Moran
Lance-Sergeant 17164, 8th Battalion, Royal Irish Fusiliers

Born	Portadown
Residence	Woodhouse Street
Enlisted	Portadown
Died	Killed in action 4 September 1916, France
Buried	No Known Grave
Commemorated	Thiepval Memorial, Somme, France. Pier and face 15A. Portadown War Memorial (246)

On 3 September 1916 part of the 8th Battalion received orders to take up positions in Casement Trench situated about 300 yards south of Bernafay Wood on the Maricourt-Longueval Road. They arrived in position at 3.00 am the next morning.

At 1.00 pm on 4 September the battalion was ordered to move up in close support of the 95th Infantry Brigade in case of an enemy attack near Leuze Wood. Positions were occupied at 7.00pm.

No sooner was the Bn in position that the enemy shelled the trenches inflicting between 20 and 30 casualties.

War Diary 8th Battalion,
Royal Irish Fusiliers

The Battle of Guillemont (3-6 September 1916)

This battle was part of the Somme campaign July-November 1916. It began at 1200 noon on 3 September with a creeping barrage. British troops captured the heavily defended village on the first day of the attack.

16th (Irish) Division Memorial, Guillemont. (Author's Collection)

Hugh Beattie
Private 43190, 7th Battalion, Royal Irish Fusiliers

Born	Portadown
Residence	Church Street
Enlisted	Belfast
Died	Killed in action

5 September 1916, France
Buried No Known Grave
Commemorated
Thiepval Memorial, Somme, France. Pier and face 15A.
Portadown War Memorial (58)

Private Hugh Beattie, Corcrain, has been missing for the past 4 weeks. He is serving with the R.I.F. and is a former Portadown postman.

Portadown News
21 October 1916

Private Beattie had previously served in the Connaught Rangers with serial number 4540.

John O'Neill
Private 18692, 7th Battalion, Royal Irish Fusiliers

Born Portadown
Parents Son of James and Jemima O'Neill of Portadown
Residence David Street
Enlisted Portadown
Died Killed in action 5 September 1916, France
Age 33
Buried Combles Communal Cemetery Extension, Somme, France. Grave IV. F. 28.
Commemorated
Portadown War Memorial (87)

John was the husband of Rosetta O'Neill of 100 Obins Street, Portadown.

Private J. O'Neill, R.I.F, Dawson's Court, Portadown is also officially reported missing.

Portadown News
21 October 1916

Joseph Lappin
Rifleman 1851, 7th Battalion, Royal Irish Rifles

Born Drumcree
Residence Obins Street
Enlisted Portadown
Died Killed in action 7 September 1916, France
Buried No Known Grave
Commemorated
Thiepval Memorial, Somme, France. Pier and face 15A & 15B.
Portadown War Memorial (186)

Joseph's widow received a letter from Private Patrick Logan

As one who was always in company with your husband, I take the liberty of writing you a few lines, as I promised to do in case anything happened to your husband. I am

sorry to say that he was killed on the 7th of the present month, while bravely doing his duty. I sincerely hope you will bear up, for God's will must be done. There was not a better or more kind-hearted soldier in the whole regiment. You have my deepest sympathy in your sad loss.

Portadown News
16 September 1916

Joseph's son William (see entry **187 William H. Lappin**) was killed in action on 10 August 1917 near Ypres in Belgium.

The Battle of Ginchy (9 September 1916)

This battle was part of the Somme campaign July-November 1916.

Rifleman Thomas James Cole
Private 2841, 7th Battalion, Royal Irish Rifles

Born	Tullylish
Residence	Castle Avenue
Enlisted	Ballykinlar
Died	Killed in action 9 September 1916, France
Buried	No Known Grave
Commemorated	Thiepval Memorial, Somme, France. Pier and face 15A & 15B. Portadown War Memorial (43)

Mrs Cole, Castle Avenue, has received intimation that her husband, Private Thomas Cole, R.I.F. is missing.

Portadown News
21 October 1916

There is a Private T. J. Cole 5th Battalion, Royal Irish Fusiliers commemorated on St. Mark's Parish Church War Memorial. However, it is unclear if this is the same person.

William Henry Lewis
Sergeant 13385, 7th Battalion, Royal Irish Fusiliers

Born	1886, Portadown
Parents	Son of Henry and Annie Lewis of 113 Hampton Terrace, Portadown
Residence	Jervis Street
Enlisted	Portadown
Died	Killed in action 9 September 1916, France
Age	30
Buried	Delville Wood Cemetery, Somme, France. Grave XV. E. 9.
Commemorated	Portadown War Memorial (138) St. Mark's Parish Church War Memorial

William had three sisters Mary Isabella, Hannah Jane and Margaret Anne and a younger brother Herbert. He married Minnie Courtney from Dungannon and the couple had two children Dorothy Alice born 1912 and William Henry, known as Harry, born 1914.

William was a member of the Ulster Volunteer Force. After enlistment William spent a few months at Tipperary Barracks undergoing training. At the front Sergeant Lewis was attached to the machine gun section of his battalion.

Sergeant William Henry Lewis. (Thelma Simpson)

It is feared that Sergeant Harry Lewis has made the supreme sacrifice. For the past four weeks no news has been received from him, and his mother has had intimation from a soldier at the front that her son has been killed in action...

Portadown News
23 September 1916

After her husband's death Minnie moved back to Dungannon residing at 17 Clare Terrace.

George Robinson MM
Corporal 17944, 9th Battalion, Royal Irish Fusiliers

Born	Portadown
Parents	Son of John and Hannah Robinson
Residence	Druminally
Enlisted	Portadown
Died	Died of wounds 12 September 1916, France
Age	30
Buried	Bailleul Communal Cemetery Extension, Nord, France. Grave II. F. 214.
Commemorated	Portadown War Memorial (298)

George's father John was a Justice of the Peace. George had a sister Ada Sinclair who resided at Canary House, Moy. Lieutenant-Colonel Stewart Blacker to his wife Eva

7 September 1916
Corpl. G. Robinson was wounded last night with the Transport, our first casualty this time in. Much Artillery activity on our side from 10p.m. last night to which the Boche didn't reply, but his M.G. fire was vicious. Corpl. Robinson was bringing up the rations, in charge of the wagon; hit in the stomach - M.G. bullet. Sounds bad, but he is away to C.C.S.

13 September 1916
Poor Robinson had died that morning.

14 September 1916
Poor George Robinson buried this morn at 8.

Seagoe Parish Magazine
1923

William John Ross
Private 11217, 1st Battalion, Royal Irish Fusiliers

Born	Armagh
Parents	Son of Robert and Maria Ross of 2 Legmore Terrace, Portadown
Residence	Atkinson's Avenue
Enlisted	1912, Armagh
Died	Killed in action 15 September 1916, Belgium
Age	21
Buried	No Known Grave
Commemorated	Ypres (Menin Gate) Memorial, Ieper, West Flaanderen, Belgium. Panel 42. Portadown War Memorial (5) Thomas Street Methodist Church War Memorial

William took part in the Retreat from Mons in August 1914 and had been subsequently wounded in action a number of times. His mother Maria received a letter from Corporal Tintz

It is my painful duty to inform you of your son William's death. He was killed instantly by a German sniper and his death was avenged by his comrades. Not long after his death we captured many Germans and found several dead. He was well liked by all in 14 Platoon and we greatly miss him. He was a good soldier and always ready to help his chums. Please accept my sincere sympathy.

Portadown News
30 September 1916

John Girvan
Private 8429, 1st Battalion, Royal Irish Fusiliers

Born	1882, Derryadd
Parents	Son of John and Annie Girvan of Derryadd
Residence	Carne
Enlisted	Lurgan
Died	Killed in action 15-16 September 1916, Belgium

Age	35
Buried	Vlamertinghe Military Cemetery, Ieper, West-Vlaanderen, Belgium. Grave IV. D. 5.
Commemorated	Portadown War Memorial (275) Seagoe Parish Church War Memorial

John was the husband of Martha Magee and the couple had six children Francis born 28 September 1909, twins Margaret and Ann born 25 October 1910, Maria born 5 August 1912, John born 5 August 1914 and Charlotte born 10 April 1916.

Private Girvan was a regular soldier and was in action with the British Expeditionary Force from August 1914. His letters and articles about his exploits at the front featured prominently in Seagoe Parish Magazine. In a letter dated 27 December 1914 Private Girvan wrote

...It is very hard to stand in mud all day, and your feet like ice. We do enjoy a smoke when we come off sentry. We have to be very careful when we are on sentry. The Germans are lying within 300 yards of us, and they keep sniping at us all day and night, if they can see even the top of your head. They attack us at night, and you can see nothing but the blaze of the rifles, and bullets whizzing all roads.

Seagoe Parish Magazine
January 1915

In a letter dated 29 May 1915 he wrote

Just a line to let you know I am well, and in good health considering the way we have to fight the Germans. I am sure you read in the papers how they gave us the gas. Well our Regiment stuck to our trenches, and when they come on our boys mowed them down, and they came no further.

Seagoe Parish Magazine
June 1915

Private Girvan was involved in numerous battles and took part in three bayonet charges and on one home leave in July 1915 he arrived direct from the front still clad in his muddy uniform complete with entrenching tools, rifle and bayonet. On this occasion he had been in the front line on 4 July before setting off on the long journey to Seagoe where he arrived on 6 July. John left on the evening of 9 July and was back in the trenches by 11 July.

His widow received a letter from Lieutenant J. H. Simpson, Field Ambulance Car

I very deeply regret to have to inform you that Private J. Girvan was killed in action serving his Trench Mortar, on the night of 15th of this month. He was one of the finest soldiers it has been my privilege to command. He gave his service as he did his life, most freely to his country. Always cool, cheerful and courageous. I enclose a gold ring, which he always wore.

Seagoe Parish Magazine
October 1916

Private John Girvan. (Seagoe Parish Magazine)

John had three brothers James, known as Jimsey, born 1879, Joseph born 1886 and Francis, known as Frank, born 1887. Frank enlisted in the Royal Irish Fusiliers and rose to the rank of Sergeant-Major. Joseph enlisted in 9th Battalion, Royal Irish Fusiliers and rose to the rank of Lance-Sergeant. He died of wounds on 4 July 1916 and is commemorated on Lurgan War Memorial.

Trevor Bonis laying a wreath at the grave of his great-grandfather. (Author's Collection)

Joseph Thompson
Private 7039, 1st Battalion, Irish Guards

Born	Portadown
Residence	Obins Street
Enlisted	10 March 1915, Belfast

Died Killed in action 15 September 1916, France
Buried No Known Grave
Commemorated
Thiepval Memorial, Somme, France. Pier and face 7D.
Portadown War Memorial (193)
St. Mark's Parish Church War Memorial

Joseph was the husband of Eliza Jane Thompson. They married in Portadown on 23 March 1909 and had four children William David born 1911, Annie born 1913, Margaret born 1914 all born in Glasgow and Joseph born 1915 in Belfast.

Joseph, who was 6' 1" tall, was employed as a driller before enlisting. He was also a footballer and played for North End.

Private Thompson sailed for France in August 1915 and joined the 1st Battalion in November.

His sister, Miss Thompson of Corcrain, received a letter from Sergeant John Milligan

I am very sorry to report that your brother Joseph was killed on 15th September. He got wounded in the arm, and while going back to the dressing station got struck again by shellfire...

Portadown News
28 October 1916

His body was recovered and buried on 30 September. Joseph's widow and children resided at 81 Solway Street, Belfast.

Robert Henry Taylor
Private 141789, 24th Battalion, Canadian Infantry, (Quebec Regiment)

Born 8 July 1891, Derrycarne
Parents Son of Robert H. and Sarah Taylor of Derrycarne
Residence Derrycarne
Enlisted 27 July 1915, Welland, Ontario, Canada
Died Died of wounds 21 September 1916, France
Age 25
Buried Puchevillers British Cemetery, Somme, France. Grave IV. D. 28.
Commemorated
Portadown War Memorial (288)
Drumcree Parish Church War Memorial

Robert Henry was employed as a clerk by Messrs Hamilton Robb Ltd before he emigrated to Canada.

On enlistment in the 76th Battalion, Canadian Infantry,

Robert's particulars were given as follows: occupation - bookkeeper, height - 5'5½", complexion - dark, eyes - grey, hair - black.

On arrival in France Joseph was transferred to the 5th Company, Machine Gun Corps which was attached to 5th Brigade, 2nd Canadian Division.

Private Taylor received a gunshot wound to his cheek on 9 June 1916 and was taken first to No. 10 Canadian Field Ambulance, then to a Casualty Clearing Station and finally by ambulance train to No. 4 General Hospital, Camiers for further treatment. On 15 June he was well enough to be taken to No. 6 Convalescent Depot at Etaples where he remained for two weeks recovering from his wounds.

On 29 June Robert rejoined his unit transferring, at his own request, to the 24th Battalion, Canadian Infantry in August 1916. On 21 September 1916 Robert received a gunshot wound to the right arm, which inflicted a compound fracture. He was taken to No. 44 Casualty Clearing Station where he died of his wounds.

George Campbell
Sergeant, 1st Battalion, Canadian Infantry (Western Ontario Regiment)

Parents	Son of John and Margaret Campbell
Residence	Church Street
Died	Killed in action 22 or 27 September 1916, France

Family grave of Sergeant George Campbell. (Author's Collection)

Commemorated
Portadown War Memorial (62)
St. Mark's Parish Church War Memorial

George's father John was a victualler and farmer. His mother Margaret died on 7 May 1894 and his father died on 17 March 1911.

The family headstone in Seagoe Cemetery, Portadown records the names of four children of John and Margaret Campbell. Annett W. died 30 April 1900, Theophilius died 13 November 1905, Robert Alexander died 20 March 1910 and George killed in France 22 September 1916.

Two other sons were David John, a butcher, of Church Place, Portadown and William James who also served with the Canadians during the Great War.

The people of Portadown have heard with deep regret that Sergeant George Campbell of the Canadians (Vancouver contingent), brother of Mr. D. J. Campbell, Church Place, has been killed in action. It is believed the sergeant - a man of splendid physique and heroic courage-formed part of the "crew" of one of the famous tanks. He received the wounds which proved fatal about 27th September.

Portadown Express
10 November 1916

Two death notices and the above newspaper report refer to George's date of death as 27 September 1916 although it is recorded as 22 September 1916 on the family headstone in Seagoe Cemetery.

It has so far been impossible to ascertain full service details of Sergeant George Campbell, Canadians, killed in action on 22 or 27 September 1916.

Maxwell Stothers
Private 14680, 9th Battalion, Royal Irish Fusiliers

Born	Portadown
Parents	Son of Ellen Stothers of 12 Bright Street, Portadown
Residence	Bright Street
Enlisted	Belfast
Died	Died 7 October 1916, France
Buried	Nieppe Communal Cemetery, Nord, France. Grave III. B. 6.
Commemorated	Portadown War Memorial (22) Seagoe Parish Church War Memorial

Maxwell was a member of the Ulster Volunteer Force.

Lt-Colonel Stewart Blacker to his wife Eva

10 October 1916
14680 M. Stothers, Portadown, was badly

injured on Saturday. He was a prisoner in the Guard tent, and a branch of a tree fell on the tent and fractured his skull.

Seagoe Parish Magazine 1923

Maxwell's brother Joseph (see entry **21 Private Joseph Stothers**) was killed in action on 1 July 1916 at the Battle of the Somme and his brother Jackson (see entry **20 Private Jackson Stothers**) died on 7 January 1917 in Dublin.

Grave of Private Maxwell Stothers.

Battle of Le Transloy (12 October 1916)

This battle was part of the Somme campaign July-November 1916. The main objective for the assault on 12 October 1916 at Le Transloy was to establish a position from which the German's frontline trenches could be attacked. The Royal Warwickshire Regiment were on the right and the 12th Infantry Brigade on the left of the 1st Battalion, Royal Irish Fusiliers.

Henry Donaghy
Private 10509, 1st Battalion, Royal Irish Fusiliers

Born	Athlone, Co. Westmeath
Parents	Son of Edward and Olive Donaghy of 6 Fowler's Entry, Portadown
Residence	Fowler's Entry
Enlisted	Portadown
Died	Killed in action 12 October 1916, Battle of Le Transloy, France
Buried	No Known Grave
Commemorated	Thiepval Memorial, Somme, France. Pier and face 15A. Portadown War Memorial (97)

St Mark's Parish Church War Memorial

Henry's father Edward was employed as a weaver and his mother Olive was a winder. She was from Sussex, England. The couple had sons Henry, Alfred John and Edward.

Edward was born in David Street, Portadown. He attended Church Street Public Elementary School and was a street artist in Belfast before the outbreak of World War Two.

Edward enlisted in the 2nd Battalion, Royal Inniskilling Fusiliers and was killed in action on 23 May 1940 during the German Blitzkrieg invasion of France and the Low countries. Fusilier Edward Donaghy, aged 32, lies buried in Hamblain Les Pres Communal Cemetery, Pas de Calais, France.

As he had moved away from Portadown and resided with his wife, Norah, at Tate's Row, Greencastle, Co. Antrim Fusilier Edward Donaghy is not commemorated on Portadown War Memorial.

Albert Graham
Private 11984, 1st Battalion, Royal Irish Fusiliers

Born	Portadown
Parents	Son of Thomas and Sarah Ann Graham of 25 Carrickblacker Road, Portadown
Residence	Carrickblacker Road
Enlisted	Armagh
Died	Killed in action 12 October 1916, Battle of Le Transloy, France
Age	26
Buried	London Cemetery & Extension, Somme, France. Grave 6. B. 21.
Commemorated	Portadown War Memorial (31) First Presbyterian Church War Memorial, Edenderry

Albert's parents Thomas and Sarah Ann Graham (nee Craig) had children Julia, Rachel, Wellington, Albert and Thomas.

News has been received that Private Albert Graham, Carrickblacker Road has been killed in action. He was employed as a bootmaker before he enlisted and is the second member of Edenderry Pipe Band to make the supreme sacrifice.

Portadown News
16 November 1916

Henry Graham
Private 7513, 1st Battalion, Royal Irish Fusiliers

Born	Portadown

Parents	Son of Thomas and Mary Jane Graham of 13 King Street, Portadown
Residence	Fox Street
Enlisted	Portadown
Died	Killed in action 12 October 1916, Battle of Le Transloy, France
Age	34
Buried	No Known Grave
Commemorated	Thiepval Memorial, Somme, France. Pier and face 15A. Portadown War Memorial (102) St Mark's Parish Church War Memorial

Private Graham was a member of 'C' Company.

Henry's three brothers Walker, David and Thomas all served during the Great War. Thomas was a Sergeant and was wounded on 25 September 1915 at the Battle of Loos. His two sisters Lavinia and Elizabeth emigrated to Dover, New Hampshire, USA.

William Hayes
Private 6042, 1st Battalion, Royal Irish Fusiliers

Born	Portadown
Parents	Son of Thomas Hayes of Sarah Street, Portadown
Residence	Sarah Street
Enlisted	Portadown
Died	Killed in action 12 October 1916, Battle of Le Transloy, France
Buried	No Known Grave
Commemorated	Thiepval Memorial, Somme, France. Pier and face 15A. Portadown War Memorial (213) St Mark's Parish Church War Memorial

News has been received that Private William Hayes, Sarah Street, has fallen in action on the Western front. His brother Jack was killed some time ago and his other brother Alexander, was wounded.

Portadown News
11 November 1916

William was one of three brothers killed during the Great War. His brothers John (see entry **212 Private John Hayes**) was killed in action on 1 July 1916 at the Battle of the Somme and Alexander (see entry **211 Private Alexander Hayes**) died on 31 July 1918 while serving in France.

Robert McLoughlin
Sergeant 3880, 1st Battalion, Royal Irish Fusiliers

Born Portadown
Parents Son of William and Elizabeth McLoughlin of 67 West Street, Portadown
Residence West Street
Enlisted Finner Camp, Co. Donegal
Died Killed in action 12 October 1916, Battle of Le Transloy, France
Age 31
Buried No Known Grave
Commemorated
Thiepval Memorial, Somme, France. Pier and face 15A. Portadown War Memorial (237) St. Mark's Parish Church War Memorial

For 10 years Robert was employed by Post Office Telephones in Glasgow. He was the husband of Annie McLoughlin of 72 Charles Street, Portadown. The couple had two children.

Sergeant R. McLaughlin, (sic) Royal Irish Fusiliers, Corcrain, Portadown, who was previously reported missing, is now announced killed. He was a member of the Orange and Black Institutions.

Portadown Express
7 September 1917

Joseph Henry Webb
Lance-Corporal 6151, 1st Battalion, Royal Irish Fusiliers

Born Portadown
Parents Son of Watson and Lizzie Webb of Mourneview Street, Portadown
Residence Mary Street
Enlisted Armagh
Died Killed in action 12 October 1916, Battle of Le Transloy, France
Buried No Known Grave
Commemorated
Thiepval Memorial, Somme, France. Pier and face 15A. Portadown War Memorial (163) St. Mark's Parish Church War Memorial

Joseph was the husband of Emma Webb (nee Crozier) and the couple had one child. The family resided at 3 Morrison's Court, Portadown.

Emma Webb received a letter from Private T. Lenard

I am very sorry to announce to you your dear husband's death. He was killed in action on the 12th October while leading his section of which I belong. I myself and all of the company that are left are very sorry to lose him as he was a brave soldier. He died as others have done before him, for those that he loved. He died fighting until the last. Goodbye and may God be with you in your sorrow.

Portadown News
11 November 1916

Mrs Webb moved to Mary Street, Portadown soon after her husband's death.

Patrick Gorman
Private 17632, 1st Battalion, Royal Irish Fusiliers

Born	Portadown
Parents	Son of Michael and Catherine Gorman of Portadown
Residence	Curran Street
Enlisted	Glasgow, Scotland
Died	Died of wounds 17 October 1916, France
Age	45
Buried	Grove Town Cemetery, Somme. Grave I. N. 6.
Commemorated	Portadown War Memorial (79)

Patrick was the husband of Elizabeth Gorman of 12 Curran Street, Portadown. They had resided in Partick, Glasgow for a time.

News is to hand that Private Patrick Gorman, Curran Street, Portadown, has been wounded in action.

Portadown News
21 October 1916

Private Gorman died of wounds received on the Somme.

Grave of Private Patrick Gorman.

William Henry Gracey
Corporal 7699, 7th Battalion, South Lancashire Regiment

Born Portadown
Parents Son of Hugh and E. J. Gracey of 9 Burnbrae Avenue, Portadown
Residence Burnbrae Avenue
Enlisted Armagh
Died Killed in action 23 October 1916, France
Buried A.I.F. Burial Ground, Flers, Somme, France. Grave XV. D. 31.
Commemorated Portadown War Memorial (23)
St Mark's Parish Church War Memorial

William was the husband of Annie Gracey. The couple resided at 5 Burnbrae Avenue, Portadown.

William fought at the Battle of Loos on 25 September 1915.

News has been received that Corporal William H. Gracey, son of Mr. Hugh Gracey, Shillington Street, has been killed in action. He belonged to the regular army and came through several fierce battles in France and Flanders. Corporal Gracey was married a few months ago.

Portadown News
18 November 1916

His brother Malcolm served in the Royal Navy during the Great War and was Fourth Engineer on HMS *Peel Castle*.

Michael Campbell
Lance-Corporal 6184, 1st Battalion, Royal Irish Fusiliers

Born Drumcree
Parents Son of Michael and Mary Campbell (nee McAusky) of Cottage Court, Callan Street, Armagh
Residence Curran Street
Enlisted Portadown
Died Died of wounds 24 October 1916, France
Age 20
Buried St. Sever Cemetery Extension, Rouen, Seine-Maritme, France. Grave O. I. C. 6.
Commemorated Portadown War Memorial (76)

Lance-Corporal Campbell died of wounds received on 14 October 1916 at the Battle of the Somme (Le Transloy).

John Collen
Second-Lieutenant,
7 Squadron, Royal Flying Corps

Born	5 February 1896, County Armagh
Parents	Son of Frederick D. and Addie Collen of Ardbrae, Portadown
Residence	Stewart Avenue
Enlisted	29 July 1915, Dublin
Died	Killed in action 25 October 1916, France
Age	20
Buried	No Known Grave
Commemorated	Arras Flying Services Memorial, Pas de Calais, France. Portadown War Memorial (218) Seagoe Parish Church War Memorial

John's father Frederick was a brick and tile manufacturer. Frederick was born in Australia and his wife Addie was from Cork. The couple had children Mary who was born in Cork and John and Freda who were born in County Armagh.

On enlistment in the 7th Battalion, Leinster Regiment as Private 7/3324 John's particulars were given as follows: occupation - bank clerk, height - 5' 4", age 19 years.

John, known as Jack, received a commission in the 7th Battalion, Royal Inniskilling Fusiliers on 5 November 1915 and was later attached to 7 Squadron, Royal Flying Corps (Royal Air Force from 1 April 1918).

The squadron was formed on 1 May 1914 and was transferred to France in April 1915 tasked with reconnaissance, tactical observation and artillery spotting duties. It was equipped with BE 2d two seater biplanes, which had a top speed of 70 miles an hour and could stay in the air for three hours.

Second-Lieutenant Collen took part in many sorties at the front sometimes flying two or three missions a day. On 25 October 1916 aircraft BE 2d serial number 5831 took off from Miraumont airfield with Second-Lieutenants William Fraser, as pilot, and John Collen on board. Whilst over Puisieux the aircraft was shot down and crashed in flames with no survivors.

When both pilots failed to return from the sortie they were officially posted as 'missing believed killed'. Their bodies were never recovered and are commemorated on the Arras Flying Memorial.

John was a member of the 'Under Age Four' crew of Portadown Rowing Club. All four of whom were killed during the Great War.

George Montgomery
Private 10867, 2nd Battalion, Royal Inniskilling Fusiliers

Born	Portadown
Residence	Castle Street
Enlisted	Belfast
Died	Killed in action 23 November 1916, France
Buried	No Known Grave
Commemorated	Thiepval Memorial, Somme, France. Pier and face 4D & 5B. Portadown War Memorial (49) Thomas Street Methodist Church War Memorial

Mrs Montgomery, 40 Castle Street, Portadown, has received official intimation that her son, Private George Montgomery, was killed in action on November 23rd 1916. He was serving with the Inniskilling Fusiliers, and was posted as missing last year.

Portadown News
2 June 1917

One of George's brothers, Joe, also served during the Great War.

George Brownlee
Private 139515, 60th Battalion, Canadian Infantry (Quebec Regiment)

Born	10 December 1887
Parents	Son of Bunting and Elizabeth Brownlee of 9 Carleton Street, Portadown
Residence	Carleton Street
Enlisted	20 July 1915, Toronto, Canada
Died	Killed in action 26 November 1916, France
Age	27
Buried	Nine Elms Military Cemetery, Thelus, Pas de Calais, France. Grave I. E. 15.
Commemorated	Portadown War Memorial (35) St Mark's Parish Church War Memorial

George's father Bunting was employed as a housepainter. His mother Elizabeth was born in County Monaghan. The couple had children Thomas, Alexander, George, Annie, Minnie, Lucy, Bunting, Albert and Charlotte.

George's mother Elizabeth remarried a Mr. Anderson and resided at Woodview Cottage, Armagh Road, Portadown.

On enlistment in the 75th Battalion, Canadian Infantry George's particulars were given as follows: occupation - painter, height

- 5' 7 3/4", complexion - dark, eyes - blue, hair - brown. He had previous service with the 10th Grenadiers and was a volunteer in the Canadian Militia.

George sailed with his unit from Halifax, Nova Scotia on the SS *Empress of Britain* on 29 March 1916, arriving in Liverpool on 9 April. He was taken on strength of the 60th Battalion, Canadian Infantry in June.

George Brownlee, age 28, formerly of Armagh, Ireland, who resided at the home of Mrs. Shields, 168 Mutual St., is to-day officially reported killed in action. Pte. Brownlee's relatives live in Ireland. He was a porter by trade and had lived in Toronto a few years. He enlisted with the 75th Battalion and went overseas with Col. Beckett's unit until June. He had been in the trenches since June.

Toronto Star
7 December 1916

We regret to learn that Pte. George Brownlee, of the Canadian Infantry, has been killed by the accidental explosion of a trench mortar.

Portadown Express
8 December 1916

George's brother Albert (see entry **34 Corporal Albert Brownlee**) died of wounds on 23 April 1918 in France.

Another brother served with the Royal Engineers during the Great War.

Samuel James Fox
Private 11664, 1st Battalion, Royal Irish Fusiliers

Born	14 October 1897, Edenderry
Parents	Son of Samuel and Louisa Fox (nee Askin) of 54 Bridge Street, Portadown
Residence	Bridge Street
Enlisted	Portadown
Died	Died of wounds 12 December 1916, France
Age	19
Buried	Grove Town Cemetery, Somme, France. Grave II. E. 15.
Commemorated	Portadown War Memorial (11) Seagoe Parish Church War Memorial

Samuel's father Samuel married Louisa Askin, daughter of James Askin, a railway labourer of Levaghery, on 2 April 1890 at Seagoe Parish Church. He was employed as a labourer at the time. The couple had nine children George born 1887, Louisa born 1891, Anne Margaret born 1893, Margaret Patton born 1895, Samuel James 1897, Mary born 1899,

Eveline born 1900, William John born 1907 and Violet Gladys born 1908.

Before the war Samuel was employed as a compositor in the offices of the Portadown News. He was a member of Seagoe Harriers and of the Ulster Volunteer Force.

Private Samuel James Fox. (Seagoe Parish Magazine)

Private Samuel Fox was posted to the Balkans where he took part in actions against the Bulgarians at Salonkia. He contacted frostbite in the mountains and was invalided home via Alexandria. On his recovery he rejoined his battalion in France. He wrote a letter to one of his sisters dated 23 November 1916

I have still got your photograph with me. It has been through some of the hardest fought battles in France. I believe they are showing the Battle of the Somme at home on the Pictures, but, believe me, they could never take a picture of it. Tell mother not to worry herself, as I am all right and out for a rest.

Seagoe Parish Magazine
January 1917

His last letter home was dated 5 December 1916

I am not too well at present, as I have a very bad cold. As long as I am able to get a smoke and something to eat I will be able to stick the hardships this winter again. It is only we out here who know what we really have to stand. I am not in form for writing. I will be in the trenches by the time you get this letter. Goodbye.

Seagoe Parish Magazine
January 1917

On 11 December 1916 Private Samuel Fox was struck in the spine by a bullet and died of wounds at No. 2 Casualty Clearing Station the following day.

His father Private Samuel Fox had served for 21 years in the army seeing action in India and Egypt. On the outbreak of war he re-enlisted in the 9th Battalion, Royal Irish Fusiliers when in his mid fifties. He served at the front until the end of 1916 when he was detailed for home service.

Samuel's brother George was wounded during the Great War.

Chapter 6
War of Attrition 1917

From February to April 1917 the Germans fell back in stages to the heavily fortified Hindenburg Line in order to shorten their front. As they withdrew they destroyed bridges, communications, buildings and everything that was of use to the Allied troops who liberated the area. They also left behind numerous booby traps to kill or injure unsuspecting Allied soldiers.

On 6 April 1917 the United States declared war on Germany and in June the first US troops began to arrive in France.

On the morning of 7 June the British detonated 19 huge mines under the German trenches and under an intense creeping barrage from 2,300 guns advanced and captured Messines Ridge. The Germans lost 24,000 men and the British 17,000 killed, wounded and missing.

The Third Battle of Ypres began on 31 July. A weeklong artillery barrage from over 3,000 guns, which expended 1,500,000 shells in the direction of the German trenches, preceded it.

On 20 November came the British attack at Cambrai, which was spearheaded, by over 350 tanks. The Germans were initially taken by surprise but recovered and in a series of counter-attacks reoccupied initial gains by the British.

William John McCardle
Rifleman 220, Scottish Rifles

Born	Seagoe
Parents	Son of Thomas and Margaret McCardle of Killycomain
Residence	Clounagh
Enlisted	21 February 1907, Armagh
Died	Killed in action 5 March 1917, France & Flanders
Commemorated	Portadown War Memorial (281) St. Mark's Parish Church War Memorial

William John enlisted in the 3rd Battalion, Royal Irish Fusiliers Special Reserve on 21 February 1907 as a Private with the serial number 4840. On enlistment his particulars were given as follows: occupation - weaver, age $17^1/_2$, height - $5'2^1/_2''$, complexion - light, eyes - blue, hair - light brown. It was also recorded that he had scars on his back. On 12 July 1908 he

reattested for a period of six years. William John and his brother, Joseph Henry, both married sisters Margaret and Hannah Jane Parks of Edenderry. The double wedding took place in Seagoe Parish Church on 10 October 1908. His age was recorded as 22, which is at variance with his age as given in his Service Records. His occupation was listed as a fireman.

The couple had a daughter Hannah born on 22 October 1909 according to his Service Records or 22 December 1909 according to Seagoe Church Records.

As part of his commitment to the Special Reserve Private McCardle had to attend annual training camps the one for 1909 was held at Finner Camp in County Donegal. The annual camp for 1910 was held at Aldershot with those for 1911 and 1912 being held at Finner Camp.

On 28 August 1912 William was arrested by the Royal Irish Constabulary and charged with "disorderly behaviour while drunk". His punishment is illegible on his Service Record. This was McCardle's first brush with authority and over the next few years he was continually in trouble with his superiors.

Private McCardle was re-engaged on 1 February 1913 and attended annual camp that summer. In 1914 he attended one more annual muster at Finner Camp before war was declared. He was mobilised on 8 August 1914 and two weeks later was confined to barracks for three days for "not being shaved on parade at 0930".

On 16 September 1914 Private McCardle deserted his post and was charged with the following offence "when on active service deserting His Majesty's Forces". A court of enquiry was convened at Ebrington Barracks, Londonderry on 5 December 1914 to investigate the "illegal absence and deficiency of kit (if any) of No. 4840 Pte McCardle, W. J of 3rd Royal Irish Fusiliers". In the meantime the search was on for his whereabouts.

On 22 February McCardle was arrested in civilian clothes by the civil police in Glasgow and on 27 February was taken into military custody by Sgt. R. McCloughlin of the 3rd Royal Irish Fusiliers. McCardle was taken to his lodging for a change of clothing and while the sergeant sat in the kitchen McCardle made good his escape.

He was rearrested in Glasgow on 11 March, once again in civilian clothes, and was brought into military custody to appear before court.

At a District Court Martial convened on 30 March 1915 Private

William John McCardle was sentenced "to undergo detention for 6 months and to be put under stoppages until deficiencies are made good".

In the roll of honour published last week the name of Private (sic) Wm. John McCardle, was omitted. He was killed in action on 5th March, 1917 while serving with the Scottish Rifles

Portadown News
4 January 1919

It has so far been impossible to ascertain full service details of Private/Rifleman William John McCardle.

His brother Joseph (see entry **280 Private Joseph Henry McCardle**) was killed in action on 25 September 1915 at the Battle of Loos. Joseph is commemorated on Seagoe Parish Church War Memorial although William is not.

George Hughes
Lance-Corporal 1203, 7th Battalion, Royal Irish Rifles

Born	Belfast
Residence	Henry Street
Enlisted	Belfast
Died	Died of wounds 24 March 1917, France
Buried	Boulogne Eastern Cemetery, Pas de Calais, France. Grave VIII. A. 180.
Commemorated	Portadown War Memorial (121) St. Mark's Parish Church War Memorial

George was the husband of Ellen Hughes and the couple had three children. The family resided at 44 Henry Street, Portadown. In his last letter to his wife he wrote

The Germans gave me a bit of a bashing with their shells. I have an iron foundry in my back, but I am hoping to be better soon, although I have not much use of my legs.

Portadown News
7 April 1917

Grave of Lance-Corporal George Hughes.

James Benson
Private 198631, 52nd Battalion, Canadian Infantry (Manitoba Regiment)

Born	10 February 1890, Portadown
Parents	Son of William and Esther Benson of Drumherriff
Residence	Drumherriff
Enlisted	27 December 1915, Sioux Lookout, Ontario, Canada
Died	Killed in action 2 April 1917, France
Age	27
Buried	Ecoivres Military Cemetery, Mont St. Eloi, Pas de Calais, France. Grave VI. A. 3.
Commemorated	Portadown War Memorial (299) Drumcree Parish Church War Memorial

James' father William was a farmer and had children William, James, David and Joseph.

James enlisted in the 94th Battalion, Canadian Expeditionary Force. On enlistment his particulars were given as follows; occupation - labourer height - 5'9½", complexion - dark, eyes - blue, hair - dark brown.

He sailed from Halifax, Nova Scotia on 28 June 1916 on the SS *Olympic* and arrived in Liverpool on 6 July. On 18 July he was taken on strength of the 32nd Battalion at Shorncliffe. Private Benson transferred to the 52nd Battalion on 17 August and landed in France the next day.

Private James Benson, 52nd Batt. Canadians, has been killed in action. He is a son of Mr. Wm. Benson, Drumherriff, Scotch Street, and brother of Mrs. Irwin, Coronation Street, Portadown.

Portadown News
14 April 1917

Grave of Private James Benson.

The Battle of Arras (9 April-16 May 1917)

An artillery barrage of nearly 3,000 guns heralded the start of the Battle of Arras on 9 April. This British and Canadian offensive was launched as a diversionary attack to draw German forces away from the French Nivelle offensive.

After initial gains the German resistance strengthened and the battle became one of attrition with further offensives launched on 23/24 April and 3 May gaining some ground. British casualties to the end of May amounted to nearly 160,000 killed, wounded, missing or prisoners.

James Faloon
Private 22122, 1st Battalion, Royal Irish Fusiliers

Residence	Fowler's Entry
Enlisted	Lurgan
Died	Killed in action 11 April 1917, France
Buried	Brown's Copse Cemetery, Roeux, Pas de Calais, France. Grave II. C. 28.
Commemorated	Portadown War Memorial (98) St. Marks Parish Church War Memorial

James was the husband of Maggie Faloon and the couple had three daughters. The family resided at Jervis Street, Portadown. Later Maggie and the children moved to 11 Fowler's Entry, Portadown. His mother and sister resided at 32 Jervis Street, Portadown.

Grave of Private James Faloon.

Peter Simpson
Private 17299, 1st Battalion, Royal Irish Fusiliers

Born	Portadown
Residence	David Street
Enlisted	Portadown
Died	Killed in action 11 April 1917, France

Buried | Brown's Copse Cemetery, Roeux, Pas de Calais, France. Grave I. E. 32.
Commemorated | Portadown War Memorial (88)

Official intimation has been received that Private Peter Simpson, David Street, Portadown, has been killed in action.

Portadown News
28 April 1917

James Henry Weir
Private 6128, 1st Battalion, Royal Irish Fusiliers

Born | Portadown
Parents | Son of James and Eliza Weir of 12 Century Street, Portadown
Residence | Meadow Lane
Enlisted | Armagh
Died | Killed in action 11 April 1917, France
Buried | Brown's Copse Cemetery, Roeux, Pas de Calais, France. Grave II. D. 14.
Commemorated | Portadown War Memorial (168) St. Mark's Parish Church War Memorial Seagoe Parish Church War Memorial

James Henry's father was employed as a general labourer and his mother Eliza was a linen weaver. The couple had six children James Henry, Joseph, Robert, Hanna, Thomas and George.

James Henry was employed as a linen weaver. He was the husband of M. B. Weir and the couple had three children. The family resided at 20 Meadow Lane, Portadown.

Private James Henry Weir was killed in action during an attack on the chemical works at Rouex.

His brothers Joseph and Robert served in the 9th Battalion, Royal Irish Fusiliers and his brother Thomas served in the 2nd Battalion, Royal Irish Fusiliers. His father James served in the Labour Corps.

His brother George (see entry **53 Private George Weir**) died on 3 October 1918 in Mesopotamia.

Peter Gilmore
Private 3930, 1st Battalion, Royal Irish Fusiliers

Born | Portadown
Residence | Curran Street
Enlisted | Portadown
Died | Died of wounds 14 April 1917, France

Buried	Haute-Avesnes British Cemetery, Pas de Calais, France. Grave C. II.
Commemorated	Portadown War Memorial (78)

On Wednesday intimation was received that Private Peter Gilbert (sic), Curran Street, Portadown had fallen in action.

Portadown News
5 May 1917

Grave of Private Peter Gilmore.

Thomas Robert Abraham
Private 253019,
102nd Battalion, Canadian Infantry (Central Ontario Regiment)

Born	11 January 1889, Co. Armagh
Parents	Son of George and Mary Ann Abraham of 36 Henry Street, Portadown
Residence	Charles Street
Enlisted	25 May 1916, Govenlock, Saskatchewan, Canada
Died	Died of wounds 17 April 1917, France
Age	18
Buried	Barlin Communal Cemetery Extension, Pas de Calais, France. Grave I. A. 34.
Commemorated	Portadown War Memorial (57)

Thomas enlisted in the 209th Battalion, Canadian Infantry. On enlistment his particulars were given as follows: occupation - labourer, height - 5'6", complexion - fair, eyes - brown, hair - light brown. It was also recorded that he had a scar on the lower left jaw and the tips of the two middle fingers on his right hand were missing.

He sailed from Halifax, Nova Scotia on 31 October 1916 on the SS *Caronia* and arrived in England on 11 November. Private Benson transferred to the 102nd Battalion on 5 December and landed in France the next day. After a few weeks at the Canadian Base Depot Thomas arrived in the field on 6 January 1917.

The 102nd Battalion took part in the assault on Vimy Ridge on 9 April 1917. The battalion attacked at 0530 hours during a heavy snowfall and managed to capture three German trench lines within the hour. The rest of the day was spent consolidating the gains made. Casualties were 125 officers and other ranks killed or died of wounds, 27 missing and 189 wounded.

Private Thomas Abraham received shrapnel wounds to the neck, back and abdomen. He was evacuated to No. 6 Casualty Clearing Station on 10 April where he died of wounds on 17 April 1917.

Thomas Robert was one of three brothers killed during the Great War. His brothers James William (see entry **56 Private James William Abraham**) and Absolom (see entry **55 Private Absolom Abraham**) were both killed in action on 1 July 1916 at the Battle of the Somme.

John Joseph Proctor
Private 32344, 15th Battalion, Royal Scots

Born	Portadown
Parents	Son of John Stevenson and Issabella Proctor (nee MacDonald) of Portadown
Residence	Harford Street
Enlisted	Glasgow, Scotland
Died	Killed in action 28 April 1917, France
Buried	No Known Grave
Commemorated	Arras Memorial, Pas de Calais, France. Bay 1& 2. Portadown War Memorial (112) Thomas Street Methodist War Memorial

The Proctor family resided in Meadow Lane and then moved to 12 Harford Street, Portadown. John's mother Issabella died on 8 April 1914. His father John Stevenson was employed as a weaver; he then ran his own fruit and vegetable business.

Private Proctor served in 'C' Company.

He had a sister Mary Elizabeth who resided in Glasgow and two brothers Ralph and Archie. He served in the Machine Gun Corps

during the Gallipoli campaign and died of pneumonia in 1921. He is not commemorated on Portadown War Memorial.

Private John Joseph Proctor, right, with his brother Ralph. (Phyllis Kerr)

Robert Whiteside
Corporal 443, 16th (Pioneer) Battalion, Royal Irish Rifles

Born	30 April 1880, Seagoe
Parents	Son of Alexander and Annie Whiteside of 27 Carrickblacker Road, Portadown
Residence	Carrickblacker Road
Enlisted	Lurgan
Died	Killed in action 18 June 1917, Belgium
Age	36
Buried	Kemmel Chateau Military Cemetery, Belgium. Grave O. 40.
Commemorated	Portadown War Memorial (32).

Corporal Robert Whiteside. (Hazel Jeffers)

Robert's father Alexander was a labourer. He and his wife Annie had children Robert born 1880, Elizabeth born 1882, Ferguson born 1887, William James born c1887, Alexander born 1888 and George born 1893. The family resided at White Row on the Carrickblacker Road, Portadown. Elizabeth emigrated to the United States of America. George died in 1915.

Robert was employed by the Great Northern Railway. He was the husband of Mary Whiteside of 112 Victoria Street, Lurgan. The couple had several children, one of whom, Billy later played football for Belfast Celtic.

Mrs Annie Whiteside received a letter from her son Ferguson

I was speaking to his platoon officer and he told me that Robert had been killed while working in the trenches. He did not suffer much pain as he died shortly after being hit. Do not fret too much about him. You have the consolation of knowing that he died for his country. I have been to see his grave. He is buried in a quiet village graveyard behind the trenches. The Captain of his company has written to his wife to let her know of his death.

Portadown Express
29 June 1917

Robert's brothers Ferguson, Alexander and William James all served during the Great War. Ferguson served in the 9th Battalion, Royal Irish Fusiliers. He married twice and had several children. He died in 1956.

Alexander emigrated to the United States of America where he lived for a time with his sister Elizabeth. He enlisted in the United States army and served in France during the Great War.

William James was a local footballer and was nicknamed the 'hat' on account of the number of hat tricks he scored while playing for junior football club Edenderry Arrows. He served in the 1st Battalion, Royal Irish Fusiliers. He was gassed at the Battle of St. Julien (2nd Ypres) in April 1915 and was permanently blinded with the loss of both eyes.

William James Whiteside, left, with comrades at St. Dunstan's. (Hazel Jeffers)

William James attended St. Dunstan's Hospital for blinded ex-servicemen where he was taught various skills such as mat making and shoe repairs. He was issued with a pair of glass eyes, which he would wear on special occasions. William James laid the wreath on behalf of Portadown's ex-servicemen at the inauguration of Portadown War Memorial on 13 November 1925. He died in 1942 the entry in Seagoe Church Records reads "Lost both eyes at the Battle of St. Julien 1915".

Thomas Robert Corkin
Rifleman 186, 16th (Pioneer) Battalion, Royal Irish Rifles

Born	Portadown
Parents	Son of James and Rachel Corkin of Ballygargan
Residence	Ballygargan
Enlisted	Lurgan
Died	Killed in action 21 June 1917, Belgium
Age	23
Buried	Wytschaete Military Cemetery, Belgium. Grave I. F. 4.
Commemorated	Portadown War Memorial (258)

Rifleman Thomas Corkin, is reported killed in action. He was the only son of Mr. And Mrs. Corkin, Knocknamuckley, Portadown.

Portadown News
7 July 1917

Grave of Rifleman Thomas Robert Corkin. (Author's Collection)

Francis Monaghan
Private 6394, 1st Battalion,
Royal Irish Fusiliers

Born Portadown
Parents Son of James and Annie Monaghan of 5 Bann Street, Portadown
Residence Bann Street
Enlisted Portadown
Died Killed in action 26 June 1917, France & Flanders
Age 20
Buried No Known Grave
Commemorated
Arras Memorial, France Bay 9.
Portadown War Memorial (6)

Before the outbreak of war Francis was employed by Messrs Spence Bryson and Co. Ltd.

Private Monaghan served in 'C' Company. On 24 June the 1st Battalion carried out a successful trench raid against enemy shell holes near the village of Roeux. The raiding party consisted of four officers and 60 other ranks. Considerable casualties were inflicted on the Germans during the operation and five prisoners were taken. Casualties were two officers killed and 14 other ranks killed or wounded.

His brother Private James Monaghan was wounded in action whilst serving with the machine gun section of the Scottish Rifles during the Great War.

James Forbes
Private 42375, 17th Battalion,
Highland Light Infantry

Born Glasgow
Residence Obins Street
Enlisted Glasgow, Scotland
Died Died of wounds 2 July 1917, Belgium
Buried Coxyde Military Cemetery, Koksijde West-Vlaanderen, Belgium. Grave I. C. 17.
Commemorated
Portadown War Memorial (185)

James previously served in the Royal Scots Fusiliers with the serial number 28967.

His father received a letter from James' commanding officer

It is with very much regret that I have to send you bad news. Your son was wounded in the head by shrapnel shell, and we all thought that it was not serious, but he subsequently passed away. I know his death will be a very sad blow to you and his mother, but it must be a great consolation to you to know that he met his death while doing his duty. Personally I regret his death very much, as he was always so willing and courageous.

Portadown News
15 September 1917

Third Battle of Ypres (31 July-10 November 1917)

On 16 July 1917 3,000 British guns opened up the preliminary bombardment of German positions. On 31 July the Second and Fifth Armies attacked but due to heavy rain the shelling had turned No Man's Land into a featureless landscape of mud and water filled craters.

The first offensive was halted on 4 August to be renewed on 16 August at the Battle of Langemarck. By the end of August of over 20 divisions, which had taken part in the fighting, 14 had to be withdrawn from the line to be reformed.

Australians, Canadians and New Zealanders were thrown into the attack in September and on 12 October came the Battle of Passchendaele. Atrocious weather conditions had dogged the battle from the onset and again the soldiers had to advance through a muddy quagmire during a storm. In two months the British and Empire forces had advanced a little over three miles and suffered enormous losses.

Total British losses were approximately 250,000 of which 70,000 were killed.

William James Benson
Lance-Corporal 14084, 10th Battalion, Royal Irish Rifles

Born	Drumcree
Parents	Son of Samuel Benson of Canagola
Residence	Canagola
Enlisted	Belfast
Died	Killed in action 6 August 1917, Belgium
Buried	New Irish Farm Cemetery, Ieper, West-Vlaanderen, Belgium. Grave XVIII. D. 1.
Commemorated	Portadown War Memorial (273) Drumcree Parish Church War Memorial Tartaraghan Parish Church War Memorial

Before the outbreak of war William had a grocery shop in Woodhouse Street, Portadown.

Lance-Corporal Benson was awarded a parchment certificate for gallantry and devotion to duty in the field.

His brother Marshall was an assistant to T. J. Montgomery, High Street, Portadown. He also served in the 10th Battalion, Royal Irish Rifles during the Great War.

Samuel Robinson Trooper 850, North Irish Horse

Born Seagoe
Residence Lisniskey
Enlisted Portadown
Died Died 9 August 1917, Belgium
Buried Mendinghem Military Cemetery, Poperinge, West-Vlaanderen, Belgium. Grave IV. B. 23.
Commemorated Portadown War Memorial (312) Seagoe Parish Church War Memorial

Trooper Robinson served with a detachment of dragoons during the South African War 1899-1902.

William Henry Lappin Private 4745, 7/8th Battalion, Royal Irish Fusiliers

Born Portadown
Parents Son of Joseph Lappin of Portadown
Residence Obins Street
Enlisted Finner Camp, Co. Donegal
Died Killed in action 10 August 1917, Belgium
Buried No Known Grave
Commemorated Ypres (Menin Gate) Memorial, Ieper, West Flaanderen, Belgium. Panel 42. Portadown War Memorial (187)

In the early hours of 8 August 1917 the 7/8th Battalion relieved the 2nd Battalion, Royal Irish Rifles in support trenches on Frenberg Road near Verlorenhoek. Over the next few days the Germans, aided by three spotter aircraft, shelled the British lines.

Enemy aerial activity continued, especially in the afternoon when over 20 aeroplanes were over our lines. During the early morning his shellfire became intense.

7/8th Battalion, Royal Irish Fusiliers War Diary 10 August 1917

At 4.30am the 7/8th Battalion went into the frontline trenches. From 8-11 August, when the Battalion went out of the trenches, casualties were 18 killed, 69 wounded and 18 missing.

William's father Joseph (see entry **186 Rifleman Joseph Lappin**) was killed in action on 7 September 1916 in France.

Samuel Gracey MM
Sergeant 8659,
Canadian Army Medical Corps

Born	8 May 1888, Portadown
Residence	Carrickblacker Road
Enlisted	22 September 1914, Valcartier, Canada
Died	Killed in action 15 August 1917, France
Age	29
Buried	Noeux Les Mines Communal Cemetery, Pas de Calais, France. Grave II. K. 7.
Commemorated	Portadown War Memorial (30) Thomas Street Methodist War Memorial

Samuel was the husband of Mary Gracey and the couple had four children. The family resided at 4 Carrickblacker Road, Portadown.

He had a brother John who resided at 89 Frances Street, Hamilton, Ontario.

Samuel enlisted in the 2nd Battalion, Canadian Army Medical Corps. On enlistment his particulars were given as follows: occupation - pipe fitter, height - 5'10 1/2", complexion - fresh, eyes - blue, hair - dark brown. His next of kin was listed as Samuel Gracey but no relationship was given.

He sailed from Quebec on 3 October 1914 on the SS *Cassandra*. On 8 February 1915 he arrived in France and on 11 December Private Gracey was taken on strength of No.2 Canadian Field Ambulance.

Private Gracey was awarded the Military Medal (London Gazette 16 August 1916) for excellent work in the field for the wounded and sick. He was promoted Corporal on 12 September and the next day was promoted Sergeant.

Sergeant Gracey was awarded a Good Conduct Badge on 23 September 1916. A week later he was hospitalised with exhaustion rejoining his unit on 7 October. He was granted leave from 9-23 December 1916.

Battle of Langemarck (Third Ypres) (16 August 1917)

Field Marshal Haig committed six Divisions of the British Fifth Army, including the 16th (Irish) and 36th (Ulster) Divisions, in the attack at Langemarck.

From 16-18 August 1916 the 36th (Ulster) Division lost 74 officers and 1,941 other ranks killed wounded and missing. Casualties for the 9th Battalion, Royal Irish Fusiliers were 35 killed in action, 323 wounded, shell shock 12, missing 83 and

missing believed killed two. The 16th (Irish) Division lost 125 officers and 2,042 other ranks.

These battles, which raged until 10 November, are collectively known as the Third Battle of Ypres.

Irish Round Tower at Island of Ireland Peace Park, Messines. (Author's Collection)

William John Campbell
Private 24952, 9th Battalion, Royal Irish Fusiliers

Born	Portadown
Parents	Son of Sarah Campbell of 24 Mourneview Street, Portadown
Residence	Mourneview Street
Enlisted	Portadown
Died	Killed in action 16 August 1917, Belgium
Buried	Bedford House Cemetery, Zillebeke, Ieper West-Vlaanderen, Belgium. Enclosure No. 4. Grave XIII. F. 9.
Commemorated	Portadown War Memorial (181) Thomas Street Methodist War Memorial St. Mark's Parish Church War Memorial

Private Campbell served in 'B' Company. William's mother received a letter from the Reverend Samuel Mayes

Your gallant boy has not been heard of since 16th August. On that day our brave lads were driven from a position they had taken early in the day, and some of the wounded were left in German hands. I hope your son is still alive as he was such a gallant soldier and beloved by all.

Portadown News
22 September 1917

His mother Sarah, brother Herbert and sister-in-law, Isobella,

emigrated to Canada after the end of the Great War and resided at Norwood, Ontario.

Joseph Clulow
Private 26914, 9th Battalion, Royal Irish Fusiliers

Born Portadown
Residence West Street
Enlisted Portadown
Died Killed in action 16 August 1917, Belgium
Buried No Known Grave
Commemorated Tyne Cot Memorial, Zonnebeke, West-Vlaanderen, Belgium. Panel 140-141. Portadown War Memorial (231) St. Mark's Parish Church War Memorial

Joseph was the husband of Eleanor Clulow. The couple had three children Joseph, James, and Ruby. The family resided at 9 Montague Street, Portadown.

Private Clulow served in 'B' Company. His brother Francis served during the Great War and another brother Edward resided at Bloomfield, Belfast. Eleanor Clulow remarried a Mr. Graham.

Joseph's two sons served during World War Two - Joseph was a Sergeant in the Royal Maritime Artillery and James (see entry **WW2-9 Sergeant James Ernest Clulow**) died of wounds on 4 August 1944 in Italy whilst serving in the North Irish Horse.

Harold Evans Cowdy
Second-Lieutenant, 9th Battalion, Royal Irish Fusiliers

Parents Son of William Laird and Nellie Evans Cowdy of Rathowen, Portadown
Residence Carrickblacker Road
Died Killed in action 16 August 1917, Belgium
Age 20
Buried No Known Grave
Commemorated Tyne Cot Memorial, Zonnebeke, West-Vlaanderen, Belgium. Panel 140-141. Portadown War Memorial (28) Thomas Street Methodist War Memorial

Harold was the only son of William Laird and Nellie Evans Cowdy and grandson of William and Mary Laird Cowdy. His father was a prominent Methodist and was the first editor of

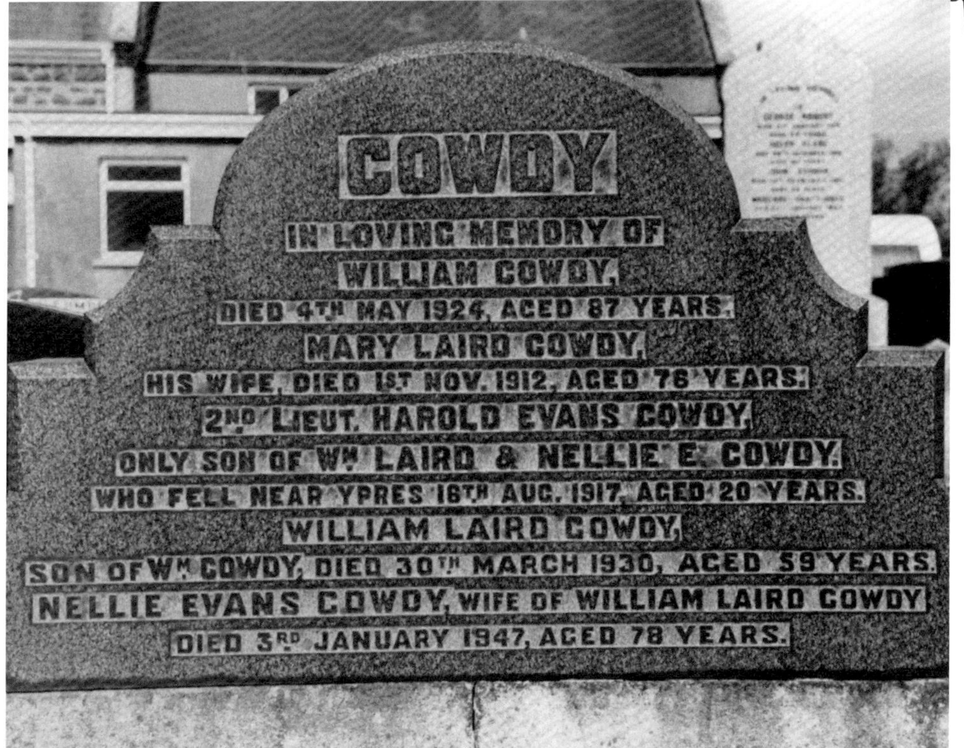

Family grave of Second-Lieutenant Harold Evans Cowdy. (Author's Collection)

Irish Christian Endeavour. He was a Justice of the Peace.

Harold was employed in the family business of Messrs William Cowdy and Son, handkerchief manufacturers, Portadown. He had a sister, Eileen who graduated from Queen's University, Belfast in 1917.

He received his commission in October 1916 through the Belfast University contingent of the Officers Training Corps. Second-Lieutenant Cowdy proceeded to the front in December 1916.

Edward Jones
Private 14363, 9th Battalion, Royal Irish Fusiliers

Born	Portadown
Parents	Son of James and Eliza Jones of Portadown
Residence	South Street
Enlisted	Portadown
Died	Killed in action 16 August 1917, Belgium
Age	38
Buried	No Known Grave

Commemorated	Tyne Cot Memorial, Zonnebeke, West-Vlaanderen, Belgium. Panel 140-141. Portadown War Memorial (217) St. Mark's Parish Church War Memorial

Edward was the husband of Maria Jones of 13 South Street, Portadown. The couple had two sons Eric and Edward Ypres - named after the place and battle where his father was killed.

Private Jones served in 'C' Company as a stretcher-bearer. His widow received a letter from the Reverend Samuel Mayes

I most deeply sympathise with you on the death of your gallant husband. He was killed instantly while carrying a wounded man back from the line. He died the death of a hero, and Portadown has every right to be proud of such sons. We miss him very much in the band, and as a stretcher-bearer. He nobly did his duty, and died like a man at his post.

Portadown News
15 September 1917

He was one of five brothers who all served in His Majesty's forces during the Great War. The brothers were David, Henry, Joseph and James. Four of the brothers served in the 9th Battalion, Royal Irish Fusiliers. James emigrated to Vancouver, Canada before the war where he was employed as a lineman. He enlisted in the 44th Battalion, Canadian Infantry in July 1915. After the war he returned to Canada and died in 1933. He was buried in the returned soldiers plot, Mountain View Cemetery, Vancouver, Canada.

He had another brother Joshua and sisters Anna and Eliza who was the wife of John Rowe. Edward also had a nephew Jim who served during the Great War.

Andrew Magowan MM Lance-Corporal 18058, 9th Battalion, Royal Irish Fusiliers

Parents	Son of William and Margaret Magowan of 63 Parkmount Terrace, Portadown
Residence	Garvaghy Road
Enlisted	Loughgall
Died	Killed in action 16 August 1917, Belgium
Age	18
Buried	Tyne Cot Cemetery, Zonnebeke, West-Vlaanderen, Belgium. Grave VIII. D. 13.

Commemorated
Portadown War Memorial (108)
First Presbyterian Church War Memorial, Edenderry

In 1917 the family resided at resided at 9 Castle Avenue, Portadown.

Lance-Corporal Magowan served in 'C' Company and was awarded the Military Medal for bravery in the field.

Alexander McCann
Private 22780, 9th Battalion, Royal Irish Fusiliers

Born	Portadown
Parents	Son of Mary and James McCann of 3 Atkinson's Avenue, Portadown
Residence	Atkinson's Avenue
Enlisted	9 November 1915, Portadown
Died	Killed in action 16 August 1917, Belgium
Buried	No Known Grave
Commemorated	Tyne Cot Memorial, Zonnebeke, West-Vlaanderen, Belgium. Panel 140-141. Portadown War Memorial (4) Thomas Street Methodist Church War Memorial

His mother Mary was a housekeeper. She was a widow and resided with her children Mark, Sarah and Alexander at 3 Atkinson's Avenue, Portadown. She also had a son George who died in 1901. Alexander was employed as a flax hackler and later as a labourer.

He enlisted in the 10th Battalion, Royal Irish Fusiliers with the serial number 10/22780. On enlistment his particulars were given as follows; occupation - labourer, height - 5'6½", age 32 years. He was described as having "slightly flat feet".

From 12-18 March 1916 Private McCann was in hospital in Belfast suffering from an eye condition known as ametropia

On 14 June Private McCann embarked from Southampton and disembarked the following day at Le Harve, France. On 13 July he joined the 9th Battalion, Royal Irish Fusiliers from Base Depot. He served in 'B' Company.

On 16 May 1917 Private McCann was admitted to No. 108 Field Ambulance suffering from furunculosis - an acute skin condition characterised by boils. On the same day he was transferred to No. 109 Field Ambulance. On 21

May he was admitted to No. 50 Casualty Clearing Station suffering from scabies and was discharged on 3 June.

He took part in the Battle of Langemarck on 16 August 1917 and was declared missing in action and presumed to have died on that date.

Author at Tyne Cot Memorial where his great uncle, Private Alexander McCann, is commemorated. (Author's Collection)

Adam McMullen
Private 14569, 9th Battalion, Royal Irish Fusiliers

Born	Donaghcloney
Parents	Son of Adam and Ellen McMullen of 120 Park Road, Portadown
Residence	Park Road
Enlisted	Portadown
Died	Killed in action 16 August 1917, Belgium
Age	30
Buried	No Known Grave
Commemorated	Tyne Cot Memorial, Zonnebeke, West-Vlaanderen, Belgium. Panel 140-141. Portadown War Memorial (196) St. Mark's Parish Church War Memorial

Adam was a member of Edenderry Pipe Band.

Private McMullen served in 'B' Company. In early 1916 it was reported that he was in a base hospital in France and later evacuated to Richmond Hospital in England.

Intimation was received on Friday last that Private Adam McMullan, R.I.F., 120 Park

Road, Portadown, who was previously reported missing has been killed in action on 16th August. Much sympathy is felt with the parents, brothers and sisters of the gallant soldier.

Portadown Express
14 September 1917

Three of his brothers, one of whom also served during the Great War, emigrated to the USA - Robert and sister-in-law Lily resided at 2 South Woodbine Street, Hartford, John and sister-in-law Jean resided at 18 Columbia Street, also Hartford, Connecticut and Joseph resided at 20 Midland Avenue, Detroit, Michigan. A sister Mary and brother-in-law John McBride resided at 54 Damascus Street, Belfast.

Henry Mortimer
Private 24909, 9th Battalion, Royal Irish Fusiliers

Born	Portadown
Parents	Son of Joseph and Mary Jane Mortimer of 136 West Street, Portadown
Residence	West Street
Enlisted	Portadown
Died	Killed in action 16 August 1917, Belgium
Buried	No Known Grave
Commemorated	Tyne Cot Memorial, Zonnebeke, West-Vlaanderen, Belgium. Panel 140-141. Portadown War Memorial (239) St. Mark's Parish Church War Memorial

Henry had previously served in the North Irish Horse with the serial number 2267. Private Mortimer served in 'C' Company.

John Quinn
Private 14625, 9th Battalion, Royal Irish Fusiliers

Born	Portadown
Parents	Son of John and Caroline Quinn of 1 Mandeville Terrace, Portadown
Residence	Union Street
Enlisted	Belfast
Died	Killed in action 16 August 1917, Belgium
Age	21
Buried	Tyne Cot Cemetery, Zonnebeke, West-Vlaanderen, Belgium. Grave VI. D. 12.
Commemorated	Portadown War Memorial (226)

St. Mark's Parish Church War Memorial

Private Quinn served in 'B' Company.

Grave of Private John Quinn. (Author's Collection)

Wilfred Laurence Reavie
Second-Lieutenant,
3rd Battalion,
Royal Dublin Fusiliers

Parents	Son of John R. and Mary Reavie of 13 Hanover Street, Portadown
Residence	Hanover Street
Died	Killed in action 16 August 1917, Belgium
Buried	No Known Grave
Commemorated	Tyne Cot Memorial, Zonnebeke, West-Vlaanderen, Belgium. Panel 144-145. Portadown War Memorial (117) Thomas Street Methodist Church War Memorial

Wilfred's father John was employed, as a clerk at the Thomas Smith owned Daisy Hill Nurseries, Newry. Previously he had worked as a clerk in the parcels office of the Great Northern Railway in Portadown Railway Station. He and his wife Mary had children Wilfred Laurence, Edwin, Victor Isaac, Gladys and Winifred.

Wilfred was a member of the Bann Lily Lodge of the British Order of Ancient Free Gardeners.

He enlisted in the North Irish Horse and rose to the rank of Sergeant. He received a commission in the Royal Dublin Fusiliers. The 3rd Battalion was a reserve battalion, which was stationed in the United Kingdom for the duration of the war. Second-Lieutenant Reavie would have been serving on attachment to another battalion or regiment when he was killed.

His mother received a letter from Captain L. C. Byrne

I cannot express to you Mrs Reavie, my sorrow or my sympathy with you in your great loss. Coming as it does so suddenly, and within such a short time of his joining the Battalion, it must be very hard to bear. You will have the consolation of knowing that your son died as I am sure you would have wished him to do - leading his men into action at Ypres on the morning of the 16th. We had some very difficult ground to attack over, and some very well defended strong points to capture. It was whilst capturing one of these that your son was killed instantaneously by a machine gun. His servant was also killed with him...

Portadown News
15 September 1917

William Robert Stevenson
Private 14674, 9th Battalion, Royal Irish Fusiliers

Born	Laurelvale
Parents	Son of Robert and Lucy Stevenson of 32 Coronation Street, Portadown
Residence	Coronation Street
Enlisted	September 1914, Portadown
Died	Killed in action 16 August 1917, Belgium
Age	19
Buried	No Known Grave
Commemorated	Tyne Cot Memorial, Zonnebeke, West-Vlaanderen, Belgium. Panel 140-141. Portadown War Memorial (74) St. Mark's Parish Church War Memorial

William was the eldest son of Robert and Lucy Stevenson. He was a member of the Ulster Volunteer Force and Dr. Kane's Crimson Star LOL 417.

He enlisted in September 1914 and underwent training at Clandeboye. Private Stevenson took part in the Battle of the Somme on 1 July 1916 and came through unscathed. Private Stevenson served in 'B' Company at the Battle of Langemarck.

Albert Wilkinson
Private 24910, 9th Battalion, Royal Irish Fusiliers

Born	Portadown
Parents	Son of John and Elizabeth Jane Wilkinson of Derrymacfall
Residence	Derrymacfall
Enlisted	Portadown
Died	Killed in action 16 August 1917, Belgium
Buried	No Known Grave

Commemorated
Tyne Cot Memorial, Zonnebeke, West-Vlaanderen, Belgium.
Panel 140-141.
Portadown War Memorial (293)
Drumcree Parish Church War Memorial

Albert's father was a farmer and had children Lizzie, Sarah, Samuel John, Marianne, Emily, Albert and Edith.

Private Wilkinson served in 'C' Company.

Patrick Bennett
Private 3920, 7/8th Battalion, Royal Irish Fusiliers

Born	Portadown
Parents	Son of Patrick and Bridget Bennett of 62 Curran Street, Portadown
Residence	Curran Street
Enlisted	Portadown
Died	Killed in action 16 August 1917, Belgium
Age	20
Buried	No Known Grave

Commemorated
Tyne Cot Memorial, Zonnebeke, West-Vlaanderen, Belgium.
Panel 140-141.
Portadown War Memorial (75)

News is to hand that private Patrick Bennett, Curran Street, Portadown, has fallen in action. He was serving in the R.I.R. (sic).

Portadown News
1 September 1917

Tyne Cot Cemetery and Memorial. (Author's Collection)

Thomas Graham Shillington Captain, 9th Battalion, Royal Irish Fusiliers

Born	9 October 1897, Ardeevin, Portadown
Parents	Son of Major David Graham and Sarah Louisa Shillington of Ardeevin, Portadown
Residence	Killycomain Road
Died	Died of wounds 18 August 1917, Belgium
Age	19
Buried	Brandhoek New Military Cemetery No. 3, Belgium. Grave II. E. 31.
Commemorated	Portadown War Memorial (153) Thomas Street Methodist Church War Memorial Family Plaque Thomas Street Methodist Church

The Shillington family was one of the most prominent families in Portadown. They were closely associated with the Methodist Church. David Graham Shillington married Sarah Louisa Collen daughter of John Collen of Killicomain House Portadown in 1895. The couple had children Gertrude Mary, Thomas Graham, Elizabeth Louise, John Graham and Robert Edward Graham.

Major Graham David Shillington, father of Captain Thomas Graham Shillington. (Author's Collection)

Thomas Graham was educated at Methodist College, Belfast and at Rossell School near Blackpool.

His father David Graham Shillington was closely associated with the Ulster Volunteer Force and when war broke out was commissioned in the 9th Battalion Royal Irish Fusiliers. Thomas' cousin Lieutenant Geoffrey St. George Shillington Cather was awarded a posthumous Victoria Cross for gallantry on 1/2 July 1916 at the Battle of the Somme.

On 21 October 1915 Second-Lieutenant Shillington, together with Lieutenant H. P. Nott of the 1/6th Gloucesters, commanded a night patrol, which consisted of 30 men. The patrol encountered a German patrol in No Man's Land and a firefight ensued.

In April 1916 he was promoted Lieutenant and was appointed Assistant Adjutant to Lieutenant Shillington Cather. He took part in the Battle of the Somme on 1 July 1916 and was wounded in action. A few days after the battle he was promoted Captain and was appointed in command of 'B' Company.

In 1916 he attended a course at anti gas school, which enabled him to instruct his men in the use of the new gas helmet.

Captain Shillington was wounded in action on 16 August 1917 at the Battle of Langemarck and died two days later at No. 3 Australian Casualty Clearing Station.

Major and Mrs David Graham Shillington donated £100 to the Ulster Volunteer Force Hospital to name two beds in memory of their son. After the war Major David Graham Shillington was elected to the Stormont Parliament as Unionist MP for Central Armagh. In 1937 he became Minister of Labour a position he held until ill health forced him to relinquish the post in 1941.

Grave of Captain Thomas Graham Shillington.

He was Governor of Methodist College, Belfast and was elected President of their Old Boys Association in 1934. Major Shillington was also President of Portadown British Legion and Portadown Music Festival. He was elected Worshipful Master of Portadown District LOL 1 in 1926, a position he held until his death in 1944.

Thomas' brother John Graham was Lieutenant-Colonel of the King's Own Scottish Borderers and served in India during World War Two.

His brother Robert Edward Graham joined the Royal Ulster Constabulary in 1933 and was appointed Chief Constable in 1970. He received a knighthood in 1972 and retired in 1973. Robert Edward Graham Shillington died in 2001.

Robert John Cordy
Private 241830,
2/5th Battalion, Kings Own (Royal Lancaster Regiment)

Born	1 March 1891, Carn
Parents	Son of David and Jane Eliza Cordy of Carn
Residence	Carne
Enlisted	Barrow
Died	Killed in action 22 August 1917, France
Age	26
Buried	Cite Bonjean Military Cemetery, Nord, France. Grave VIII. D. 29.
Commemorated	Portadown War Memorial (274) Seagoe Parish Church War Memorial

Robert was a member of Tamnificarbet LOL 17.

In his last letter home to his father, dated 18 July 1917, he ended with the words

My Boss will be over seeing you from Barrow. Let him see that you are proud to have a son fighting for the old Homestead, as he likes a true Ulster man.

Seagoe Parish Magazine
December 1917

Grave of Private Robert John Cordy.

His mother received a letter from Captain W. E. Burdet

It is my melancholy duty to inform you of the death of your gallant son, Private R. J. Cordy, who was killed by a shell while sleeping in his dug-out. I can only hope that it will be some slight consolation to you to know that he died without pain or suffering. I beg to express not only my own deep sympathy with you in your bereavement, but also that of all officers and men of his company. We had no better soldier, nor more popular man among us than your son.... It is a great loss to me personally, for as one of the company runners, your son had discharged arduous duties in a way that made him almost indispensable.

Portadown News
26 October 1918

Battle of Passchendaele (Third Ypres) (12 October-10 Nov. 1917)

On 12 October the Battle of Passendaele began with attacks by Australians and New Zealanders. On 26 October and again on 6 November it was the turn of the Canadians. Passchendaele was finally captured on 10 November. These battles, which raged until 10 November, are collectively known as the Third Battle of Ypres.

James Williams
Private 40984, 1st Battalion, South Staffordshire Regiment

Born	Portadown
Parents	Son of Joseph and Mary Williams of 19 Needham Street, Newry
Residence	Montague Street
Enlisted	Newry
Died	Killed in action 26 October 1917, Belgium
Buried	No Known Grave
Commemorated	Tyne Cot Memorial, Zonnebeke, West-Vlaanderen, Belgium. Panel 90-92 & 162-162A. Portadown War Memorial (178)

James previously served in the Army Service Corps with the serial number T4/142343.

The name of Private James Williams, Staffordshire Regiment, late of Montague Street, Portadown, who was posted as missing in 1917, and officially announced dead late last year, was inadvertently omitted from the Roll of Honour published in a recent issue of the "News".

Portadown News
11 January 1919

William Allen
Private 2345, 2nd Battalion, Australian Imperial Force

Born	15 January 1889, Moy, Co. Tyrone
Parents	Son of Richard and Anne Allen of 39 Carleton Street, Portadown
Residence	Carleton Street
Enlisted	5 May 1915, Singleton, New South Wales, Australia
Died	Killed in action 27 October 1917, Belgium
Age	28
Buried	Belgian Battery Corner Cemetery, Belgium. Grave II. H. 5.
Commemorated	Portadown War Memorial (33) St. Mark's Parish Church War Memorial

William served for four years in the Royal Irish Fusiliers militia. He was employed as a labourer and emigrated, aged 23, to Singleton, New South Wales, Australia.

On enlistment in the 7th Reinforcements, 2nd Battalion, Australian Imperial Force, his particulars were given as follows: occupation - labourer, height - 5'6", complexion - dark, eyes - brown, hair - dark, age 26 years and three months. He had tattoos on both arms.

Private Allen embarked for service on HMAT *Orsova* and arrived at Gallipoli on 4 November 1915. He sailed from Gallipoli on the *Huntsgreen* and arrived at Alexandria on 28 December.

On 19 February 1916 Private Allen was admitted to No. 3 Field Ambulance at Tel-el-Kebir suffering from sickness and was transferred to No. 2 Australian Stationary Hospital with a foreign body in his left thigh. After two days he was discharged to duty and rejoined his battalion on 26 February.

On 22 March he embarked on the troopship *Invernia* at Alexandria and disembarked on 28 March at Marseilles from where he proceeded to the front.

Private Allen was wounded in action in France when he received a gunshot wound to the leg and cheek on 22 July. He was admitted to No. 44 Casualty Clearing Station from where he was transferred to No. 23 General Hospital at Etaples. As his wounds were severe he was transferred on the hospital ship *Dieppe* to England and forwarded to No. 1 Northern General Hospital at

Newcastle-upon-Tyne. In September 1916 Private Allen attended Delhi Hospital for an eye test.

In October Private Allen was posted to No. 3 Commonwealth Depot at Bovington and in January 1917 was transferred to No. 4 Commonwealth Depot based at Wareham.

From March until August 1917 Private Allen served with the 61st Battalion in England before returning to the 2nd Battalion, which was attached to the Overseas Training Brigade at Perham Downs.

On 5 September he proceeded overseas to France arriving at the 1st Australian Divisional Base Depot at Le Havre the next day. From here Private Allen journeyed to the front arriving in the field on 29 September. On 3 November 1917 he was killed in action in Belgium.

William's sister Lila and brother-in-law William Holland resided at 7426 Ottawa Road, Cleveland, Ohio, USA.

Intimation has been received that Private Wm. Allen has been killed in action. He was a son of Mr. Richard Allen, Carleton Street, Portadown, and fell in action while serving with the Australian Imperial Force on the Western front.

Portadown News
17 November 1917

He had two brothers who served during the Great War and a cousin Bert Allen was killed in action while serving with the Australian forces.

John Henry Grayson
Lieutenant, 6th Battalion, Royal Irish Regiment

Parents	Son of John J. and Margaret E. Grayson of Delmaine, Malahide
Residence	High Street
Enlisted	Portadown
Died	Killed in action 20 November 1917, France
Age	20
Buried	Croiselles Railway Cemetery, France. Grave I. D. 7.
Commemorated	Portadown War Memorial (126) St. Mark's Parish Church War Memorial

John Henry's father John was employed by the Bank of Ireland. He transferred to the Drogheda branch in 1917. He was a member of Portadown Golf Club. John Henry was employed in the office of the Scottish Widows Fund Society, Belfast.

Lieutenant Grayson was injured by a gunshot wound to the thigh in 1916 and was evacuated to a hospital in Rouen.

John's sister served in France with the Voluntary Aid Detachment of the St. John Ambulance during the Great War.

Grave of Lieutenant John Henry Grayson.

Samuel Malcolmson
Private 14454, 9th Battalion, Royal Irish Fusiliers

Born — Portadown
Parents — Son of Joseph and Caroline Malcolmson of 56 Jervis Street Portadown.
Residence — Jervis Street
Enlisted — Portadown
Died — Killed in action 23 November 1917, France
Age — 23
Buried — No Known Grave
Commemorated — Cambrai Memorial, Louveral-Nord, France. Panel 10. Portadown War Memorial (139) St. Mark's Parish Church War Memorial

Private Malcolmson served in 'B' Company. His mother received a letter from a comrade of her son

It is with grief I write to inform you of the death in action of your dear son Samuel, who was killed on 23 November by a German sniper. I was speaking to him just a few days before his death, and he was very cheerful and happy then. He suffered no pain, death being instantaneous. I know it is a great loss to you, but he died a hero fighting for his King and country. I will miss him very much, as he was one of my best chums. May God comfort you in your great sorrow, and help you to bear the loss of one you so dearly loved.

Portadown News
15 December 1917

Samuel had a brother Willie and sister-in-law Harriett who resided

in Tandragee, a sister Sarah and brother-in-law James Wilson who resided at 109 Hemlock Street, South Manchester, Connecticut, USA and another sister Emily and brother-in-law William James Pepper who resided at 48 Jervis Street, Portadown.

Cambrai Memorial.

George Flavelle
Rifleman 175, 8/9th Battalion, Royal Irish Rifles

Born	Armagh
Residence	Corbrackey
Enlisted	Belfast
Died	Killed in action 5 December 1917, France
Buried	Fifteen Ravine British Cemetery, Villers-Plouich, Nord, France. Grave IV. D. 20.
Commemorated	Portadown War Memorial (283) Drumcree Parish Church War Memorial

There are newspaper reports in the Portadown News 17 November 1917 and Portadown Express 23 November 1917 regarding a George Flavelle who was wounded in action serving with the Canadians. It is not clear if this is the same person.

Grave of Rifleman George Flavelle.

Chapter 7
Victory and Armistice 1918-19

In the spring and summer of 1918 the Germans planned to launch a series of five offensives on the Western Front, which it was hoped, would bring ultimate victory over the Allies.

The first and largest was codenamed Operation Michael, which became known as the 'Kaiser's Battle'. After initial successes and gains of up to 30 miles the offensive was eventually stopped by determined British resistance. The other four offensives failed to make a war-winning breakthrough although one - Operation Blucher-Yorck brought the Germans to within 40 miles of Paris. With the defeat of these five offensives went any chance of Germany winning the war. The Allies now had the resources and manpower to advance to victory.

With morale collapsing on the frontline and with riots, mutinies and revolution taking place in their homeland the Germans sued for peace. An armistice was signed in a railway carriage at Compiegne, which came into effect at 1100 hours on 11 November 1918. The Great War had come to an end.

Meanwhile in Pasewalk Hospital near Stettin, Pomerania a little known corporal was undergoing treatment for the affects of mustard gas poisoning. His name was Adolf Hitler.

Joseph Aston Annesley
Private 204585, 15th Battalion, Canadian Infantry (Central Ontario Regiment)

Born	6 June 1894, Portadown
Parents	Son of John and Elizabeth Annesley of The Rocks, Portadown
Residence	Ballyfodrin
Enlisted	27 March 1916, Saskatoon, Canada
Died	Killed in action 7 February 1918, France
Age	23
	Buried Fosse No. 10 Communal Cemetery Extension, Pas de Calais, France. Grave III. A. 12.
Commemorated	Portadown War Memorial (257)

Drumcree Parish Church War Memorial

Joseph's father John was a farmer and had children John, Mary Jane, Sarah, Arthur, George, Elizabeth, Margaret Anne, James and Joseph Aston.

He was the husband of Louisa Annesley and the couple resided at 1134 Avenue South, Saskatoon, Canada.

On enlistment in the 96th Battalion, Canadian Infantry, Joseph's particulars were given as follows: occupation fireman, height - 5'10", complexion - fresh, eyes - grey, hair - light brown.

Grave of Private Joseph Aston Annesley.

He sailed with his unit from Halifax on the SS *Laconia* on 27 September 1916, arriving in Liverpool on 6 October. Two days after arrival in England he was transferred to the 92nd Battalion and on 4 January 1917 was taken on strength of the 5th Reserve Battalion.

Private Annesley proceeded to France on 9 April 1917 and was taken on strength of the 15th Battalion on 18 April. He was attached to 3 Brigade Headquarters for two weeks in December 1917 and from 15 January until 31 January 1918 he was on home leave when he was able to visit his family in Portadown.

His brother the Reverend James Annesley resided at Hamilton, Ontario, Canada.

Joseph's wife Louisa who in late 1917 resided at 607 Avenue North, Saskatoon, later remarried a Mr. Roberts.

Operation Michael (21 March-29 April 1918)

At 0440 on 21 March the Germans unleashed a five-hour barrage of artillery shells containing high explosives, shrapnel, phosgene and mustard gas on the British Third and Fifth Armies. At 0930 specially trained storm troopers equipped with machine guns, grenades and flamethrowers rushed from their trenches and advanced on the British lines.

Initially British units at the front were overwhelmed with the ferocity of the attack. By the end of the first day the Germans had advanced five miles, had taken 20,000 prisoners of war and killed 7,000 British soldiers.

Heavy fighting continued throughout March and April but the Germans failed to achieve a breakthrough and on 29 April the German High Command called off the offensive.

Richard Fulton
Private 17788, 36th Battalion, Machine Gun Corps

Born	Drumcree
Parents	Son of Nicholas and Elizabeth Fulton of 42 Henry Street, Portadown
Residence	Henry Street
Enlisted	Portadown
Died	Killed in action 21 March 1918, France
Age	31
Buried	No Known Grave
Commemorated	Pozieres Memorial, Somme, France. Panel 90 - 93. Portadown War Memorial (119) St. Mark's Parish Church War Memorial

Richard's father Nicholas and mother Elizabeth were employed as weavers. His parents had children Edward, Richard, Mathew and Ellen. All the children, except Ellen, were employed in the linen industry with Richard working as a spinning mule assistant when aged 16 years.

He was the husband of Hannah Fulton (later Beattie) of 6 and later 10 Henry Street, Portadown. The couple had four children.

Private Fulton had previously served in the Royal Irish Fusiliers with the serial number 14269.

James Hughes DCM, MM
Sergeant 4517, 9th Battalion, Royal Irish Fusiliers

Born	Portadown
Parents	Son of John and Elizabeth Hughes of 15 John Street, Portadown
Residence	John Street
Enlisted	Finner Camp, Co. Donegal
Died	Killed in action 21 March 1918, France
Age	30
Buried	Roye New British Cemetery, Somme, France. Grave IV. B. 1.

Commemorated
Portadown War Memorial (147)
St. Mark's Parish Church War Memorial

James was an instructor in the Ulster Volunteer Force. He also played football.

He was wounded in both jaws in 1916 and was awarded the Military Medal and the Distinguished Conduct Medal.

The King has been graciously pleased to approve of the award of the Distinguished Conduct Medal to the under mentioned 4517 Sergeant J. Hughes MM, Royal Irish Fusiliers (Portadown).

For conspicuous gallantry and devotion to duty. He went forward with a Lewis gun and knocked out an enemy machine gun, which was firing on our right flank. When his team were disabled, although wounded himself, he kept the gun in action until reinforcements came up.

Portadown News
14 September 1918

2 a.m. Intensive enemy barrage opened on our positions for a depth of from 4-6 Kilometres. At 6 a.m. enemy attacked. Bn. Moved to Bdge H.Q. just east of village. 2 Lt. Prenter and 4 O.Rs killed 2 Lt. Perkins and 16 Platoon missing. Part of 2 Platoons of A Coy. missing.

9th Battalion, Royal Irish Fusiliers
War Diary 21 March 1918

James Lamb
Private 4626, 1st Battalion, Royal Irish Fusiliers

Born	Portadown
Parents	Son of James and Sarah Lamb of 27 Foundry Street, Portadown
Residence	Foundry Street
Enlisted	Finner Camp, Co. Donegal
Died	Killed in action 21 March 1918, France
Age	27
Buried	No Known Grave

Commemorated
Pozieres Memorial, Somme, France. Panel 76 & 77.
Portadown War Memorial (94)
Seagoe Parish Church War Memorial
Thomas Street Methodist Church War Memorial

James was a local footballer who played for the 'Reds'.

Private Lamb served in 'B' Company and served in France from August 1914. At one time he was buried for three hours in a trench, which collapsed after a German shell exploded nearby.

Pozieres Memorial.

It was at 4.30 a.m. that the stillness was suddenly broken by the commencement of a terrific bombardment by artillery of all calibres and trench mortars, in which a good proportion of gas shells was employed, especially against artillery positions.... The long expected German offensive had begun, and the troops of the Fifth Army braced themselves to meet it.

The 1st Battalion Faugh-A-Ballaghs in the Great War

George Moore Smyth
Lance-Corporal 18002,
2nd Battalion,
Royal Munster Fusiliers

Parents	Son of George Smyth of Fairview Terrace, Portadown
Residence	Church Street
Enlisted	Whitehall, London
Died	Killed in action 21 March 1918, France
Buried	No Known Grave
Commemorated	Pozieres Memorial, Somme, France. Panel 78 & 79. Portadown War Memorial (67) St. Mark's Parish Church War Memorial

George Moore's father George was the principal of Park Road National School, Portadown.

George Moore, who resided in London, previously served in the Royal Dublin Fusiliers with the serial number 27316.

Enquiries regarding his son's fate brought George's father a response from the Red Cross. The organisation had received a report from Corporal J. Shannon, Labour Corps, the report stated that a Corporal T. Conlan

Saw Lance-Corporal Smyth killed by a hand grenade in our trenches at Epehy in the morning. He was hit by the same grenade. We retired the same day, and his body was left.

Portadown Express
4 October 1918

James Tedford
Private 25204, 1st Battalion, Royal Irish Fusiliers

Born	Portadown
Residence	Margaret Street
Enlisted	Portadown
Died	Killed in action 21 March 1918, France
Buried	No Known Grave
Commemorated	Pozieres Memorial, Somme, France. Panel 76 & 77. Portadown War Memorial (156)

Private James Tedford, R.I.F., Margaret Street, is reported missing.

Portadown Express
12 July 1918

Casualties reported for the 1st Battalion, Royal Irish Fusiliers on 21 March 1918 were 10 other ranks killed, one officer and 55 other ranks wounded and nine officers and 275 other ranks missing.

Thomas James Smyth
Rifleman 1795, 12th Battalion, Royal Irish Rifles

Born	Portadown
Residence	Mahon
Enlisted	Hamilton, Scotland
Died	Killed in action 21 March 1918, France
Age	19
Buried	No Known Grave
Commemorated	Pozieres Memorial, Somme, France. Panel 74 - 76. Portadown War Memorial (314)

By 5a.m. all communications with the 12th Royal Irish Rifles in the forward area were cut. This gallant battalion fought on to the end, and sacrificed itself in delaying the enemy infantry attacks, which surged forward like huge waves, overwhelming the isolated defended posts like sand castles on the beach.

The 1st Battalion Faugh-A-Ballaghs in the Great War

The surname appeared as Smith on Portadown War Memorial until the year 2000 when it was corrected at the request of Dennis Wiggins of Australia, a grand nephew of the deceased.

William James Topping
Rifleman 995, 16th (Pioneer) Battalion, Royal Irish Rifles

Parents	Son of James Topping of Ballydougan
Residence	Fowler's Entry
Enlisted	Lurgan
Died	Killed in action 21 March 1918, France
Buried	No Known Grave
Commemorated	Pozieres Memorial, Somme, France. Panel 74 - 76. Portadown War Memorial (101) St. Mark's Parish Church War Memorial

News has been received in Gilford that Rifleman Wm. James Topping, Royal Irish Rifles, was killed in the recent heavy fighting. Rifleman Topping enlisted in the Portadown Battalion of the Rifles shortly after its formation.

Portadown Express
26 April 1918

Recreated trench system, Tommy's Bar, Pozieres. (Author's Collection)

Samuel S. Woodhouse
Rifleman 20593, 12th Battalion, Royal Irish Rifles

Residence	Breagh (Drumcree Parish)
Enlisted	Belfast
Died	Killed in action 21 March 1918, France
Buried	No Known Grave
Commemorated	Pozieres Memorial, Somme, France. Panel 74 - 76. Portadown War Memorial (269) Drumcree Parish Church War Memorial

The 1901 Census Return lists the Woodhouse family of Breagh (Drumcree) Parish as follows

Thomas James, head of family, aged 28, a fowl dealer
Myria, wife, aged 23, a dressmaker
Henrietta, daughter, aged 4
Samuel, son, aged 2 months

The family's religious denomination is listed as Church of Ireland. It is not clear if this entry refers to Samuel S. Woodhouse.

Another Woodhouse family of Breagh (Drumcree) Parish listed in the 1901 census returns was George and Elizabeth Woodhouse. They had eight children one of whom was also called Samuel. This family had a son Thomas (see entry **268 Private Thomas Woodhouse**) who was killed in action on 21 October 1914. It is not clear if the Samuel S. Woodhouse listed above had any connection with this family.

Samuel previously served in the Army Service Corps with the serial number MT/266226.

Richard Edmond Watt
Private 24853, 1st Battalion, Royal Irish Fusiliers

Born	Tartaraghan
Residence	Drumannon
Enlisted	Portadown
Died	Killed in action 24 March 1918, France
Buried	No Known Grave
Commemorated	Pozieres Memorial, Somme, France. Panel 76 & 77. Portadown War Memorial (295) Tartaraghan Parish Church War Memorial

Private R.E. Watt, Royal Irish Fusiliers, son of Mrs. Watt, Drumannon, Portadown, who was previously reported missing, is now officially announced killed.

Portadown Express
27 September 1918

On 24 March 1918 the Germans continued their advance occupying Golancourt. After heavy fighting they took the village of Villeselue but were repulsed after a charge by 3rd Cavalry Division supported by 1st and 9th Battalions, Royal Irish Fusiliers. Later the Germans renewed their advance.

In a Casualty Return dated 4 September 1918 Private Watt was presumed killed on the statement of Private 43331 A. Warren who witnessed his colleague being killed in action. Private Warren managed to escape the German advance and report to his unit.

Samuel Edward McClatchey Captain, Royal Army Medical Corps, Attached 18th Battalion, Welsh Regt.

Parents	Son of Robert and Mary McClatchey of 34 Woodhouse Street, Portadown
Residence	Woodhouse Street
Enlisted	Portadown
Died	Killed in action 25 March 1918, France
Age	37
Buried	No Known Grave
Commemorated	Arras Memorial, France. Bay 10. Portadown War Memorial (245) St. Mark's Parish Church War Memorial

Samuel's father Robert was Town Clerk of Portadown. His mother Mary died on 2 May 1916 and was buried in Drumcree Churchyard. Samuel married Gladys Edith Scaife, only daughter of Samuel Scaife of Manchester, on 8 September 1917 at the Parish Church, Buxton. He was employed in Preston before the outbreak of war.

After gaining his commission in the RAMC Captain McClatchey served with the British Hospital Staff in Serbia arriving in February 1915. He was mentioned in despatches for his bravery in the field and was awarded the Order of St. Sava 5th Class by Serbia.

Captain McClatchey was attached to the 18th Battalion, Welsh Regiment. The battalion was in the line at a crossroads near Judas Farm, south of Arras. The area was the focus of an attack by the German Seventeenth Army as part of the Northern flank of the 21 March offensive. The battalion was given orders to withdraw and as it left the village of Ervillers, 10 miles south of Arras, at 2.00pm on the afternoon of 25 March, it suffered heavy casualties as a result of German shelling.

Arras Memorial.

In the early hours of 26 March the withdrawal continued via Courcelles, Le Comte, Ayette, Moncy to Sombrin where the casualty returns stated that the Battalion had lost 23 killed, 120 wounded and 79 missing. Captain McClatchey was one of those killed in action; he was attending to the wounded in a dugout when it received a direct hit from an enemy shell. He was killed instantly.

Samuel's widow remarried a Mr. Restall and they resided at Woodhouse, Faringdon, Berkshire. He had a brother Matthew A. W. McClatchey who was Town Clerk of Portadown.

Thomas Ernest England
Rifleman 130, 11/13th Battalion, Royal Irish Rifles

Born	Portadown
Parents	Son of William John and Elizabeth England of Mount Verdant, Kilkenny
Residence	Church Street
Enlisted	Belfast
Died	Died of wounds 27 March 1918, France
Age	22
Buried	No Known Grave
Commemorated	Pozieres Memorial, Somme, France.

Panel 74 - 76.
Portadown War Memorial (64)
St. Mark's Parish Church War Memorial

Thomas was the third son of William John and Elizabeth England of Portadown, who later moved to Kilkenny, and the grandson of Henry England of Knocknamuckley. He was employed as an apprentice engineer at the Falls Foundry, Belfast.

Thomas enlisted in the Royal Irish Rifles and proceeded to France in October 1915. He took part in a number of engagements and was gassed in the summer of 1917. He was attached to the 22nd Entrenching Battalion.

Two of his brothers Second-Lieutenant A. J. England, Royal Dublin Fusiliers and Sergeant R. H. England, RAMC served during the Great War.

Norman Sydney Holmes
Driver 100913, 15th Divisional Ammunition Column, Royal Field Artillery

Born	4 December 1894, Portadown
Parents	Son of David and Sarah Jane Holmes of Killycomain
Residence	Killycomain
Enlisted	Armagh
Died	Died of wounds 31 March 1918, France
Age	23
Buried	Duisans British Cemetery, Pas de Calais, France. Grave V. F. 76.
Commemorated	Portadown War Memorial (304) Seagoe Parish Church War Memorial

Norman Sydney was educated at Seagoe School and was a regular worshipper at church and Sunday school. He married Rachel Gates, the daughter of William Gates, a shoemaker of Edenderry, on Christmas Day 1915 at Seagoe Parish Church. She was employed as a weaver.

Driver Holmes and a comrade Jack Howard were ordered to recover some ammunition, which was within artillery range of the German guns.

They had just reached the ammunition when a shell wounded Howard's horse. He called to Holmes to bring him one of his own, and as he was bringing it another shell fell just beside them, wounding both of them. Holmes was the more severely wounded. They were both brought to the same

Casualty Clearing Station, and were placed in beds beside each other. In the morning it was clear that Holmes could not live. His chum asked that he might be allowed to hold Holmes' hand, and pushing back the screen that surrounded the bed of his dying friend he grasped his hand and held it until the end came. Holmes' last words were of his wife and home.

Seagoe Church
Magazine May 1918

Norman's brother Thomas Henry (see entry **305 Private Thomas Henry Holmes**) was killed in action on 1 July 1916 at the Battle of the Somme.

Grave of Driver Norman Sydney Holmes.

Richard Sherman
Corporal 14673, 9th Battalion, Royal Irish Fusiliers

Born	Portadown
Parents	Son of Isabel Sherman of Portadown
Residence	Montague Street
Enlisted	Portadown
Died	Died of wounds 1 April 1918, France
Age	27
Buried	St. Sever Cemetery Extension, Rouen, France. Grave P. VII. E. 9A.

Grave of Corporal Richard Sherman.

Commemorated
Portadown War Memorial (177)
Thomas Street Methodist Church War Memorial

Richard had two sisters Hannah and Lillie.

He was wounded on 1 July 1916 at the Battle of the Somme. Corporal Sherman was severely injured in the stomach and succumbed to his wounds at No. 5 General Hospital, Rouen.

Miss Sherman, Montague Street, returned home from France on Monday after visiting the grave of her brother Richard.

Portadown News
18 April 1918

Richard's cousin Ephraim (see entry **176 Private Ephraim Sherman**) was killed in action on 6 July 1916 at the Battle of the Somme.

John George Brew
Major, 9th Battalion, Royal Irish Fusiliers

Born	14 December 1876, Gateshead, Durham
Parents	Son of John George and Jane Isabella Brew of Carrickblacker Road, Portadown
Residence	Carrickblacker Road
Enlisted	15 September 1914, Portadown
Died	Died of wounds 6 April 1918, France
Age	41
Buried	Roye New British Cemetery, Somme, France. Grave IV. D. 9.

Commemorated
Portadown War Memorial (26)
First Presbyterian Church War Memorial, Edenderry

John George Brew senior married Jane Isabella Chater, the daughter of John Chater a foreman at a locomotive department, on 15 July 1872 in Gateshead. They had seven children William born 1872 and who died in 1874 aged 19 months, John born 1874 and who died aged 11 days, John George born 1876, Thomas born 1878 and who died aged 12 weeks, Albert born 1879, Ernest born 1883 and who died aged 12 weeks and Leonard Septimus born 1887.

John George senior was employed for several years by the North Eastern Railway Company before going to sea as a third engineer on the steamship *Opah* in 1873. He became a 2nd Class Marine

Engineer in 1875 and two years later earned his certificate as a 1st Class Engineer. John George died on 15 October 1886 when his ship SS *Castleton* sank in a storm in Bideford Bay. His wife Jane Isabella died on 25 September 1897 in South Shields.

Their son John George first went to sea in 1893 on the barque *Charles Cotesworth*. In 1897 he joined G. Heyn and Sons of Belfast, also known as the 'Headline' as the company named its ships after headlands. He saw service on the steamships *Rathlin Head, Torr Head* and *Teelin Head*.

Major John George Brew. (Steve Brew).

John George Brew married Annie Moffat Clow, daughter of William Moffat Clow JP, of Feddal House, Portadown on 19 April 1905. His brother Leonard, an apprentice engineer in Liverpool, was witness to the wedding. The couple had three children William who died of scarlet fever on 17 December 1911 aged 5 years 10 months and was buried in Seagoe Cemetery, John Kenneth born 17 January 1909 and Winifred Marion born 3 September 1911. The family resided at Rathlin, Carrickblacker Road, Portadown.

On enlistment as Private 13975 his particulars were given as follows occupation - ship's master, height - 5' 8", complexion - sallow, eyes - brown, hair - dark. He was commissioned as a Second-Lieutenant on 1 December 1914.

On 26 March 1918, during the German Spring Offensive, Major Brew, together with Colonel M.J. Furnell, Colonel Green and a driver, were travelling in a staff car when advancing German troops captured them. As they were being escorted back to the German lines enemy soldiers who did not realise that they had already been captured fired upon them. Major Brew was wounded in the lung and died of wounds on 6 April 1918.

Major J. G. Brew, Royal Irish Fusiliers, Portadown is believed to have been captured by the Germans in the recent fighting. He is a son-in-law of Mr. W. M. Clow J.P., Feddal House, Portadown and a partner in the firm of Messrs. James Clow and Co., corn millers. He was a member of the Portadown U.V.F. and joined the Royal Irish Fusiliers on the outbreak of war.

Portadown Express
12 April 1918

John George Brew was a member of Masonic Lodge No. 219, Portadown. His brother-in-law Malcolm Clow (see entry **27 Conducteur Malcolm Percy Clow**) died on 11 July 1917 in Serbia.

James Murray
Private 5481, 1st Battalion, Royal Irish Fusiliers

Born	Portadown
Parents	Son of John and Margaret Murray of Portadown
Residence	Woodhouse Street
Enlisted	Portadown
Died	Killed in action 11 April 1918, France & Flanders
Age	26
Buried	No Known Grave
Commemorated	Tyne Cot Memorial, Zonnebeke, West-Vlaanderen, Belgium. Panel 140-141. Portadown War Memorial (247)

James was the husband of Mary Murray and the couple resided at 34 Woodhouse Street, Portadown. He was an amateur boxer.

For nearly a week he was a prisoner, but escaped and rejoined his regiment.

Portadown News
8 May 1915

His brother Patrick also served in the Royal Irish Fusiliers and was wounded in action during the Great War.

Thomas Edward Chapman Crosbie MC & Bar
Captain, 9th Battalion, Royal Irish Fusiliers

Born	30 May 1897, Portadown
Parents	Son of Francis E. and Elizabeth Crosbie of Mahon House, Portadown
Residence	Mahon
Died	Died of wounds 15 April 1918, France & Flanders
Age	20
Buried	No Known Grave
Commemorated	Tyne Cot Memorial, Zonnebeke, West-Vlaanderen,

Belgium.
Panel 140-141.
Portadown War Memorial (313)
First Presbyterian Church War Memorial, Edenderry
Family Memorial Plaque, First Presbyterian Church, Edenderry
Lurgan College War Memorial

Francis was head of the family dairy firm Messrs. Crosbie Bros. From 1914 until 1920 he was a representative of Portadown Rural Division on the Lurgan Rural Council and was also on the Lurgan Board of Guardians. He had three sons - Thomas, Ernest and Kenneth. Ernest went on to practise medicine in Liverpool.

Thomas Edward was educated at Lurgan College and Queen's University. He was a cadet in the 10th Battalion, Royal Irish Fusiliers and a member of Queen's University Officers Training Corps. He was commissioned in December 1916 and completed his training at Moore Camp, Fermoy.

In 1917 Second-Lieutenant Crosbie was awarded the Military Cross for gallantry in action when he

Displayed signal bravery in charge of a party which set out to blow a gap in the enemy wire. He cut his way through the second belt, and drove the enemy out of shell holes. Subsequently he brought in a wounded man under heavy fire, and searched No Man's Land for missing men.

Portadown Express
26 April1918

Memorial to Captain Edward Chapman Crosbie, First Presbyterian Church, Edenderry. (Author's Collection)

In 1918 Captain Crosbie was awarded a bar to the Military Cross

For conspicuous gallantry and devotion to duty during a retirement. He handled his

company with great coolness and by his fine disregard of personal danger encouraged them to successfully cover the retirement of the battalion. He saw to the evacuation of all wounded under heavy artillery and machine gun fire, and throughout set a splendid example of courage and determination.

Portadown News
21 September 1918

His father received a letter from the Reverend Andrew Gibson, Forces Chaplain

I write with deep sorrow to tell you of the death in action of your son, Captain Crosbie MC on the 15th inst. One sees so many of his comrades and friends laying down their lives, but there are always a few among these whose death touches one more closely, because the bond of friendship is stronger and more tender. Thus it is with me for your son. He was a gallant soldier and one of the best of friends. His death was in keeping with his life. We had been heavily shelled and then attacked. Some positions had been temporarily lost, and he had gone forward to re-establish the line. He fell gallantly leading his men. He was severely wounded and died soon after he was brought into the first aid post. I am very sorry I was not there when he was brought in. I had left it some time before, so I did not see him. I assure you of my deep sympathy, and join with you in your sorrow...

Portadown Express
3 May 1918

William J. Redmond Lance-Corporal S/40807, 5th Battalion, Queen's Own Cameron Highlanders

Born Portadown
Residence Curran Street
Enlisted Glasgow, Scotland
Died Killed in action 16 April 1918, Belgium
Buried No Known Grave
Commemorated
Tyne Cot Memorial, Zonnebeke, West-Vlaanderen, Belgium.
Panel 136-138.
Portadown War Memorial (84)

Mrs. Redmond, Curran Street, has received intimation that her son, Private William Redmond, has been killed in action. He was serving with the Argyle and Sutherland Highlanders (sic).

Portadown News
11 May 1918

Lance-Corporal Redmond previously served in the Lovat Scouts with the serial number 3328.

Albert Brownlee
Corporal 6370, 1st Battalion, Royal Irish Fusiliers

Born	Portadown
Parents	Son of Bunting and Elizabeth Brownlee of 9 Carleton Street, Portadown
Residence	Carleton Street
Enlisted	Portadown
Died	Died of wounds 23 April 1918, France
Age	19

Grave of Corporal Albert Brownlee.

Buried	Etaples Military Cemetery, Pas de Calais, France. Grave XXIX. L. 3A.
Commemorated	Portadown War Memorial (34) St. Mark's Parish Church War Memorial

Albert's brother George (see entry **34 Private George Brownlee**) was killed in action on 26 November 1916 in France.

James Taylor
Pioneer 282271, Royal Engineers, attd. 41st Brigade, Royal Garrison Artillery

Born	Portadown
Parents	Son of James and Susannah Taylor of Battlehill
Residence	Jervis Street
Enlisted	Belfast
Died	Died of wounds 25 April 1918, Belgium
Age	36
Buried	Mendinghem Military Cemetery, Belgium. Grave X. C. 17.
Commemorated	Portadown War Memorial (140)

St. Mark's Parish Church War Memorial

James was the husband of Elizabeth Taylor and they resided at 55 Jervis Street, Portadown.

Pioneer Taylor served in the Royal Engineers Signal Section and was attached to the 41st Brigade, Royal Garrison Artillery. He died of wounds at No. 64 Casualty Clearing Station, France.

Mrs. L. Taylor, Battlehill, Portadown has received official information that her husband, Pioneer James Taylor, R.E., Signal Section, has died of wounds at the 64th Casualty Clearing Station. He leaves a wife and six small children.

Portadown News
18 May 1918

Thomas Flannigan
Private 34462, Canadian Army Medical Corps

Born	2 February 1895, Portadown
Parents	Son of John and Mary Anne Flannigan of 21 Bridge Street, Portadown
Residence	Hanover Street
Enlisted	19 September 1914, Montreal, Quebec, Canada
Died	Killed in action 19 May 1918, France
Age	23
Buried	Etaples Military Cemetery, Pas de Calais, France. Grave LXVI. D. 2.
Commemorated	Portadown War Memorial (114) St. Mark's Parish Church War Memorial Seagoe Parish Church War Memorial

Thomas was the husband of Eliza Hanna, daughter of Wilson Hanna, of Portadown. They had a daughter.

On enlistment in the No. 1 Canadian General Hospital, CAMC, his particulars were given as follows: occupation labourer, height - 5'6", complexion - dark, eyes - grey, hair - brown.

He sailed for England on the SS *Scandinavian* on 3 October 1914 and embarked for France at Southampton on 13 May 1915. Private Flannigan was based at Etaples - a huge military camp and hospital complex.

He was hospitalised from 11 August until 20 August 1915 when he accidentally fractured his little finger on his right hand. From 26 February until 18 March 1917 he was hospitalised due to influenza.

Late on the evening of 19 May 1918

German aircraft attacked an important railway near Etaples and bombs fell on the nearby military barracks including two of the hospitals. Wards six and seven of No. 9 Canadian Stationary Hospital received direct hits with six patients being killed and 32 wounded. Nine bombs fell within the No. 1 Canadian General Hospital complex, which at the time housed 1200 patients. A total of 64 patients and staff were killed or later died of wounds and 80 were wounded.

With her husband at the front Eliza and her daughter resided with her mother and father at 44 Hanover Street Portadown. She received a letter from, John A. Buchanan, No. 1 Canadian General Hospital

It is with the deepest sympathy that I write in an endeavour to console you in your great bereavement in the loss of your dear husband Thomas Flannigan. He was a splendid fellow, and I feel that I have lost a friend who can never be replaced. He was always like a younger brother to me ever since we enlisted together at Montreal, and no one had a nobler, truer friend that he was. I am not alone in my grief at his loss. His many other friends in the unit with whom he was so popular send you their heartfelt sympathy. There was only one Tommy in my life since I lost my own brother Tom, who was killed in the Aegean Sea, and now I have lost the other one who was just the same to me.... I may say that Tommy never suffered at all as his death was instantaneous. I hope that I may have the pleasure in seeing you in the near future either in Ireland or Canada to shake hands with you over the memory of my best friend and comrade.

Portadown News
8 June 1918

Grave of Private Thomas Flannigan.

Thomas Ellis
Rifleman 7353, 2nd Battalion, Royal Irish Rifles

Born	Seagoe
Parents	Son of Thomas and Mary Jane Ellis of 82 Bridge Street, Portadown
Residence	Bridge Street
Enlisted	1914, Portadown
Died	Died of wounds 24 June 1918, Stendal, Germany
Age	25
Buried	Berlin South-Western Cemetery, Brandenburg, Germany. Grave I. B. 8.
Commemorated	Portadown War Memorial (9) St. Mark's Parish Church War Memorial Seagoe Parish Church War Memorial

Thomas enlisted in 1914 and served at Gallipoli and the Western Front. He was twice wounded in action and was a prisoner of war.

Rifleman Thomas Ellis died from pneumonia in a PoW camp in Germany.

His brother Harry served with the 9th Battalion, Royal Irish Fusiliers during the Great War and was wounded in action on three occasions.

James McCullough
Driver 119976, 18th Division Ammunition Column, Royal Field Artillery

Born	Drumcree
Parents	Son of Elsie McCullough of 23 Henry Street, Portadown
Residence	Henry Street
Enlisted	Portadown
Died	Died 30 July 1918, France
Age	18
Buried	Argoeuves Communal Cemetery, Somme, France.
Commemorated	Portadown War Memorial (122)

Alexander Hayes
Private 714, 2nd (Garrison) Battalion, Royal Irish Regiment

Born	Kilmore
Parents	Son of Thomas Hayes of Sarah Street, Portadown
Residence	Sarah Street
Enlisted	Finner Camp, Co. Donegal

Died	Died 31 July 1918, France
Buried	Longuenesse (St. Omer) Souvenir Cemetery, Pas de Calais, France. Grave V. D. 18.
Commemorated	Portadown War Memorial (211) St. Mark's Parish Church War Memorial

Private Hayes previously served in the Royal Irish Fusiliers with the serial number 4792. He received shrapnel wounds in the arm when off duty at the beginning of 1915. He spent six weeks in hospital and was allowed home on leave in February 1915.

Private Alexander Hayes, Edgarstown, Portadown has died in an overseas hospital. He was serving with the R. I. F., and held the Mons Star. He was a well-known local footballer, and is the third member of his family to give his life for his country.

Portadown News
10 August 1918

Alexander was one of three brothers killed during the Great War. His brother John (see entry **212 Private John Hayes**) was killed in action on 1 July 1916 at the Battle of the Somme and his brother William (see entry **213 Private William Hayes**) was killed in action on 12 October 1916 at the Battle of Le Transloy.

Grave of Private Alexander Hayes.

The Advance To Victory (8 August-11 November 1918)

On 8 August the Allies launched a major offensive at Amiens. By 10 August the Allies had captured almost 25,000 prisoners and hundreds of artillery pieces.

Towards the end of August German forces withdrew to the

defences of the Hindenburg Line and went purely on the defensive for the rest of the war. On 9 November Kaiser Willhelm II went into exile with riots and revolution sweeping his country and with his generals in peace talks. On 10 November Canadian troops entered the Belgian town of Mons, scene of the British Army's epic 'Retreat from Mons' in August 1914. The next day 11 November 1918 the guns fell silent at 1100 hours.

In June 1919 came the Treaty of Versailles, which formally brought hostilities to an end.

Nicholas England
Private 754285, 58th Battalion, Canadian Infantry (Central Ontario Regiment)

Born	9 April 1888, Portadown
Parents	Son of David and Elizabeth England of 1 Goban Street, Portadown
Residence	Bridge Street
Enlisted	27 January 1916, Webbwood, Ontario, Canada
Died	Died of wounds 10 August 1918, France
Age	30
Buried	Hourges Orchard Cemetery, Domart Sur La Lure, Somme, France. Grave B. 15.
Commemorated	Portadown War Memorial (10) Thomas Street Methodist Church War Memorial

Nicholas' father David had a smallholding and was employed as a handloom weaver and then a scutch mill operator. He and his wife Elizabeth, who were devout Methodists, resided in the townland of Knocknamuckley. They had 14 children. In the 1901 census return the following children are listed - Margaret, Sarah, Elizabeth, David, Annie, Nicholas, William, Ellen, John, Edith and Robert. All were recorded as Methodists except David whose religious affiliation is given as Salvation Army. As the family grew they moved into Portadown.

Most of the family were employed in W.D. Robb's linen factory - three of the girls worked there for over 50 years and a son William Nicholas' twin brother, was employed at the factory for 58 years and was awarded the British Empire Medal. David England died on 14 February 1910 and was buried in Knocknamuckley Church of Ireland Churchyard, Portadown.

Nicholas travelled to Canada on a

number of occasions before returning home to enlist in the Royal Irish Fusiliers. After three years service with the colours he left home once more for Canada where he settled in Ontario. Nicholas was the husband of Jane England and the family resided in Webbwood, Ontario, Canada where Nicholas managed a farm.

On enlistment in the 119th Battalion, Canadian Infantry, his particulars were given as follows: occupation - farmer, height - 5'9", complexion - fair, eyes - brown, hair - black.

He sailed from Halifax on the SS *Metagama* on 8 August 1916 and arrived in Liverpool on 19 August. He was appointed Corporal on the same day he landed in England and reverted to Private on 31 August. On 7 September he was appointed Lance-Corporal and ten days later was promoted Corporal. On 1 February 1917 Nicholas was promoted Sergeant and on 20 February he reverted to Corporal.

A week later Nicholas reverted to Private in order to serve overseas and set off for France. He was taken on strength of the 58th Battalion and joined the unit in March 1918. On 8 August 1918 he was wounded in action and died of his injuries two days later. A colleague wrote to his mother

Private England fought on until too weak to go farther. Then he turned to go back to the dressing station and while on the way he saw two of the men of his own battalion lying wounded. He went over to them and

Family grave of Private Nicholas England. (Author's Collection)

stooped to help them as best he could when a shell came and killed all three.

Portadown News
7 September 1918

Nicholas' widow moved to the United States and resided at 472 Front Street Chicapsee, and later at 340 Dickinson Street, Springfield, both in Massachusetts.

His brother Robert resided at Bulyea, Saskatchewan and was studying for the Methodist ministry. He was also a volunteer in the Canadian Militia, serving in the 95th Saskatchewan Rifles. Robert gained a commission in the 203rd Battalion, Canadian Expeditionary Force in April 1916 and later served in the Royal Canadian Rifles, Nova Scotia Regiment. He was seriously wounded in action in the legs and right arm in August 1917. Lieutenant Robert England was awarded the Military Cross

For conspicuous gallantry and devotion to duty during the operations near Cambrai from 27th September to 1st October 1918. During the night prior to the attack he reconnoitred a village, and later returned with a party and mopped up enemy posts. During the operations as scout officer he kept the battalion commander accurately informed of the situation, being wounded in obtaining information.

Portadown News
10 October 1919

Nicholas' brother David emigrated to New England and Canada before returning to Portadown where he became a Justice of the Peace and a Methodist lay preacher.

His brother John was educated at Marlborough Street Technical College in Dublin and became a school principal and later President of the Methodist Church in Ireland.

Willoughby Frazer
Private 9852, 9th Battalion, Royal Irish Fusiliers

Born	Portadown
Parents	Son of David and Elizabeth Frazer of 12 Windsor Road, Belfast
Residence	Bridge Street
Enlisted	Lurgan
Died	Died of wounds 16 August 1918, France
Age	30
Buried	Arneke British Cemetery, Nord, France. Grave III. C. 13.
Commemorated	Portadown War Memorial (12) Seagoe Parish Church War Memorial

Willoughby was the eldest son of David and Elizabeth Frazer.

Formerly of Edenderry they had moved to Belfast. He was a former member of Seagoe Church Lads' Brigade.

...Pte. Frazer, who came from India with a battalion of the R.I.F shortly after the outbreak of war, took part in a number of fierce engagements, being at one time seriously wounded.

Portadown News
24 August 1918

Patrick Prentice
Private 2115, 8th Battalion, Royal Irish Regiment

Grave of Private Patrick Prentice.

Residence	Breagh (Seagoe Parish)
Enlisted	Belfast
Died	Died of wounds 23 August 1918, France
Buried	Bagneux British Cemetery, Gezaincourt, Somme, France. Grave V. A. 4.
Commemorated	Portadown War Memorial (270)

Patrick previously served in the Royal Irish Fusiliers with the serial number 3755.

Samuel Robinson
Private 2137998, 72nd Battalion, Canadian Infantry (British Columbia Regiment)

Born	14 October 1892, Portadown
Parents	Son of Ann Robinson of Drumherriff
Residence	Drumherriff
Enlisted	7 November 1917, Vancouver, Canada
Died	Killed in action 2 September 1918, France
Age	25
Buried	Beaurains Road Cemetery, Pas de Calais, France. Grave B. 31.

Commemorated
Portadown War Memorial (300)

On enlistment in the 2nd Depot Battalion, British Columbia Regiment, his particulars were given as follows: occupation - Able Seaman SS *Princess Sophia*, height - 5'10 1/2", complexion - fresh, eyes - hazel, hair - brown. He had a scar on the back of his right hand.

Grave of Private Samuel Robinson.

He sailed from Halifax on the SS *Tunisian* on 9 April 1918 and arrived in Liverpool on 19 April. He was taken on strength of 1st Canadian Reserve Battalion at Seaford on 20 April and preceded on draft to the 29th Battalion on 20 August. He arrived in France on 23 August and transferred to the 72nd Battalion, joining the regiment on 28 August 1918.

James Hewitt
Private 14306, 1st Battalion, Royal Irish Fusiliers

Born	Portadown
Residence	West Street
Enlisted	Belfast
Died	Killed in action 4 September 1918, France & Flanders
Buried	No Known Grave
Commemorated	Ploegsteert Memorial, Comines Warneton Hainaut, Belgium. Panel 9. Portadown War Memorial (232) St Mark's Parish Church War Memorial

Private Hewitt was wounded on 4 September 1918 and died on his way to the dressing station.

Portadown Express
14 February 1919

James William Sharpe
Private 5851, 9th Battalion, Royal Irish Fusiliers

Born: Laurelvale
Parents: Son of John and Maggie Sharpe of 30 James Street, Portadown
Residence: James Street
Enlisted: Newry
Died: Killed in action 4 September 1918, France & Flanders
Age: 21
Buried: No Known Grave
Commemorated: Ploegsteert Memorial, Comines Warneton Hainaut, Belgium. Panel 9. Portadown War Memorial (131) Seagoe Parish Church War Memorial

James had a brother John.

Thomas Henry Allen
Private 3417, 8th Battalion, Royal Irish Regiment

Born: Annaghmore
Residence: Mourneview Street
Enlisted: Armagh
Died: Killed in action 6 September 1918, France & Flanders
Age: 22
Buried: No Known Grave
Commemorated: Ploegsteert Memorial, Comines Warneton Hainaut, Belgium. Panel 4. Portadown War Memorial (179) St. Mark's Parish Church War Memorial

Private Allen previously served in the Royal Irish Fusiliers with the serial number 11552.

Thomas' family resided at 33 Mournview Street, Portadown. A sister Margaret resided at North 2nd Street, Philadelphia, USA and a sister Annie and brother-in-law John Craig, resided at 38 Charles Street, Portadown. Another sister, Sarah and brother-in-law Richard J. Pentland, resided in Drumnakelly.

William Partridge
Rifleman 53960, 13th Battalion, Kings Royal Rifle Corps

Born: Drumgor
Parents: Son of William Partridge of 7 Sarah Street, Portadown
Residence: Sarah Street
Enlisted: Portadown
Died: Killed in action 13 September 1918, France

Buried No Known Grave
Commemorated
Vis-en-Artois Memorial, Pas de Calais, France. Panel 9.
Portadown War Memorial (214)
St. Mark's Parish Church War Memorial

William had a brother and three sisters.

Rifleman Partridge previously served in the Royal Irish Rifles with the serial number D/21795. His father received a letter from Lieutenant S. T. Haney

Rifleman William Partridge. (Shirley Branyan)

I am deeply grieved to have to write and inform you of the death of your son in action. The company was attacking a strong German position, and your son was killed instantaneously while fighting in the front ranks, which had penetrated well into the German lines. I am sure that it will be a small consolation to you to know that your son did his duty nobly to the last. He was always regarded by the officers and men as one of the very best.

Portadown News
5 October 1918

William Henry Preston Private 3080368, 5th Battalion, Canadian Mounted Rifles (Quebec Regiment)

Born 26 September 1892, Portadown
Parents Son of Thomas and Elizabeth Preston of Portadown
Residence Henry Street
Enlisted 19 November 1917, Montreal, Canada
Died Died of wounds 14 September 1918, France
Age 25
Buried Ligny St. Flochel British Cemetery, Averdoingt, Pas de Calais.
Grave IV. D. 24.
Commemorated
Portadown War Memorial (124)

Thomas Street Methodist Church War Memorial

On enlistment in the 1st Depot Battalion, 1st Quebec Regiment, his particulars were given as follows: occupation - silk beamer, height - 6'1½", complexion - fair, eyes - brown, hair - dark. He developed a sore throat and was admitted to Montreal General Hospital on 3 January 1918 with tonsillitis. He was discharged from hospital on 16 January and spent four days recuperating in the Grey Nuns Convalescent Home, Montreal.

Private Preston sailed from Halifax on the SS *Grampian* on 3 February 1918 and arrived in England on 16 February. On 27 February he was taken on strength of the 23rd Reserve Battalion based at Bramshott and at the end of May was posted to the 5th Canadian Mounted Rifles.

On 26 August 1918 he was dangerously wounded in the right arm by shrapnel and was evacuated to No. 10 Canadian Field Ambulance. Private Preston was transferred to No. 7 Casualty Clearing Station, on 31 August where he died of wounds on 14 September 1918.

William's sisters Lizzie Stannage, Amelia and brother-in-law James Whitten, resided at 27 Florence Street, South Manchester Connecticut, USA. His sister Minnie and brother-in-law Dan Hall resided at 5 Sarah Street, and later at 22 Union Street, Portadown. A brother Thomas resided at 30 David Street, Portadown.

Grave of Private William Henry Preston.

Patrick Joseph McVeigh
Private 3/6960 2nd Battalion, Argyll & Sutherland Highlanders

Born	Portadown
Parents	Son of John and Mary Ann McVeigh of 107 Obins Street, Portadown

Residence	Obins Street
Enlisted	June 1914, Glasgow, Scotland
Died	Killed in action 24 September 1918, France
Buried	Villers Hill British Cemetery, Villers-Guislain, Nord, France. Grave VII. C. 13.
Commemorated	Portadown War Memorial (192)

Grave of Private Patrick Joseph McVeigh.

Patrick enlisted in June 1914 and took part in the retreat from Mons in August 1914. He had been previously wounded in action on three occasions and spent a short time on home leave in February 1915 recovering from frostbite in his feet.

James McKeown
Private 4811, 5th Battalion, Royal Irish Fusiliers

Born	Portadown
Parents	Son of Patrick and Elizabeth McKeown of 2 Obins Street, Portadown
Residence	Obins Street
Enlisted	Finner Camp, Co. Donegal
Died	Killed in action 29 September 1918, France
Age	27
Buried	Sailly-Labourse Communal Cemetery Extension, Pas de Calais. Grave L. 11.
Commemorated	Portadown War Memorial (191)

James' father Patrick was employed as a weaver. He and his wife Elizabeth had children Mary, Lizzie, James, John, Henry and Patrick.

James was the husband of Teressa McKeown.

He served in 'C' Company and was wounded in 1915. Private McKeown's wife received a letter from Lieutenant T. H. Corrigan

It is with the greatest sorrow that I have to write and inform you of the death of your husband. Will you please accept my sincere sympathy with yourself and your children in your sad bereavement. He was killed by a shell which fell in the trench beside him and three of his comrades. I can assure you, small consolation though it be, that his death was absolutely instantaneous, and he suffered no pain. This took place in the early morning of the 30th September about 5:30 am. His funeral took place yesterday afternoon and was attended by his comrades in the company and by myself. The service was conducted by the Rev, Father Delaney, C.F. and was conducted with all the rites of the Roman Catholic Church and with full military honours....He was always a good soldier, cheerful even in hardships, and kind hearted and generous to all.

Portadown News
12 October 1918

After the death of her husband Teressa moved to Union Place, Dungannon.

James' three brothers also served in the Royal Irish Fusiliers during the Great War. Patrick served in the 2nd Battalion and was wounded in the hand in 1917, Henry was seriously wounded in the side in 1915 and John was also wounded in action.

Grave of Private James McKeown.

James Cullen MC
Second-Lieutenant, 1st Battalion, Royal Irish Fusiliers

Parents	Son of James and Kate Cullen of 45 Thomas Street, Portadown
Residence	Thomas Street
Died	Died of wounds 3 October 1918, Belgium
Age	26

Buried Haringhe (Bandaghem) Military Cemetery, Belgium. Grave III. A. 8.

Commemorated Portadown War Memorial (220)

James was wounded in action on two occasions and rose to the rank of Company Sergeant-Major. Late in 1917 he gained his commission.

Second-Lieutenant Cullen was awarded the Military Cross in 1918 the citation stated

For conspicuous gallantry and devotion to duty while in command of a platoon during an enemy attack. He showed fine courage and handled his men skilfully, inflicting heavy casualties on the enemy and delaying his advance.

Portadown Express
2 August 1918

Marshall Wright
Lance-Corporal 22990, 9th Battalion, Royal Irish Fusiliers

Born Portadown

Parents Son of Marshall and Jane Wright of 29 Jervis Street, Portadown

Residence Jervis Street

Enlisted Portadown

Died Killed in action 3 October 1918, Belgium

Age 28

Buried Dadizele New British Cemetery, Belgium. Grave IV. B. 26.

Commemorated Portadown War Memorial (141)

Mrs Wright, Irwin Street, has received official intimation on Wednesday that her son Private Marshall Wright, is wounded, but it is not known into which hospital he has been admitted.

Portadown News
2 November 1918

Unofficial news has reached Portadown that Private Marshall Wright, Irwin Street, has been killed in action. He was previously reported wounded, but no further news was heard of him, until a local soldier wrote home stating that he had attended the burial service.

Portadown News
9 November 1918

Joseph Weir
Private 6107/A, 3rd Battalion, Australian Pioneers, Australian Imperial Force

Born Portadown

Parents Son of Joseph and Elizabeth Weir

Residence Cornamuckley

Enlisted 11 March 1916 Bathurst, New South Wales, Australia

Died Died of wounds
7 October 1918,
France
Age 20
Buried St. Sever Cemetery
Extension, Rouen,
France.
Grave S. II. L. 17.
Commemorated
Portadown War
Memorial (285)

Joseph was educated at Richmount School and was 13 years old when the family moved to Australia to settle in Mudgee, New South Wales, Australia. He was employed as a farmer near the town, which was situated about 100 miles north west of Sydney.

Joseph enlisted in 'A' Company, Depot Battalion, Bathurst. On enlistment his particulars were given as follows: occupation - labourer, height - 5'6½", complexion - dark, eyes - brown, hair - beech. Age 18 years and 11 months. He had served with the cadets at Mudgee.

He transferred to 'A' Company, 1st Battalion, Bathurst on 18 April 1916 and soon transferred to the 3rd Battalion. Private Weir embarked from Sydney, New South Wales on the troopship *Wiltshire* on 22 August and arrived at Plymouth on 13 October.

On 13 December he proceeded overseas from Folkestone on the SS *Arundel* and arrived at the 1st Australian Divisional Base Depot at Etaples the following day. On 12 January 1917 he was taken on strength of the 1st Battalion and on 14 July was transferred to the 3rd Pioneer Battalion.

Private Weir was wounded in action on 20 October 1917 when the Germans bombarded the Australian trenches with mustard gas shells. He was admitted to No. 11 Australian Field Ambulance and then transferred to No. 3 Australian Casualty Clearing Station. Two days later Private Weir was evacuated by ambulance train and admitted to the No. 24 General Hospital at Etaples. On 28 October he was embarked on the hospital ship *Pieter de Cornick* and admitted to the County of Middlesex War Hospital for specialised treatment for the affects of mustard gas.

Private Weir was hospitalised from the end of October 1916 until New Year's Eve when he was granted a fortnight's furlough, which he spent at No 1 Command Depot at Sutton Veny. He remained at No. 1 Command Depot until June 1918.

On 26 June Private Weir was mustered for the Overseas Training Brigade and on 30 July preceded to

France from Folkestone. In mid August he was once more in the field.

Grave of Private Joseph Weir.

On 1 October 1918 Private Weir was wounded in action for the second time when he received gunshot wounds to the back and abdomen. He was taken to No. 10 Australian Field Ambulance and transferred to No. 53 Casualty Clearing Station. The next day he was evacuated on No. 2 Ambulance Train and admitted to No. 12 General Hospital at Rouen. Private Joseph Weir died of wounds at 1540 hours on 7 October 1918.

His sister Mrs E. A. Hardy resided in Denison Street, Mudgee, another sister Miss M. Weir resided at Lawson Street, Mudgee and a brother William, resided in Nurbridge.

Abraham Cush
Private S/2541, 1/5th Battalion, Seaforth Highlanders

Born	Drumcree
Parents	Son of Michael and Elizabeth Cush of Drumherrif, Scotch Street, Portadown
Residence	Cornamuckley
Enlisted	1914, Kelty, Fifeshire, Scotland
Died	Died of wounds 15 October 1918, France
Age	26
Buried	Iwuy Communal Cemetery, Nord, France. Grave A. 16.
Commemorated	Portadown War Memorial (284) Drumcree Parish Church War Memorial

Abraham's mother Elizabeth was employed as a farm servant and had children Emma, Rachel, Anna Bella and Abraham.

His mother received a letter from Lieutenant Beake, Seaforth Highlanders

It is indeed with much regret that I have to inform you that your son was killed by a shell on October 15th, he was with me at the time with a party of men in a village, when a shell fell in the middle of the group. Your son was very badly wounded and died almost immediately. On behalf of the company, I tender you our deepest sympathy. He was a favourite with us all, and a good soldier. He was buried in a cemetery behind our lines.

Portadown News
2 November 1918

David Morton
Sapper 64389, 150th Field Company, Royal Engineers

Born	Portadown
Parents	Son of James and Rebecca Morton of 122 Thomas Street, Portadown
Residence	Thomas Street
Enlisted	Belfast
Died	Died of wounds 15 October 1918, Belgium
Age	31
Buried	Duhallow A.D.S. Cemetery, Belgium. Grave IV. E. 4.
Commemorated	Portadown War Memorial (222) Armagh Road Presbyterian Church War Memorial

David, the youngest son of James and Rebecca Morton, came home from Canada to enlist after the outbreak of war. He had a brother Jim.

He proceeded to the front with the 36th (Ulster) Division to which he was attached. He was seriously wounded in October 1916 and spent four months in hospital recovering from his injuries.

Sapper Morton was wounded in action on 15 October 1918 and was evacuated to No. 44 Casualty Clearing Station where he succumbed to his injuries later the same day.

Wilson J. Teggart
Rifleman 2307, 15th Battalion, Royal Irish Rifles

Born	Portadown
Parents	Son of William and Emily Teggart of 18 Burnbrae Avenue, Portadown
Residence	Burnbrae Avenue
Enlisted	Belfast
Died	Killed in action 20 October 1918, Belgium
Age	22
Buried	No Known Grave

Commemorated
Tyne Cot Memorial, Zonnebeke, West-Vlaanderen, Belgium.
Panel 138-140 to 162A & 163A.
Portadown War Memorial (24)
St. Mark's Parish Church War Memorial

Wilson's mother received a letter from an officer of her son's regiment

Allow me, who knows the loss of a brother and who understands the love of a mother for her son, to offer you my deepest sympathy. May God enable you to bear the terrible blow and take comfort from the thought "Greater love hath no man than this, that he gave his life for his friends".

Portadown News
2 November 1918

Wilson had two brothers who also served during the Great War.

Edward Breen
Rifleman 54218, 2nd Battalion, Kings Royal Rifle Corps

Parents	Son of William Breen of Fara
Residence	Fara
Enlisted	Glasgow, Scotland
Died	Died of wounds 27 October 1918, France
Buried	St. Sever Cemetery Extension, Rouen, France. Grave S. II. T. 6.
Commemorated	Portadown War Memorial (302)

Rifleman Breen previously served in the Royal Irish Rifles with the serial number D/22932. He died of wounds at No. 1 Australian Hospital in Rouen, France.

Grave of Rifleman Edward Breen.

William Ernest Hall
Private 25333, 7th Battalion, Royal Irish Regiment

Born	26 August 1896, Portadown
Parents	Son of Thomas J. and E.M. Hall of Windsor Terrace, Portadown
Residence	Bridge Street
Enlisted	Dublin
Died	Died of wounds 28 October 1918, Hassenheide, Germany
Age	22
Buried	Berlin South Western Cemetery, Brandenburg, Germany. Grave VI. D. 1.
Commemorated	Portadown War Memorial (14) Lurgan College War Memorial Seagoe Parish Church War Memorial

William was educated at Lurgan College. He was a member of Portadown Rowing Club.

Private Hall had previously served in the South Irish Horse with the serial number 1309. He was wounded in action in 1918 and taken to Germany as a prisoner of war.

With the signing of the Armistice on 11 November 1918 British PoWs were repatriated and William's family awaited his arrival. His mother received a letter from her son dated 17 October 1918 in which he seemed to be in good spirits and he concluded the letter with the words "I am going to stick it". As the days and weeks went by there was no further news of Private William Ernest Hall.

In January 1919 his mother received a letter written in German, from a German doctor who had tended her son in a military hospital at Hasenheide, Germany. The letter stated that William had died of wounds in hospital on 28 October 1918.

His brother Lieutenant Fforde Hall served with the 9th Battalion, Royal Inniskilling Fusiliers during the Great War and was also a prisoner of war in Germany.

He had been employed as an apprentice in Messrs Spence Bryson and Co. before enlisting. Private Fforde Hall rose through the ranks to Quartermaster Sergeant before gaining his commission. Like his brother he was also a member of Portadown Rowing Club.

William Copeland
Sergeant 100520, 398th Battery, Royal Field Artillery

Born	Portadown
Parents	Son of Robert and Mary Copeland of 24 Hanover Street, Portadown
Residence	Hanover Street
Enlisted	Belfast
Died	Died of wounds 1 November 1918, France
Age	24
Buried	St. Sever Cemetery Extension, Rouen, France. Grave S. II. JJ. 21.
Commemorated	Portadown War Memorial (113) First Presbyterian Church War Memorial, Edenderry

William was employed as a clerk in Bannview Weaving Factory before the outbreak of war. He was a member of Portadown Rowing Club.

William was the husband of Alice Killops, daughter of W.J. Killops, who served in the Army Service Corps. She died on 4 April 1917 at her mother's residence, 2 Little Victoria Street, Belfast and was buried in Seagoe Cemetery.

tSergeant Copeland received a gunshot wound to the head on 21 October 1918 and was evacuated to No. 6 General Hospital in Rouen where he died of wounds on 1 November 1918.

His brother Robert, goods station foreman for the G.N.R. and sister-in-law Margaret, resided at 42 Hanover Street, Portadown. He had a sister Edith and brother-in-law Robert Dawson and another sister Nellie and brother-in-law Robert Johnston resided at 43 Spencer Road, Londonderry.

Grave of Sergeant William Copeland.

James Totton Gardiner
Second-Lieutenant, 1st Battalion, Royal Irish Rifles

Born	2 April 1899, Portadown
Parents	Son of Thomas and Hannah Gardiner of Annagh House, Portadown
Residence	Annagh
Died	Died of wounds 1 November 1918, Antwerp, Belgium
Age	19
Buried	Schoonselhof Cemetery, Antwerp, Belgium. Grave 54.
Commemorated	Portadown War Memorial (250) First Presbyterian Church War Memorial, Edenderry Lurgan College War Memorial

James Totton's father Thomas was a librarian and rate collector. His mother Hannah became a librarian at the Free Library in Edward Street, Portadown. She was secretary of the Free Library Committee. They had five children James, Charles, Robert Davison, Thomas and Mary who was a teacher at Edenderry Public Elementary School. In 1901 the family resided at 27 Carleton Street, Portadown. Their son James Totton was educated at Lurgan College.

On 16 August 1917 James joined the Inns of Court Officers Training Corps with the serial number D/11865. He was sent to No. 3 Officers Cadet Battalion on 8 February 1918 and was commissioned in the 1st Battalion, Royal Irish Rifles on 30 July.

Second-Lieutenant Gardiner was involved in some of the last actions of the Great War. During the night of 20 October 1918 his unit had reached the Gaverbek Stream and captured a 6" naval gun and Daimler tractor. The following day the 1st Battalion reached the line northwest of Knock to the Gaverbek Stream and dug in to await support.

During the engagement one officer was killed and two others including Second-Lieutenant Gardiner were seriously injured. He was captured as a prisoner of war and died of wounds on 1 November 1918 in a German hospital in Antwerp.

James Black
Private 19209, 6th Battalion, Royal Inniskilling Fusiliers

Born	Portadown
Parents	Son of Benjamin Black of Artabrackagh

Residence	Artabrackagh
Enlisted	Airdrie
Died	Killed in action 5 November 1918, France
Age	23
Buried	St. Souplet British Cemetery, Nord, France. Grave II. B. 1.
Commemorated	Portadown War Memorial (253) LOL 371 War Memorial, Drumnahuncheon Orange Hall

James was a member of Drumnahuncheon LOL 371. He was the nephew of Jane Wright of Drumnasoo, Mary Bulla of 35 Mourneview Street, Portadown and Alice Black of Drumnasoo.

Private Black had over four years service and had seen action at Gallipoli, Salonika, Egypt and France.

There is a Private J. Black 3rd Battalion, Royal Inniskilling Fusiliers commemorated on St. Mark's Parish Church War Memorial. However, it is unclear if this is the same person.

John Woods
Private 9969, 3rd Battalion, Canadian Infantry (Central Ontario Regiment)

Born	21 May 1894, Chicago, Illinois, USA
Parents	Son of Margaret Wylie (formerly Woods) and stepson of Thomas Wylie of 42 Jervis Street, Portadown.
Residence	Woodhouse Street
Enlisted	22 September 1914, Valcartier, Canada
Died	Died 11 January 1919, Bonn, Germany
Age	24
Buried	Brussels Town Cemetery, Belgium. Grave X. I. 9.
Commemorated	Portadown War Memorial (248) Thomas Street Methodist Church War Memorial

John's stepfather Thomas died in the USA. His mother Maggie Wylie resided at 42 Jervis Street, Portadown.

On enlistment in the 3rd Battalion, Canadian Infantry, John's particulars were given as follows: occupation - sales clerk, height -

5'7", complexion - dark, eyes - blue, hair - dark brown. He was attached to the transport section. The 3rd Battalion disembarked at St. Nazaire, France on 11 May 1915.

Private Woods was admitted to No. 1 Canadian Field Ambulance with influenza in January 1917.

In January 1918 he was granted permission to marry Amelia, known as Maggie, and they resided at 16 Charles Street, Portadown.

On 4 January 1919 Private Woods was admitted to No. 1 Canadian Casualty Clearing Station with influenza and he died on 11 January 1919. His widow received a letter from Captain M.D. Murdoch

It is with the greatest sorrow that I offer you, not only my sympathy, but the sympathy of all the men in the battalion transport, in the great loss you have sustained in the death of your husband, Jack. I really cannot tell you how sorry we all were when the sad news reached us. It was a terrible shock and awfully hard to believe. I can truthfully and honestly say that Jack was one of the finest chaps I had in my section, and I thought a great deal of him....We took up a collection and with the money bought a wreath and placed it on his grave. Also some of the chaps who are Orangemen took up a collection and bought another wreath, which they placed on his grave.

Portadown News
1 February 1919

In Loving Memory of
My Dear Husband,
Private JOHN WOODS,
3rd Batt First Canadians,
Who Died on 11th January, 1919.
Interred in Poppelsdorfer Cemetery,
Bonn, Germany.
Aged 25 Years.

16 Charles Street,
Portadown.

Memorial card for Private John Woods. (Portadown Times)

A memorial card issued by his widow Amelia refers to Private John Woods being buried in Poppelsdorfer Cemetery, Bonn, Germany. His body was later removed from Germany and reinterred in Brussels Town Cemetery, Belgium.

John's brother, Arnold, served in the 9th Battalion, Royal Irish Fusiliers during the Great War. After the war he was a District Commandant of the Portadown Ulster Special Constabulary. Arnold was awarded the MBE.

Original grave of Private John Woods. (Portadown Times)

Chapter 8
The Far Flung Fields of Empire

Although the main military effort throughout the Great War was in France and Flanders it was the world's first global conflict and involved fighting in Western and Eastern Europe, Africa, the Middle and Far-East, India, the Balkans, Italy, Greece and Turkey. The war on the Eastern Front fought on a colossal scale between the Central Powers and Russia and the campaigns in Italy and the Balkans are outside the scope of this book.

With an Empire to defend, sea-lanes to police and Allies to protect Britain and her Empire was committed to a war on many fronts.

Gallipoli

After an abortive attempt to force the Dardenelles in February/March the Allies landed on the Gallipoli coast on 25 April 1915. The British 29th Division landed at Cape Helles on the southern tip of the peninsula whilst the Anzacs (Australian and New Zealand Army Corps) landed 15 miles north on the western side of Gallipoli at place soon to be renamed Anzac Cove. On 6 August new landings took place at Suvla Bay, five miles north of Anzac Cove and three fresh divisions were thrown into the campaign but to no avail.

In October it was decided to evacuate all the Allied troops from Gallipoli. The evacuations began in early December 1915 and were completed by 9 January 1916 by which time 150,000 Allied troops had been withdrawn.

Helles Memorial, Turkey.

British casualties were 19,000 killed or died of disease and over 46,000 wounded; Anzacs 11,000 killed or died of disease and over 22,000 wounded and India 1,400 killed or died of disease and 3,500 wounded. A further 7,500 British troops were taken prisoner of war and many of these died in captivity.

Charles Garvey
Private 10789, 1st Battalion, Royal Dublin Fusiliers

Born	Tirgarvey, Armagh
Parents	Son of Henry and Elizabeth Garvey of 136 Park Road, Portadown
Residence	Montague Street
Enlisted	Lurgan
Died	Killed in action 26 April 1915, Cape Helles, Gallipoli
Age	22
Buried	V Beach Cemetery, Gallipoli, Turkey. Special Memorial A. 62.
Commemorated	Portadown War Memorial (172)

Charles' father Henry was employed as a labourer. He and his wife Elizabeth had children Harry, Michael and Charles. The family resided at 39 Montague Street, Portadown.

Charles had five years service in the army and was stationed in India when war was declared. He was a marksman and had received awards for his shooting.

The 1st Battalion, Royal Dublin Fusiliers landed, with very heavy casualties, at Sedd El Bahr on Cape Helles from the troopship *River Clyde* and numerous small cutters.

Charles' brother Michael also served during the Great War and lost a leg when wounded. He resided in Park Road and his wife was the sister of well-known local junior footballer Joe Reavy.

John Boseman
Trooper 631, 1st Australian Light Horse, Australian Imperial Force

Born	Drumena
Parents	Son of Thomas and Mary Margaret Boseman of Drumena
Residence	Drumenagh
Enlisted	1 September 1914, Roseberry Park, New South Wales, Australia
Died	Killed in action 7 August 1915, Gallipoli
Buried	No Known Grave

Commemorated
Lone Pine Memorial, Turkey. I.
Portadown War Memorial (297)
Drumcree Parish Church War Memorial

John's father Thomas was a farmer and had children Elizabeth, May Margaret, Richard, John, William George, David and Joseph. John emigrated to Sydney, New South Wales, Australia.

On enlistment in the 1st Australian Light Horse, Australian Imperial Force, his particulars were given as follows: occupation - farmer, height - 5'8", complexion - fresh, eyes - grey, hair - light brown, age 23 years and 4 months. He served in 'A' Troop.

Trooper Boseman embarked from Sydney on 20 December 1914 and proceeded to join the Mediterranean Expeditionary Force on 9 May 1915.

On 7 August 1915 the 1st Light Horse Regiment took part in an offensive against a Turkish position known as the 'Chessboard' and suffered 147 casualties out of a strength of 200.

His sister Mrs S. N. McKelvey resided at 39 Phillip Street, Balmain, Sydney, New South Wales, Australia.

Patrick Morgan
Private 2174, 3rd Battalion (New South Wales), Australian Imperial Force

Born	Portadown
Residence	Marley Street
Enlisted	Sydney, New South Wales, Australia
Died	Killed in action 7-12 August 1915, Gallipoli
Age	40
Buried	Lone Pine Cemetery, Anzac, Turkey.Special Memorial A. 14.
Commemorated	Portadown War Memorial (159)

Patrick was educated at Curran Street National School, Portadown. He was employed as a postman and also a ship's fireman. He emigrated to Sydney, New South Wales, Australia aged 29.

Private Morgan was 'mentioned in despatches' for gallant conduct during the Gallipoli campaign.

His sister Mrs M. A. McDonnell of 9 Marley Street, Portadown received a letter from Lieutenant-Colonel M. D. Graham, Assistant Military Secretary

I have it in command from His Majesty the King to inform you, as next of kin of the late Private Patrick Morgan, No. 1174 (sic) of the 3rd Battalion (New South Wales)

Australian Imperial Force, that this Private was mentioned in a Despatch from General Sir Ian Hamilton dated 11th December 1915, and published in the Supplement to the "London Gazette" dated 28th January, 1916 for gallant and distinguished service in the field.

I am to express to you the King's high appreciation of these services and to add that His Majesty trusts that their public acknowledgement may be of some consolation in your bereavement.

Portadown News
12 August 1916

James Hamilton Power
Private 12005, 5th Battalion, Royal Inniskilling Fusiliers

Born	Drumcree
Residence	Meadow Lane
Enlisted	Glasgow, Scotland
Died	Killed in action 15 August 1915, Kiretch Tepe, Gallipoli
Buried	No Known Grave
Commemorated	Helles Memorial, Turkey. Panel 97 - 101. Portadown War Memorial (167) St. Mark's Parish Church War Memorial

James Campbell
Private 18218, 6th Battalion, Royal Irish Fusiliers

Born	Portadown
Residence	Baltylum
Enlisted	Portadown
Died	Killed in action 15 August 1915, Kiretch Tepe, Gallipoli
Buried	No Known Grave
Commemorated	Helles Memorial, Turkey. Panel 178 -180. Portadown War Memorial (263)

On 7 August 1915 the 6th Battalion, Royal Irish Fusiliers disembarked from minesweepers HMS *Honey-suckle* and HMS *Snaefell* at Salt Lake Bay. Over the next few days they were in action at Hill 53 and Hill 70.

On 12 August the battalion was in support trenches at Karakol Dagh and on 15 August were ordered to dig new trenches and strengthen existing positions. The battalion came under enemy fire and moved into the frontline.

5 pm. Bn. Heavily engaged with enemy infantry, which lasted during the night intermittently, sustaining in proportion slight casualties.

6th Battalion, Royal Irish Fusiliers
War Diary 15 August 1915

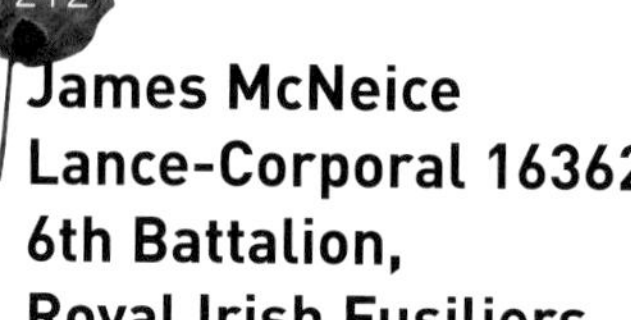

James McNeice
Lance-Corporal 16362,
6th Battalion,
Royal Irish Fusiliers

Born — Loughgall
Parents — Son of Sarah Ann Devlin of David Street, Portadown
Residence — David Street
Enlisted — Portadown
Died — Killed in action 15 August 1915, Kiretch Tepe, Gallipoli
Age — 28
Buried — No Known Grave
Commemorated — Helles Memorial, Turkey. Panel 178 - 180. Portadown War Memorial (85)

David George Dunlop
Private 11574, 5th Battalion,
Royal Irish Fusiliers

Born — Portadown
Parents — Son of Joseph and Mary Dunlop of 45 Meadow Lane, Portadown
Residence — Meadow Lane
Enlisted — Armagh
Died — Killed in action 16 August 1915, Kiretch Tepe, Gallipoli
Buried — No Known Grave
Commemorated — Helles Memorial, Turkey. Panel 178 - 180. Portadown War Memorial (164) St. Mark's Parish Church War Memorial Seagoe Parish Church War Memorial

Seagoe Parish Church War Memorial. (Author's Collection)

David was employed as a weaver before the outbreak of war. He was the husband of Ann Jane Dunlop (nee Campbell). The couple had two children Elsie Eveline born 5 September 1912 and Eileen who was baptised on 1 May 1915. Ann Jane Dunlop, who was aged 22, died on 31 March 1915 a few days after giving birth to her second daughter.

The 5th Battalion, Royal Irish Fusiliers sailed from England on 12 July 1915 on the HMT *Andania* and arrived at Mudros on 25 July. On 7 August the battalion landed at Suvla Bay from the SS *Osmanieh*. On 15/16 August the battalion advanced along the ridge at Kiretch Tepe and suffered many casualties.

Many casualties during the day and great difficulty in bringing wounded out of action owing to lack of stretchers and the difficulties of the paths.

5th Battalion, Royal Irish Fusiliers
War Diary 16 August 1915

Private Dunlop wrote to his mother-in-law the day before he was killed in action

Just a line to let you know I am getting on well. I got the cigarettes you sent me alright, also your letter. I am glad to hear of you and the children being well. Remember me to my father and mother and all the rest. I have nearly all my chums as yet. We have not lost very many of them. Jeffers is alright and Archie Proctor. We are all together as yet, and having a good time sniping the Turks down. I only got your letter on Saturday, 14th August, so I answer it as soon as I can. I think this is all for this time only. D. G. D. Write soon.

Seagoe Parish Magazine
October 1915

Private David Jeffers wrote concerning the deaths of his own brother Private James Jeffers (see entry **99 Private James Jeffers**) and of Private Dunlop who were both killed in action at Gallipoli on 16 August 1915

I remember the 16th August last. We were on a ridge about 9:15 in the morning, and were only twenty minutes there till it was packed with dead and wounded. My brother-in-law, Private David Dunlop, was killed just on my left. He never spoke as he got shot through the heart, and dropped a yard from me.

Portadown News
20 May 1916

James Jeffers
Private 11838, 5th Battalion, Royal Irish Fusiliers

Born	Portadown
Residence	Fowler's Entry
Enlisted	Portadown
Died	Killed in action 16 August 1915, Kiretch Tepe, Gallipoli

Buried No Known Grave
Commemorated
Helles Memorial, Turkey.
Panel 178 - 180.
Portadown War Memorial (99)
St. Mark's Parish Church War Memorial

James and his wife resided at 26 Fowler's Entry, Portadown.

Private Jeffers served in 'D' Company. Mrs Jeffers received a number of letters concerning the death of her husband; one was forwarded from the British Red Cross Society

We have received from Private Michael Smith (15090) now in hospital abroad, a report as follows - "In an attack on 16th August Jeffers was wounded below the heart, and I and others carried him back on our rifles for about a quarter of a mile. We were then ordered to retire, and as we could not carry him with us down the hill and it was dark, we had to leave him under the side of a boulder, where he would have protection from shellfire. He had been wounded early in the day".

Portadown Express
19 November 1915

Private Jeffers was killed in the same incident as Private David George Dunlop (see entry **164 Private David George Dunlop**).

Henry Patrick Blacker Private 11667, 5th Battalion, Royal Irish Fusiliers

Born Portadown
Parents Son of Henry and Annie Blacker of Portadown
Residence John Street
Enlisted Portadown
Died Died of wounds 19 August 1915, Mediterranean Sea
Age 23
Buried No Known Grave
Commemorated
Helles Memorial, Turkey.
Panel 178 - 180.
Portadown War Memorial (142)

Lance-Corporal (sic) Harry Blacker, who resided in John Street, Portadown, is officially reported killed in action. He volunteered for service about twelve months ago, and was attached to the 5th Battalion, Royal Irish Fusiliers, which has done such noble fighting at the Dardenelles. His brother Hugh, died from wounds a few weeks ago.

Portadown News
11 September 1915

His brother Hugh (see entry **143 Private Hugh Blacker**) died of wounds on 28 August 1915 at Netley Hospital, England.

Francis Currie
Private 11730, 5th Battalion, Royal Irish Fusiliers

Private Francis Currie. (Seagoe Parish Magazine)

Born	Portadown
Parents	Son of James and E. A. Currie of Queen Street, Portadown
Residence	Ormond Street
Enlisted	Portadown
Died	Died of wounds 29 August 1915, Gallipoli
Age	27
Buried	No Known Grave
Commemorated	Helles Memorial, Turkey. Panel 178 - 180. Portadown War Memorial (194) Seagoe Parish Church War Memorial

Francis was a member of Seagoe Church Lads' Brigade.

Thomas James Neill
Private 11666, 5th Battalion, Royal Irish Fusiliers

Born	Portadown
Parents	Son of William and Sarah Jane Neill of 33 David Street, Portadown
Residence	David Street
Enlisted	Portadown
Died	Died of wounds 9 September 1915, Mediterranean Sea
Age	30
Buried	No Known Grave
Commemorated	Helles Memorial, Turkey. Panel 178 - 180. Portadown War Memorial (86) St. Mark's Parish Church War Memorial

Thomas' father William was a shoemaker by trade and his mother Sarah Jane was a winder. The couple had children Thomas James, Jemima, Elizabeth, Sarah

Margaret and William. Thomas James and his sister Jemima were both employed as weavers.

Family grave of Private Thomas James Neill. (Author's Collection)

David Mason
Private 2644,
1/7th (Blythswood) Battalion, Highland Light Infantry

Parents	Son of Richard and Sarah Mason of 5 Fox Street, Portadown
Residence	Fox Street
Enlisted	Glasgow, Scotland
Died	Died of wounds 12 December 1915, Gallipoli
Age	27
Buried	Lancashire Landing Cemetery, Turkey. Grave H. 68.
Commemorated	Portadown War Memorial (103) Thomas Street Methodist Church War Memorial

David's father Richard was employed as a cloth passer and his mother Sarah was a housekeeper. The couple had children Richard, Elizabeth, Robert, Sarah, David, Martha and Susan.

Before the outbreak of war David was employed as a railway guard. David was the husband of Eleanor Mason (nee Mills) of 23 Mourneview Street, Portadown. The couple resided at 86 Main Street, Shettleston, Glasgow. They had four children. Mrs Mason later moved to 706 Shettleston Road, Shettleston, Glasgow.

Private Mason died of wounds at No. 17 Stationary Hospital, Cape Helles. His widow received a letter from the Reverend Mr. Burrow, Methodist Chaplain

He bore up very bravely against the pain and discomfort. I went in each day to see him, and we all did what we could for him. He passed away very peacefully on Sunday afternoon, December 12th. He was laid to rest on the following day at 2p.m. Rev Dr Ewing, a Presbyterian chaplain conducted the funeral service...

Portadown News
26 February 1916

Grave of Private David Mason.

William John Law Croix de Guerre Lieutenant-Colonel, 7th Battalion, Lancashire Fusiliers

Born	Portadown
Parents	Son of Thomas Law of Margretta Terrace, Portadown
Residence	Edward Street
Died	Killed in action 19 December 1915, Gallipoli
Age	38
Buried	Twelve Tree Copse Cemetery, Turkey. Special Memorial C. 305.
Commemorated	Portadown War Memorial (90) St. Mark's Parish Church War Memorial

William's father Thomas was assistant petty sessions clerk of Portadown and resided in Margretta Terrace, Portadown. William was the brother of Mrs D. G. Loughery of Cathedral Schools, Dromore. He was a graduate of Trinity College, Dublin and was a keen sportsman playing for Lansdowne XV on two occasions when they won the senior cup. He also played when he was at university.

After graduation he received a Home Office appointment as an inspector of factories in the Manchester area where he became involved with the 7th Battalion, Lancashire Fusiliers in 1909. He was married with one son.

In September 1914 the 7th Battalion was sent to Egypt and landed at 'W' beach, Gallipoli on 5 May 1915. From May until June the 7th Battalion was in and out of the front line. Lieutenant-Colonel William John Law was slightly wounded on 10 June and was hospitalised on 18th June due to sickness. On 2 November 1915 he returned from a further spell in hospital in Egypt.

Lieutenant-Colonel Law was 'mentioned in despatches' on three occasions - London Gazette 5 November 1915 on this occasion for services from 5 May to the end of June, 28 January 1916 and 13 July 1916 on this occasion "For gallant and distinguished service in the

field". He was also awarded the French Croix de Guerre - London Gazette 24 February 1916.

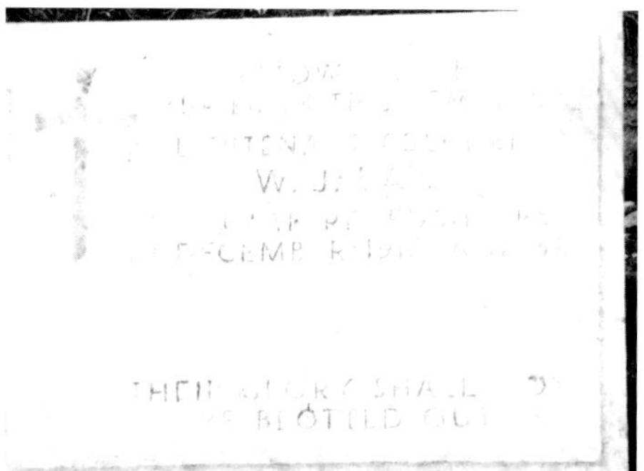

Grave of Lieutenant-Colonel William John Law.

During the evacuation operations from the Gallipoli peninsula Lieutenant-Colonel William John Law was charged with directing a rearguard action against the Turks. On 19 December 1915, two hours before the commencement of the operation, he was shot in the head and killed instantly.

Major-General Sir William Douglas on hearing the news of his death wired

Tell the 7th Lancashire Fusiliers that I deeply deplore Major Law's death; he has done such gallant work throughout the campaign, and his name and that of his gallant battalion were mentioned in army corps orders for the good work done by them, thus adding laurels to the 42nd East Lancashire Division, which has already earned a great name.

Portadown Express
4 February 1916

Malta

With the outbreak of the Great War the fortress island became a major naval base for the British and French Mediterranean fleets. As the war progressed Japanese, United States, Italian and Greek naval forces joined their Allies operating from the island.

The island played a crucial role in the treatment of wounded service personnel from Gallipoli, Salonika, Egypt, Palestine and other Middle Eastern battlefields and during the war 15 new military hospitals were built.

Samuel Clayton
Private 17909, 6th Battalion, Royal Irish Fusiliers

Born	Portadown
Parents	Son of Mary Jane Clayton of 3 Century Street, Portadown
Residence	Century Street
Enlisted	Armagh
Died	Died of wounds 2 October 1915, Malta
Age	23
Buried	Pieta Military Cemetery, Malta. Grave B. XVII. 2.
Commemorated	Portadown War Memorial (51)

St. Marks Parish Church War Memorial
Seagoe Parish Church War Memorial

Private Clayton was wounded in the chest at Gallipoli on 3 September 1915 and was evacuated to Malta.

The Rector of Seagoe, the Reverend James Archer, made enquiries on behalf of the Clayton family and he received a letter from the Reverend Maurice A. Farren, Forces Chaplain

Private Clayton was admitted to Tigne Hospital on September 11th, and died on October 2nd. He had a gunshot wound in chest and back and also pneumonia. He was buried in the Military Cemetery here. A photo of the Cemetery has been or will be sent to his Mother. He was buried with full Military Honours. The coffin was covered with a Union Jack, and on the coffin rested a Helmet, Belt, and Bayonet, and a Wreath with the following inscription, "Malta's Tribute to Dead Heroes".

Seagoe Parish Magazine
December 1915

Samuel had a brother William who served with the 2nd Battalion, Royal Irish Fusiliers during the Great War.

Salonika

France and Great Britain sent considerable forces to Salonika in northern Greece, which at that time was neutral (Greece came into the war on the Allied side in June 1917). By early 1916 the British had six divisions, including the 10th (Irish) Division, which had landed in October 1915.

Over 400,000 British and Empire troops served in Salonika where sickness was rife. Casualties were 10,000 killed or died of wounds or sickness, 16,500 battlefield injuries and 2,500 PoWs.

Wesley Bleakley
Private 11735, 5th Battalion, Royal Irish Fusiliers

Born Portadown
Parents Son of R. Bleakley of Clounagh, Portadown
Residence Russell Street
Enlisted Portadown
Died Killed in action 7 December 1915, Battle of Kosturino, Salonika
Age 29
Buried No Known Grave
Commemorated
Doiran Memorial, Greece.
Portadown War Memorial (208)
St. Mark's Parish Church War Memorial

Wesley was employed in a factory at Tavanagh, Portadown before the outbreak of war. He was the husband of Mary Bleakley who later resided at 86 Methven Street, Belfast.

The 5th Battalion, Royal Irish Fusiliers, part of the 10th (Irish) Division, disembarked at Salonika on 15 October 1915. The next few weeks was spent training. On 1 December 1915 the battalion took up positions on Rocky Peak west of the town of Kosturino.

At 0500 hours on 7 December 1915 the Bulgarians attacked Rocky Peak. Within half an hour they had occupied the battalion's positions with the battalion withdrawing to Memesli, south of Rocky Peak.

Wesley's sister Mrs Hobson of Castle Street received a letter from the British Red Cross Society

Dear Madam-We have the following report from Private Wm. Kearney, 12355, 5th Battalion, Royal Irish Fusiliers, C. Co., West London Hospital, Hammersmith. Informant states that on December 7th, 1915, the Division retired from "Rocky Peak" to lake Dorian by night. The Battalion had about 50 casualties, and the missing would probably have been wounded and left behind in the dark. Informant did not see Bleakley during the retirement. He was himself wounded and taken to No. 4 Canadian General Hospital, Salonika. Company Sergt-Major Wm. Rowe, 5th Battalion, Royal Irish Fusiliers, now at Salonika, may know something about Bleakley. We are continuing our enquiries and shall at once forward you any further information we succeed in obtaining.

Portadown News
18 March 1916

Robert Joseph McGaughey
Private 11536, 5th Battalion, Royal Irish Fusiliers

Born	Portadown
Parents	Son of William and Moira McGaughey of 32 Brownlow Terrace, Lurgan
Residence	Coronation Street
Enlisted	Portadown
Died	Killed in action 7 December 1915, Battle of Kosturino, Salonika
Age	19
Buried	No Known Grave
Commemorated	Doiran Memorial, Greece. Portadown War Memorial (71) St. Mark's Parish Church War Memorial

Private Joseph McCaughey, (sic) Royal Irish Fusiliers, Coronation Street, Portadown, is reported by the War Office to be missing.

Portadown Express
14 January 1916

Joseph Robinson
Private 5/11553, 5th Battalion, Royal Irish Fusiliers

Born Lurgan
Parents Son of Thomas and Susan Robinson of 6 Coronation Street, Portadown
Residence Coronation Street
Enlisted Armagh
Died Died 1 June 1916, Salonika
Buried Kirechkoi-Hortakoi Military Cemetery, Greece. Grave 3.
Commemorated
Portadown War Memorial (72)
St. Mark's Parish Church War Memorial

Private Robinson's father received a letter from Company Quarter-Master Sergeant C. Wiggins

I am writing to you on behalf of myself and my company to offer you our deepest sympathy for the loss of your son, who died on the 1st June. We were all very sorry to lose him, as he was a very good soldier, and was liked by all the officers, N.C.O's and men of the company. We can understand that this will be a terrible blow to you and therefore we hope you will accept our deepest sympathy. He was buried on the 2nd with full military honours, and a full burial service conducted by our own chaplain. The funeral was attended by the whole company, and by every man in the regiment from Portadown. He was buried in the British Military Cemetery here and today Sergeant Hobson and two of his comrades have erected a wooden cross over the grave with the following inscription - In Memory of No. 11553 Pte J. Robinson, 5th Royal Irish Fusiliers.

Portadown Express
23 June 1916

James Wilson
Driver TASR/04498, 34th Reserve Park, Army Service Corps

Born Drumcree
Residence Castle Street
Enlisted Belfast
Died Died of wounds 5 August 1916, Salonika
Buried Salonika (Lembet Road) Military Cemetery, Greece. Grave 296.
Commemorated
Portadown War Memorial (50)
St. Mark's Parish Church War Memorial

James was employed by Mr. James Grew JP as a busman before the outbreak of war. He was the husband of Sarah Wilson and the couple had one child. They resided at 5 Castle Street, Portadown.

Driver James Wilson died of a contusion to the abdomen.

David Porter
Private 11858, 6th Battalion, Royal Irish Fusiliers

Born	11 May 1890, Portadown
Parents	Son of Henry and Sarah Porter of 1 James Street, Portadown
Residence	James Street
Enlisted	Portadown
Died	Killed in action 30 September 1916, Salonika
Age	26
Buried	No Known Grave
Commemorated	Doiran Memorial, Greece Portadown War Memorial (130) Seagoe Parish Church War Memorial Thomas Street Methodist Church War Memorial

David had a brother William John and sisters Ruth, Elizabeth, Ann and Sarah. He was a member of the Ulster Volunteer Force.

Private Porter served in 'C' Company. He took part in the landing at Suvla Bay at 5.00am on 6 August 1915 and was wounded in the heel of the right hand two hours later. He was evacuated to a hospital near Alexandria, Egypt.

The 6th Battalion, Royal Irish Fusiliers, part of the 10th (Irish) Division, was then posted to Salonika in October 1915.

In September 1916 the battalion was involved in digging new trenches and positions and on 29 September occupied positions on the northern bank of the Komarjan bridgehead.

Casualties were LT. J. C. McCutcheon, seriously wounded, 1 W.O. wounded and missing, 1 O.R died of wounds. 2 O.R Missing and wounded. 1 Missing believed killed and 3 O.R. wounded. Owing to close and heavy fire it was not possible to remove all the wounded.

6th Battalion, Royal Irish Fusiliers
War Diary 30 September 1916

William John Craig
Corporal 9975, 2nd Battalion, Royal Irish Fusiliers

Born	Shankill, Lurgan
Parents	Son of William and Elizabeth Craig of 195 Upper Meadow Street, Belfast
Residence	Atkinson's Avenue
Enlisted	Lurgan
Died	Died of wounds 10 November 1916, Salonika

Age	24
Buried	Salonika (Lembet Road) Military Cemetery, Greece. Grave 674.
Commemorated	Portadown War Memorial (2) St. Mark's Parish Church War Memorial

Corporal Craig was a regular soldier and was stationed in India when war was declared. He served on the Western Front for several months before being posted to Salonika. Corporal Craig's parents received letters from two officers

I have a very high opinion of him not only as an extremely capable N.C.O. but also as a straightforward, conscientious and clean-living man, who was a splendid example to the other men. When he was hit he was doing his duty under fire, fearlessly and well, like the good soldier he had always proved himself to be. He had been hit with shrapnel in the left shoulder and arm, but so far as we could make out not badly, for as he went down the trench he was laughing and saying that he was bound for England. The company was indeed greatly surprised, and sorry to hear of his death, as no more popular N.C.O. ever served in 'D' Company. He was not only a general favourite, but respected by all ranks for his courage, consideration, and efficiency.

Portadown News
20 January 1917

Corporal Craig was brought to No. 29 General Hospital but succumbed to his wounds. His younger brother Rifleman Robert J. Craig Royal Irish Rifles was twice wounded in action - the second occasion so severely that he was medically discharged from further service.

Johnston McAfee Company Quarter-Master Sergeant 6717, 2nd Battalion, Royal Irish Fusiliers

Born	Portadown
Parents	Son of Mrs McClatchey of 111 Donegall Road, Belfast
Residence	Bridge Street
Enlisted	Portadown
Died	Died 3 January 1917, Salonika
Age	36
Buried	Salonika (Lembet Road) Military Cemetery, Greece. Grave 760.
Commemorated	Portadown War Memorial (16) Seagoe Parish Church War Memorial

Johnston was the husband of Elizabeth Jane McAfee who later resided at Portland School House, Burr, Co Tipperary. He had served during the South African War 1899-1902 and was stationed in India when war was declared.

CQMS McAfee died as a result of burns received accidentally.

Serbia

In August 1914 Austria invaded Serbia in a punitive expedition in revenge for the assassination of Archduke Franz Ferdinand.

The suffering of the Serbian people was well publicised in the United Kingdom and became a *cause celebre*. The British and French Red Cross sent medical aid, doctors and nursing staff to the area.

Malcolm Percy Clow
Conducteur, French Red Cross

Born	Portadown
Parents	Son of William Moffat and Eva Clow of Feddal House, Portadown
Residence	Carrickblacker Road
Died	Died 11 July 1917, Serbia
Age	32
Buried	Serbia
Commemorated	Portadown War Memorial (27) First Presbyterian Church War Memorial, Edenderry

The Clow family were originally from the southern part of Perthshire, Scotland. On a tombstone in the Parish of Braco is recorded the death in 1818 of a "James Clow of the Miln of Feddal". Feddal was the name given to the family residence in Portadown.

The Clow family were millers and James' grandson, also called James came, with three sons, to manage Caledon Mill in 1854. One of his sons was William Moffat Clow, who was born in Glasgow in 1852.

In 1885 William Moffat Clow set up in the milling business in Portadown. He married Eva Thompson, daughter of William Thompson, of Saintfield. The couple had two sons William Thompson and Malcolm Percy, and two daughters Nellie and Ann Moffat Clow.

Mrs Eva Clow died on 27 January 1902 and was buried in Seagoe Cemetery. William Moffat Clow remarried Emily Robertson from Scotland.

Besides being the head of the family business William Moffat Clow was also an elder in the First Presbyterian Church, Edenderry from 1886, and was Chairman of the Portadown Technical Instruction Committee from 1902. He was

appointed a Justice of the Peace in 1906 and from 1905-1911 he served on the Urban Council. He took a keen interest in agriculture, sport and animal welfare and compiled a history of First Presbyterian Church, Edenderry.

His son, Malcolm, was interested in music and the arts and excelled in theatrical drama. He was a member of the Armagh Bohemian Club. In 1914 Malcolm won the Miller and Beattie Cup at the Londonderry Feis. A silver challenge cup was later donated to the Londonderry Feis in his memory.

On the outbreak of war he tried repeatedly to enlist but was turned down for medical reasons. Malcolm eventually volunteered as an ambulance driver, with the title of Conducteur in the French Red Cross and served in Salonika, Macedonia and Serbia.

In letters home Malcolm vividly described the treacherous conditions he experienced in tending to the wounded troops and civilians injured in the bitter fighting in the mountain peaks of the Balkans. His unit was often within sight and sound of battle and had also to contend with the poor weather conditions in the mountains especially in the winter months.

We are now 14 kilometres further up the mountains, at a height of 4,000 feet. Our last camp was about 2,000 feet up, so you see we are now carrying our wounded along a road 14 kilometres long and descending 2,000 feet in the journey... I really am of the opinion that we are working one of the most dangerous and difficult roads in the Balkans. We have the honour, too, of being the first ambulances behind the lines. Our journeys down are the worst, and there is scarcely a day that some of us do not at times feel like the man who wanted the trousers of his new uniform in advance when he first saw the big guns go off!

When it was decided to come here, Capt. R. took us all into the mess-tent and made a straightforward and manly speech to us. The Medicin Divisionaire had put the case to him in such a way that we hadn't any other course open to us but to obey. Men's lives were being lost through delay...but the lives must be saved. Capt. R. pointed out to us our dangers, and the need for the greatest care and patience, and asked us to do our very best for him and our reputation, but especially for the poor suffering souls.

Portadown Express
27 July 1917

Conducteur Malcolm Clow died of dysentery, which he contracted after visiting a dying friend. In his last letter home he wrote

As in the beginning so now there is a great deal of growling going on among some of the men here. Personally when I begin to think earnestly and count up my blessings they are far in excess of any grievances. In

comparison with millions the lines have fallen to me in pleasant places. The risks as days go by seem of smaller and smaller account. I miss many, very many of the luxuries of home, but I have enough to spare....

While in the main we are happy we never cease to talk of home. Daily we conjure up what we shall do when that great day of peace shall dawn...Much water will pass under the bridges before then, and there is much to do in the meantime, work which will daily bring us near to suffering and self sacrifice, and teach us perhaps some lessons in unselfishness and bring us nearer to finding our souls. On the whole there is renewed courage out here, and the hope of a brighter....

(Here the letter breaks off abruptly with the writer's death).

Daily Express
21 August 1917
Portadown Express
24 August 1917

The letter, which was originally reproduced in full in the Daily Express, and then in the Portadown Express, was also the subject of favourable comment in the Editorial of the London newspaper under the banner "A Soldier of Humanity"

We print in another column a letter from a young soldier, dead at Salonika and happy in his death, knowing that he had done all in his power, quietly, humbly, and thankfully, for the land he loved and for the people in it. In its beautiful serenity is conveyed a message which should solemnly be taken to heart by all at home, especially by those who fancy they have grave wrongs and intolerable grievances, and who are so intent on standing up for what they call their "rights" that one would think them content to see their country perish rather than endure a minute's privation or an hour's extra labour.

Malcolm Clow, who was too feeble in health to pass the recruiting sergeants, and who wound up his life as a humble motor-driver in the service of the French Red Cross, will rank as high in the future as a corps commander or the head of a mighty Department of State. But he did not consider himself a hero; neither did he look upon himself as a martyr. "In comparison with millions" this true soldier of humanity writes, "my lines have fallen in pleasant places".

Daily Express
21 August 1917
Portadown Express
24 August 1917

Malcolm Clow was a member of Masonic Lodge No. 219, Portadown.

In 1925 William Moffat Clow was elected President of Portadown Chamber of Commerce and in 1929 he was appointed High Sheriff of County Armagh. William Moffat Clow died aged 81 on 21 July 1933 and was buried in Seagoe Cemetery.

Malcolm's brother-in-law John George Brew (married to his sister

Ann Moffat) died of wounds on 6 April 1918 in France (see **26 Major John George Brew**).

Egypt and Palestine

In October 1914 Turkey joined the war on the side of the Central Powers. Her strategic position posed a major threat to the Suez Canal, which was vital to Britain's interests. The British under T. E. Lawrence (Lawrence of Arabia), aided the Arab Revolt against the Turks in occupied Arabia and Palestine.

The British launched offensives at Gaza on 26 March and 17-19 April 1917 which both failed to make a major breakthrough. Under a new commander, General Sir Edmund Allenby, the British attacked again from 27 October-7 November 1917. The third battle resulted in a victory with the British continuing their advance northwards into Palestine capturing Jerusalem by Christmas.

On 1 October 1918 the Australians, with Arab support, captured Damascus. On 25 October British forces reached Aleppo and five days later an armistice was signed with the Turks bringing the campaign to an end. British and Empire losses amounted to 20,000 killed, 40,000 wounded and 3,500 prisoners of war.

John Broadwood Atkinson Captain, 5th Battalion, Royal Irish Fusiliers

Parents	Son of Joseph and Ann Edith Atkinson of Crowhill
Residence	Crowhill
Enlisted	September 1914
Died	Died 24 December 1915, Egypt
Age	21
Buried	Alexandria (Chatby) Military and War Memorial Cemetery, Egypt. Grave E. 91.
Commemorated	Portadown War Memorial (286) Tartaraghan Parish Church War Memorial

John was the third son of John Atkinson DL. He was educated at Mourne Grange, County Down and at Ourdale School, Northamptonshire.

Captain Atkinson was wounded in action on 6 August 1915 in the Gallipoli campaign.

Lieutenant (sic) Atkinson is a son of Mr. Joseph Atkinson, D.L., of Crowhill near Portadown, who, as our readers know, is the senior representative of a family which came to Ireland at the time of the Cromwellian settlement, and every member of which is held in high esteem throughout the county. We shall be glad to learn of Lieut. Atkinson's speedy recovery.

Portadown Express
20 August 1915

Captain Atkinson died in hospital at Alexandria, Egypt of enteric fever after a three-month illness.

Henry May
Private 5/12051, 5th Battalion, Royal Irish Fusiliers

Born	Portadown
Parents	Son of James May of Drumlellum
Residence	Drumlellum
Enlisted	Inverkeithy, Fife, Scotland
Died	Killed in action 7 November 1917, Third Battle of Gaza, Hureira, Palestine
Buried	Gaza War Cemetery, Israel. Grave VIII. D. 7.
Commemorated	Portadown War Memorial (301) Drumcree Parish Church War Memorial

Intimation has been received by Mr. James May, Drumlellum, Portadown, that his son, Private Harry May, R.I.F., has been killed in action while serving in Egypt. Mr. May has two other sons serving with the Canadians.

Portadown News
2 March 1918

The 5th Battalion, Royal Irish Fusiliers, part of the 10th (Irish) Division, was posted to Egypt and Palestine in September 1917.

During the Third Battle of Gaza on 7 November 1917 the 5th Battalion, together with the 2nd Battalion, Royal Irish Fusiliers and the 6th Battalion, Royal Inniskilling Fusiliers assaulted the Hureira Redoubt occupying a strategic position on the Gaza to Beersheba Road. 200 Turkish soldiers supported by trench mortars and 30 machine guns defended the Redoubt.

Casualties were one officer and five other ranks killed and two officers and 36 other ranks wounded.

Henry's brother James a railway switchman, served in the 42nd Regiment, Canadian Infantry during the Great War. James was born in 1889 and emigrated to Canada where he resided with his sister Minnie at 100 St. Matthew Street, Montreal. James' place of birth is recorded as "Portadeon Township, Dumallewyn" in his service records.

Samuel James Finnegan
Private 17385, 2nd Battalion, Royal Irish Fusiliers

Born	Portadown
Parents	Son of William and Anne Finnegan of 18 Jervis Street, Portadown.

Residence Jervis Street
Enlisted Portadown
Died Died of wounds 7 November 1917, Third Battle of Gaza, Hureira, Palestine
Buried Gaza War Cemetery, Israel. Grave XX. A. 6.
Commemorated
Portadown War Memorial (135)
St. Mark's Parish Church War Memorial

Samuel's father William was employed as a carter. He and his wife Anne had children Elizabeth, Samuel James, William, Frances, Mary Margaret and Martha.

Samuel James was employed as a weaver. He was the husband of Minnie Finnegan and the couple had a daughter. The family resided at 5 Jervis Street, Portadown. His brother William resided in the USA.

Edward Magee
Private 18158, 5th Battalion, Royal Irish Fusiliers

Residence Curran Street
Enlisted Portadown
Died Killed in action 10 March 1918, Battle of Tell 'Asur, Palestine
Buried No Known Grave Jerusalem Memorial, Israel. Panel 45.
Commemorated
Portadown War Memorial (81)

Private E. Magee, Royal Irish Fusiliers, Portadown, is officially reported killed in action.

Portadown Express
19 April 1918

The Battle of Tell 'Asur was fought from 9-12 March 1918 in the mountains north of Jerusalem. It involved the 53rd, 74th, 75th and 10th (Irish) Divisions. The 5th Battalion, Royal Irish Fusiliers formed part of 31st Brigade of the 10th (Irish) Division, which was allocated positions on the right centre. On 9 March the battalion captured Ras El Tarfii and Attara coming up against slight resistance.

On 10 March the battalion came under heavy enfilade fire but managed to capture Aliuta where they killed 30 Turks and one German. Later that day they captured Jiljilia, which was undefended. Casualties were three officers wounded and 11 other ranks killed and 33 wounded.

Thomas Sprott Sergeant Dispenser 37082, 143rd (Indian) Combined Field Ambulance, RAMC

Born	1888, Portadown
Parents	Son of Samuel and Jane Sprott of Carraboo, Portadown
Residence	Killicomain Road
Enlisted	Londonderry
Died	Died 11 October 1918, Ludd, (Arimathea), Palestine
Age	30
Buried	Ramleh War Cemetery, Israel. Grave Z.60.
Commemorated	Portadown War Memorial (154) First Presbyterian Church War Memorial, Edenderry Family Memorial Plaque, First Presbyterian Church, Edenderry

Samuel Sprott, together with Mr. H. W. McCammon, set up a curing business in Castle Street, Portadown. After a few years and a move to new premises Samuel continued his curing business on his own. He married Jane McClelland from County Down and the couple had children Jeanie, Samuel, Thomas, William, May and R. McClelland. In 1901 the family resided in Hanover Street, Portadown.

Thomas' brother Sergeant R. McClelland Sprott, Legion of Frontiersmen New Zealand, had previous service in the Royal Navy. In 1915 he was appointed as a recruiting officer for Port Ahuriri, New Zealand.

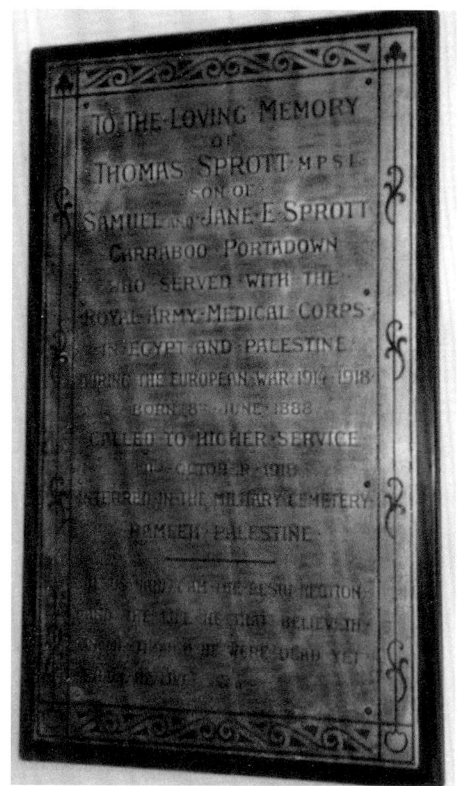

Memorial to Sergeant Dispenser Thomas Sprott, First Presbyterian Church, Edenderry. (Author's Collection)

His brother Samuel born 1887 emigrated to Montreal, Canada and another brother William resided at Arden, Thomas Street, Portadown. William married Jeannie Stevenson, daughter of James Stevenson of Parkmount, on 27 April 1916 at the First Presbyterian Church, Portadown. Jeanie married Samuel S. Corbett of Quarrybank, Killicomaine.

Sergeant Sprott arrived in Egypt in June 1915 and later served at Ludd in Palestine, which was the site of a number of medical units. The Indian Combined Field Ambulance, with which he served, was converted from the British Field Ambulance. Sergeant Dispenser Thomas Sprott died of pneumonia.

David John Grimley
Private 9911, 2nd Battalion, Royal Irish Fusiliers

Born	Portadown
Parents	Son of John and Mary Grimley of 38 Meadow Lane, Portadown
Residence	Meadow Lane
Enlisted	Portadown
Died	Died 10 November 1918, Palestine
Buried	Deir El Belah War Cemetery, Israel. Grave B. 199.
Commemorated	Portadown War Memorial (165) St. Mark's Parish Church War Memorial

David's father John was employed as a weaver and his mother Mary was a winder. The couple had children David John, Julia and Mary Jane.

Private Grimley had served for eight years in the army and was in India when war was declared. He saw service on the Western Front and in Salonika.

Letters received from Salonika state that David John Grimley, (Meadow Lane), of the 2nd Battalion, Royal Irish Fusiliers, has been recommended for a high distinction, but no official notification has yet come to hand...

Portadown Express
30 June 1916

Private Grimley died of peritonitis.

Mesopotamia

Nearly 900,000 British and Empire troops served in the Mesopotamia campaign. Total battle casualties amounted to 70,000 killed, wounded and missing with a further 10,000 prisoners of war many of whom died in captivity. British Army losses were 7,500 killed or died of wounds. Many troops suffered from disease including dysentery, beri beri and malaria as well as having to contend with the extreme heat of the desert sun. Non-battle casualties included over 8,000 British Army deaths from sickness.

John Greenaway
Corporal 8552, 6th South Lancashire Regiment

Born	Drumcree
Residence	John Street
Enlisted	Portadown
Died	Died of wounds 16 February 1917, Mesopotamia
Buried	Amara War Cemetery, Iraq. Grave XXI. L. 13.
Commemorated	Portadown War Memorial (146) St. Mark's Parish Church War Memorial

Corporal Greenaway was a regular soldier and had served in India and France before the outbreak of war.

In February 1917 the 6th South Lancashire Regiment was involved in heavy fighting with Turkish forces in and around the Dahra Bend on the River Tigris.

His brother Francis (see entry **145 Private Francis Greenaway**) died of wounds on 28 April 1915 in France.

John Andrews Walker
Corporal 148682, 15th Divisional Signal Company, Royal Engineers

Born	Portadown
Parents	Son of John and Martha Andrews Walker of Portadown
Residence	Annagh
Enlisted	Belfast
Died	Died 12 July 1917, Mesopotamia
Age	20
Buried	Baghdad (North Gate) War Cemetery, Iraq. Grave V. B. 7.
Commemorated	Portadown War Memorial (252) Armagh Road Presbyterian Church War Memorial

John Andrews was an only son. His father John was Clerk of Petty Sessions in Portadown and died on 13 January 1915. John Andrews took over as Clerk of Petty Sessions from his late father.

Soon after his appointment John volunteered for active service and became a despatch rider in the Royal Engineers.

On 2 July 1916 Corporal Walker was thrown from his motorcycle by the explosion of a shell. He was knocked unconscious and remained so until the following day. He was

Family grave of Corporal John Andrews Walker. (Author's Collection)

evacuated to hospital and spent a month at a convalescent home at Epsom recovering from shell shock.

Deep regret, too, will be felt in Portadown at the news of the death of Mr. John A. Walker, which took place on 12th inst. in Mesopotamia from heart exhaustion.

Portadown Express
20 July 1917

After the death of her husband and with her son at the front Martha and her daughters moved to Hawarden, Bloomfield in Belfast.

George Weir
Private M344819, 1020th Mechanical Transport Coy., Army Service Corps

Born	Seagoe
Parents	Son of James and Eliza Weir of 12 Century Street, Portadown
Residence	Century Street
Enlisted	Belfast
Died	Died 3 October1918, Basra, Mesopotamia
Age	20
Buried	Tehran War Cemetery, Iran. Grave V. D. 16.
Commemorated	Portadown War Memorial (53) Seagoe Parish Church War Memorial

Private George Weir, Century Street, has died in hospital in Egypt from sickness contracted on service. He is a son of Mr. James Weir who served in France himself, whose five sons joined the colours after the outbreak of war. James was killed, George has died from sickness as already stated, Thomas and Robert have been discharged owing to wounds, and Joseph is still serving in France.

Portadown News
October 1918

Private Weir died of sandfly fever at Basra, Mesopotamia.

His brother James (see entry **168 Private James Henry Weir**) was killed in action on 11 April 1917 in France.

South Africa

In August 1914 Prime Minister Louis Botha and General Jan Smuts declared war on Germany. This was not to the liking of some South Africans including General Manie Maritz who declared his support for the Germans. On 9 October 1914 Maritz and 500 supporters crossed into German South West Africa to plan a rebellion. Eventually over 10,000 Boers and a number of Boer generals rallied to his support. The rebellion was defeated on 30 January 1915.

Charles Milling Anderson
Trooper, Kimberley Central Commando, (Scott's Horse)

Parents	Son of Robert and Margaret Anderson of High Street, Portadown
Residence	Church Street
Enlisted	28 October 1914, Kimberley, South Africa
Died	Died 29 July 1917, South Africa
Age	21
Buried	Kimberley, South Africa
Commemorated	Portadown War Memorial (61) St. Mark's Parish Church War Memorial

Robert Anderson was originally from the Derryhale area. He entered the drapery business of Mr.Averell Shillington before starting with his own premises in Mandeville Street, Portadown. He was a member and later Chairman of Portadown Urban Council. Robert held a host of chairmanships and his interests included welfare, library services, schools, tourism and employment.

A prominent member of the Church of Ireland he was a member of the Select Vestry of St. Mark's Parish Church from 1893 and a member of the General Synod. Robert and his wife Margaret who was from County Londonderry had children Daisy, Herbert, Julia, Samuel, Evaline, Lucy, Robert, Charles Milling and Winifred.

Robert graduated as a medical doctor from Trinity College, Dublin and on the outbreak of war gained a commission in the Royal Army Medical Corps. He had a distinguished military career during the Great War. He served in the

Gallipoli Campaign in 1915 and after a severe illness contacted in the Dardenelles was posted to the South of England where he was attached to the 16th Reserve Squadron, Royal Flying Corps.

Captain Robert Anderson married Margaret Jane Gibson of Prenton, Birkenhead on 31 May 1916 at St. Paul's Church Birkenhead. He was appointed Deputy Assistant Director of Medical Services and later in the same year was posted to India, where remained until 1918 and the end of hostilities.

Robert was appointed Lieutenant-Colonel on 7 July 1939 serving as Assistant Director of Hospitals, Northern Command and as Commanding Officer, Field Ambulance, South Coast. In 1941 was appointed Commander of the General Hospital in Bangor.

His brother Charles also had ambitions to be a doctor and had entered Trinity College, Dublin, but was unable to pursue his studies as he contracted the lung disease tuberculosis. On medical advice he emigrated to Kimberley, South Africa.

With the outbreak of war Charles volunteered his services enlisting in the Kimberley Central Commando. The unit was comprised of 300 men who could ride and shoot and was also known as Scott's Horse.

The Kimberley Central Commando was involved in trekking down the rebels who were operating near the border with German South West Africa. The unit took part in four main so-called trekking operations against the enemy. In many letters home Trooper Anderson has left a unique insight into this irregular or guerrilla type warfare.

1) 11 November - 23 December 1914 Upington - Kakamas Trekking Operations

At any rate, after 18 long weary days we arrived at Upington, a dirty weary column, and hungry! Upington is a principal town in that district, some 18 miles from the German border, and made a military base with a large hospital by the authorities. We lay at Upington for some time, about 3 weeks. Our journey here was for the purpose (which we afterwards discovered) of cutting off one of the rebel leaders with 700 or 800 men who were making for the German border, there to join his friends. Needless to say we never saw him, and so he escaped. After moving from Upington we went to Kakamas, and then started a ceaseless track against the rebels. We tracked to and fro incessantly, always on the lookout for rebels, who never came - or rather they came, but we arrived generally about 2 hours too late.

Portadown Express
9 May 1915

2) 23 December 1914 - 17 January 1915 Keinoes - Bivouac and Trekking Operations

We trekked all through the night, and early in the morning came to Keinoes. There we learnt the reason for our hurry. The rebels under Kemp and Maritz were nosing round that district on the lookout for loot and supplies, and were expected to attack the town. There we spent Xmas. Bullybeef and biscuits, dust and filthy water was the menu of our Xmas dinner. For over three weeks we stayed here.

Portadown Express
9 May 1915

Trooper Charles Milling Anderson. (Portadown Times)

3) 17 January - 22 January 1915 Lodz Pitts - Keinoes Trekking Operations

The Colonel had got word the rebels were about to attack a small force of ours at Lodz Pitts. So this night again we trekked through the whole night; at sunrise we off saddled for two hours, and then on again. About 2 o'clock in the afternoon we arrived at Lodz Pitts, to find the fight over and our men routed.

Portadown Express
9 May 1915

4) 24 January - 30 January 1915 Upington Trekking Operations

Maritz and Kemp and Stadler, the three rebel leaders were marching on Upington with 1,500 rebels and a number of artillery... On Sunday morning the 24th January about 10 minutes before dawn broke, the first canon shot was fired...
We are going into action at last. My heart jumped. We are off, one long line over a mile long, 4 yards between each man. We had not gone two miles until we were under fire, shells whistling over me and bullets whizzing all round...Next section from me a horse and man falls; I look back the man rises unhurt, but his horse has been shot. We pass on....We advance on foot about 300 yards. "Take cover". We are down to it. "At 1200 yards' independent firing - carry on". I put my rifle to my shoulder, take sight; I can't pull the trigger. My heart beats faster and faster. I fear a sort of faintness. Again I raise my rifle, and this time I fire. Immediately I feel as if a weight is lifted from off me. I snuggle down into a more comfy

position, and now fire coolly and methodically. Shooting to the best of my ability....An officer sits at my feet with glasses. I am beside two chums. Suddenly the officer says "Anderson! Peters! Here! Look that man on horseback!" Dimly we see a man galloping like fury from behind the enemy's lines. He is probably an orderly. Instantly about 16 rifles (half our troop) are pointed at him, including my own. Then ring! - Phut! He falls; we wonder whose bullet has hit him. We continue once more firing at the enemy's lines.

Portadown Express
9 May 1915

Later Trooper Anderson, who was attending to some horses, was slightly wounded in the hand when he and his unit came under sustained shellfire from the enemy

The shells were lighting all round in amongst our horses. I was holding four horses, and you have to lie down to do it, so it was jolly uncomfortable. One shell burst about 3 feet behind my horses, and a piece of shrapnel entered No. 2 horse in the side. It made an awful wound about 18 inches long and you could put your head into the hole... I myself felt something hit my right hand, and it was bleeding, but only a graze on the knuckles. As soon as the smoke cleared away the Captain came up and said "Hurt Anderson!" I said not, but showed him the wounded horse; he was lying down, and did not seem in much pain, but the Captain said he had better finish him and shot him outright with his revolver.

Portadown Express
9 May 1915

Charles Anderson died of tuberculosis on 29 July 1917, with his sister Daisy by his side, at the Bend Hotel, Sydney, Kimberley, South Africa.

His father Robert died on 10 October 1942 and was buried in Drumcree Churchyard. Charles' brother Herbert (Herbie) was Chairman of Portadown Football Club in the 1960s.

Crosbie Weir
Captain,
Royal Army Medical Corps

Parents	Son of William J. and Minnie Weir of Ashgrove House, Portadown
Residence	Ballinagone
Died	Died 15 November 1918, South Africa
Buried	Peddie, Cape Province, South Africa.
Commemorated	Portadown War Memorial (255) Drumcree Parish Church War Memorial

Crosbie was the eldest son of William and Minnie Weir and the grandson of W. J. Crosbie of Dawson's Grove, Portadown. He was educated at Cookstown Academy under the late Harry

Lindsay and afterwards continued his studies under the Reverend W. H. T. Tilson.

On 17 June 1909 he enrolled in Trinity College, Dublin. After graduation Crosbie doctored at Mercer's Hospital, Dublin before being appointed Resident House Surgeon of County Londonderry and City Infirmary.

On 2 October 1916 he gained a commission in the Special Reserve of Officers of the Royal Army Medical Corps. He was stationed at Birr, King's County. After training he was posted to Basra, Mesopotamia, arriving in May 1917, where he was placed in charge of the Base Hospital in the city. After a severe illness he was granted six months leave in England and to aid his recovery was given permission by the War Office to spend three months in South Africa.

He had two sisters and his brother, William, was engaged in the farming industry.

Captain Crosbie Weir contacted Spanish Influenza (the pandemic that swept the world in 1918 and 1919), and died of pneumonia at Peddie, Cape Province, South Africa.

India

On the outbreak of the Great War many British Army regiments were hastily recalled from India for the Western Front. India supplied many famous and superb regiments for the Indian Army and they fought on the Western Front and in the Middle East, Gallipoli, East Africa and Mesopotamia. A total of over one and a half million Indian troops were raised for the war effort. Casualties were over 62,000 killed, died or missing in all theatres including 24,000 killed in Mesopotamia and 7,000 on the Western Front.

Garrison battalions, made up from veterans who had rejoined the colours and who were unfit or too old for duty in the front line trenches, were dispatched to India to replace the drain on British and Indian Army troops bound for the front.

Robert Edward Reville
Sergeant-Major G/13181, 1st (Garrison) Battalion, Royal Irish Fusiliers

Born	Devonport
Parents	Son of William Reville
Residence	Church Street
Enlisted	Armagh
Died	Died 17 April 1917, India

Buried No Known Grave
Commemorated
Kirkee 1914-1918 Memorial, India. Face E.
Portadown War Memorial (66)

Robert was the second son of William Reville from Kilkenny who was a Quarter-Master Sergeant and was born in Monaghan. He was the husband of Isabella Reville and the couple and their children resided at 43 Church Street, Portadown.

Sergeant-Major Reville served for a number of years on the Monaghan Regiment permanent staff. He was discharged from the army in 1908 when the regiment was disbanded and took up employment as a postman in Portadown.

On the outbreak of war he volunteered for service with the 1st (Garrison) Battalion, Royal Irish Fusiliers which was formed in September 1915 in Dublin.

Sergeant-Major Reville was stationed in Armagh, Tipperary and Dublin before the battalion sailed for India in February 1916 to take up garrison duties.

He died of malaria in Colaba War Hospital, Bombay, India.

Burma

Burma was located on the eastern periphery of India and was garrisoned in the same way.

William Milligan
Private G/14481,
1st Garrison Battalion,
Royal Irish Fusiliers

Born	Magheralin
Parents	Son of Isaac Milligan
Residence	Century Street
Enlisted	Belfast
Died	Died 10 February 1918, Burma
Age	38
Buried	No Known Grave
Commemorated	Taukkyan Memorial, Burma. Portadown War Memorial (52) Seagoe Parish Church War Memorial

William was the husband of Mary Milligan and the couple resided at 8 Century Street, Portadown.

It is believed that William enlisted in the 9th Royal Irish Fusiliers and served and was wounded at the Battle of the Somme 1916. On recovery Private Milligan was posted to the 1st (Garrison) Battalion, Royal Irish Fusiliers. The battalion was posted to Burma in May 1917 and performed the same

duties as it had in India. It sailed for the United Kingdom in November 1919.

His eldest son Sergeant John Milligan, who resided in Woodhouse Street, Portadown, served in the Irish Guards during the Great War. He was 'mentioned in despatches' for gallant and devoted service in the field, was awarded the Italian Bronze Star and twice received certificates for gallantry in the field. He was also wounded in action on two occasions. One of the certificates, signed by Major General A. Jennings, read

This is to certify that No. 3235 Sergt. John Milligan, Second Bn. Irish Guards, performed this deed of bravery. On 15th March 1917, the enemy left their front trenches in St. Perrie Waast Wood, and our troops penetrated into the outskirts of the Wood. It was imperative to find out the position, which they held. All over the wood there were snipers and in some places machine guns. The orders were to push gradually on, so as to obtain the whole wood. This sergeant for three consecutive days worked with his section, reconnoitring the position, and taking every possible advantage of the retirement of the enemy. His energy and courage have before been brought to notice, and he was mentioned in despatches on the 1st January 1917, for consecutive good work. He has however never received any British Military reward.

Portadown News
19 January 1918

He joined the Royal Irish Constabulary after the end of the Great War. Two other sons Private Robert Milligan 9th Battalion, Royal Irish Fusiliers and Sergeant William Milligan, Machine Gun Corps, were wounded in action during the Great War.

Private William Milligan, who was on his way home after a recovering from a serious illness, died from injuries received in a train collision.

Chapter 9
The Home Front

Almost 60,000 Irishmen were serving in the Crown forces when war was declared on 4 August 1914. During the Great War approximately 150,000 Irishmen enlisted making a total contribution of 210,000. All were volunteers, as conscription, introduced in 1916/17 on the British mainland, did not apply to Ireland.

Three infantry divisions were raised in Ireland 10th (Irish), 16th (Irish) and 36th (Ulster) Division. Many Irishmen also enlisted in the forces of the Empire - Canada, Australia, New Zealand, India and South Africa, although there are no figures available. Irishmen also served in the United States forces and a small number also served in Allied forces such as the French and Serbian Red Cross. It has been estimated that around 240,000 Irishmen in total served in British, Empire and Allied forces during the Great War of which 35,000 lost their lives.

Royal Navy personnel from Portadown who lost their lives during the Great War are included in this section as they died protecting their country in home waters.

For a number of servicemen their troubles did not end with their demobilisation as they still bore the scars and injuries received at the front and diseases contacted while on service at home or abroad. As they died after being discharged from the services their names are not included in the Soldiers Died or CWGC Debt of Honour Registers. It was decided by the Portadown War Memorial Committee that their names should be included on Portadown War Memorial.

Hamilton John Robb
Lieutenant, Royal Marine Light Infantry, HMS *Sutlej*

Born	31 January 1894, Edenderry House
Parents	Son of Hamilton Robb of Edenderry House, Portadown
Residence	Bridge Street
Enlisted	1 January 1912
Died	Died 10 November 1914, Queenstown (Cobh)
Age	20
Buried	No Known Grave
Commemorated	Portadown War Memorial (18) Drumcree Parish Church War Memorial

Lurgan College War Memorial

Hamilton John's father Hamilton owned the Hamilton Robb Weaving Factory in Edenderry. He had two children Hilda and Hamilton John. Gertrude Baxter a school governess from Bradford educated them.

Hamilton John was educated at Lurgan College and enrolled at the Naval College, Greenwich in January 1912. From June until September 1912 he attended the Royal Marine Depot at Deal in Kent. From 1 October 1912 until 16 June 1913 he was attached to the Royal Marine Artillery Division where he received instruction in gunnery and the electric torpedo. From 17 June until 14 December 1913 he spent six months on board HMS *Donegal* being trained in practical naval subjects before joining the Portsmouth Division.

Lieutenant Robb served with the Portsmouth Battalion of the 3rd Royal Marine Brigade which was involved in operations in support of the Belgian army's defence of Ostend from 27 - 31 August 1914.

He joined HMS *Sutlej* on 19 September 1914. HMS *Sutlej* was a Cressy Class cruiser of 12,000 tons launched in 1899 at Clydebank. She was armed with two 9.2" and twelve 6" guns and had a top speed of 21 knots.

Family grave of Lieutenant Hamilton Robb. (Author's Collection)

Lieutenant Robb was drowned when the boat he was in capsized and sank bringing crew members back to from Queenstown to HMS *Sutlej*.

The late Lieutenant Robb was an officer of the Marine Light Infantry on HMS Sutlej, and had just arrived at Queenstown after a cruise in the Atlantic. On Tuesday, with five other officers of the ship, he went ashore

and spent the evening in Cork. On the return journey they arrived at Queenstown shortly before midnight, and engaged two boatmen to row them to the ship, which was in mid channel. When some distance from the shore, clear of the headland, a squall caught the boat, which was a small one, and capsized it, leaving the occupants struggling in the water. When the craft reappeared they all got hold of it, but realizing that it had not sufficient buoyancy to keep them all afloat Lieutenant Robb and four others volunteered to try and swim ashore. Their shouts for help were heard on shore, and a rowboat from a vessel at the quay was despatched and picked up two of the officers - Surgeon Monahan and Paymaster Gillespie. Four others were also rescued, but there was no trace of Lieutenant Robb and one of the boatmen - a man named Hurley - who were drowned.

Portadown Express
13 November 1914

The names of the drowned are - Lieutenant Robb, RN and Boatman Hanley. Those saved were Lieut. Daniels, Surgeon Symms, Captain Davenport, RN, Dr. Moynihan, RN, Paymaster Gillespie and Boatman Forde.

Portadown News
14 November 1914

Lieutenant Hamilton Robb's details were not included in the CWGC Register. In 2004, as a result of the research of the author, his details have now been added to the CWGC Debt of Honour Register. The author received a letter from the CWGC

I am pleased to tell you that the Ministry of Defence, having examined the non-commemoration of Lieutenant Hamilton John Robb, have agreed that the cause of his death was attributable to his war service and that he should therefore be treated as a war casualty.

Commonwealth War Graves
Commission 13 April 2004

James Keinzley
Private 5276, 1st Battalion, Royal Irish Fusiliers

Born	Portadown
Parents	Son of James and Bridget Keinzley of 9 John Street, Portadown
Residence	John Street
Enlisted	Portadown
Died	Died of wounds 20 March 1915, Lurgan
Age	23
Buried	Drumcree Roman Catholic Churchyard, Portadown
Commemorated	Portadown War Memorial (148)

James' father James was a blacksmith by trade. His mother Bridget was from County Cavan. The couple had boys Robert, Thomas and James.

Private Keinzley served in 'C' Company.

Private James Kingsley (sic), R.I.F., whose relatives reside in John Street, died in Lurgan Infirmary on Saturday last, and was buried on Monday. The deceased had been invalided home from the front, having spent some months in the battle line.

Portadown Express
25 March 1915

Grave of Private James Keinzley. (Author's Collection)

Robert H. Porter
Driver T4/059074,
Army Service Corps

Born	Portadown
Parents	Son of Samuel and Elizabeth Porter of Knocknamuckley
Residence	Knocknamuckley
Enlisted	Belfast
Died	Died 11 May 1915, United Kingdom
Age	21
Buried	Knocknamuckley Church of Ireland Churchyard, Portadown
Commemorated	Portadown War Memorial (309)

On Friday evening last the remains of Driver R. H. Porter, Army Service Corps, were laid to rest in Knocknamuckley burying ground, in the presence of the largest attendance ever seen at a funeral there. A detachment of the deceased comrades, under the command of Sergeant-Major Brown, travelled from Belfast to pay military honours, and the pipers of the 16th Battalion, Royal Irish Rifles played the remains from the house to the place of interment. The scene at the graveside was most impressive, a firing party from the Rifles firing three volleys over the grave, and the bugles sounding the Last Post. Deceased had only been in the army a short time when he was taken ill and removed to hospital, where he died.

Portadown Express
21 May 1915

Grave of Driver Robert H. Porter. (Author's Collection)

William Henry Sloan
Private 3426, 4th Battalion, Royal Irish Fusiliers

Born	Portadown
Parents	Son of William John Sloan of Ballinagone
Residence	Ballinagone
Enlisted	Belfast
Died	Died 16 May 1915, United Kingdom
Age	16
Buried	Drumcree Church of Ireland Churchyard, Portadown
Commemorated	Portadown War Memorial (254) Drumcree Parish Church War Memorial

Private Sloan, Ballinagone, Portadown, who was attached to the Ulster Division and had been ill for some time, passed away in the early part of the week.

Portadown News
22 May 1915

Grave of Private William Henry Sloan. (Author's Collection)

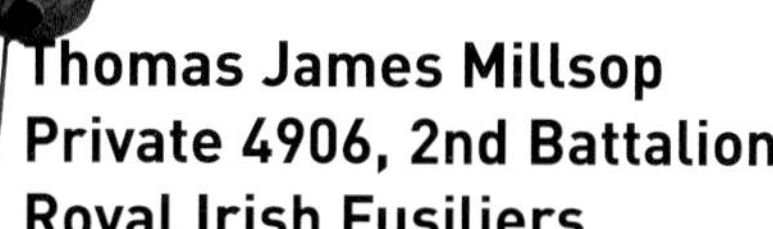

Thomas James Millsop Private 4906, 2nd Battalion, Royal Irish Fusiliers

Born	Portadown
Parents	Son of Robert and Mary Ann Millsop of Portadown
Residence	Montague Street
Enlisted	Finner Camp, Co. Donegal
Died	Died of wounds 30 May 1915, Sheffield
Age	25
Buried	Seagoe Cemetery, Portadown
Commemorated	Portadown War Memorial (175) St. Mark's Parish Church War Memorial

Thomas James' father Robert was employed as a general labourer. He and his wife Mary Ann had children Lizzie Ann, Maggie, William, Thomas, Sarah and Susan. In 1901 the family resided in Union Street, Portadown.

Lizzie Ann and Maggie were employed as flax spinners while in their youth William and Thomas were employed as tidy doffers.

Thomas was a reservist and was called up after the outbreak of war. On 2 May 1915 he was wounded in action in the chest with a shrapnel bullet. Private Millsop was evacuated to a hospital in England and died from wounds at the Royal Infirmary, Sheffield.

Grave of Private Thomas James Millsop. (Author's Collection)

Samuel McCutchen Bailey Engine Room Artificer 4th Class, M/11615, Royal Navy, HM Torpedo Boat *10*

Born	2 July 1892, Lurgan
Parents	Son of William and Minnie Bailey of 55 Mourneview Street, Portadown
Residence	Mourneview Street
Enlisted	19 January 1915, Chatham, England

Died	Lost at sea 10 June 1915, HMTB *10*, North Sea
Age	22
Buried	No Known Grave
Commemorated	Chatham Memorial, Kent. Panel 11. Portadown War Memorial (180) Thomas Street Methodist Church War Memorial

Samuel was the husband of Martha Bailey.

On enlistment in the Royal Navy his particulars were given as follows: occupation - fitter and turner, height - 5' 2", complexion - fresh, eyes - brown, hair - brown.

Samuel began his naval career at HMS *Pembroke II* and within three months was posted to HMS *Undaunted* - an Arethusa Class light cruiser displacing 3,520 tons and armed with two 6" and six 4" guns. He spent a further three weeks at the shore station before being posted to HM Torpedo Boat *10*. She displaced 250 tons, had a complement of 35 and had been built in 1906-07 by Thorneycrofts.

Increased German U-boat activity in the Thames Estuary area had caused the Admiralty to deploy five destroyers from the Nore Defence Flotilla, a number of armed trawlers from the Auxiliary Patrol and six Torpedo Boats including HMTBs *10* and *12* in pursuit.

At 0330 on 10 June 1915 a large explosion rocked HMTB *12*. HMTB *10* took HMTB *12* in tow with three destroyers standing by keeping a lookout for German U-boats. Soon afterwards HMTB *10* was also rocked by an explosion, which broke her in two. She sank within minutes. At 1055 HMTB *12* also sank. There were 41 survivors out of a combined complement of 70. ERA Bailey was one of those who did not survive.

At the time the Admiralty issued a communiqué stating that the two torpedo boats had been torpedoed by a German U-boat but it later transpired that both vessels had been the first victims of undersea mines laid by specially built U-boat minelayers.

He had brothers Alfred and Robert. His sister-in-law Eva resided at 72 Thomas Street, Portadown.

Hugh Blacker Lance-Corporal 15780, 6th Battalion, Royal Irish Fusiliers

Born	Portadown
Parents	Son of Henry and Annie Blacker
Residence	John Street
Enlisted	Portadown

Died — Died of wounds 28 August 1915, England
Buried — Drumcree Roman Catholic Churchyard, Portadown
Commemorated — Portadown War Memorial (143)

Lance-Corporal Blacker was shot in the head and was evacuated to Netley Hospital, England where he died of wounds.

The remains of Lance-Corporal Hugh Blacker arrived in Portadown on Sunday night. He was seriously wounded at the Front, and subsequently died in Netley hospital. The funeral took place on Monday to Drumcree R. C. burying ground, and was largely attended. A good many soldiers followed the remains, and the coffin was covered in the Union Jack. Deceased volunteered for service towards the end of last year. At the graveside, Rev. F. Kerr C. C. paid an eloquent tribute to the deceased soldier's devotion to duty and the noble example he had set in joining the Army to fight for his King and country in the terrible struggle in which the empire is at present involved.

Portadown News
4 September 1915

His brother Henry (see entry **142 Private Henry Patrick Blacker**) died of wounds received at Gallipoli on 19 August 1915.

Grave of Lance-Corporal Hugh Blacker. (Author's Collection)

George Grimason
Able Seaman 235183, Royal Navy, HMS *Illustrious*

Born — 17 July 1888, Portadown
Parents — Son of John and Mary Grimason of 14 Carleton Street, Portadown
Residence — Carleton Street
Enlisted — 5 November 1905, Devonport, England

Died Died 9 October 1915, Grimsby, England
Age 27
Buried Grimsby (Scartho Road) Cemetery, Lincolnshire, England.
Grave 42. D. 3.
Commemorated
Portadown War Memorial (37)

George was the husband of Ada Grimason of 11 Union Street, Plymouth.

On enlistment, as a Boy Sailor, his particulars were given as follows: occupation - blacksmith's assistant, height - 5' 5", complexion - fresh, eyes - blue, hair - light brown. He had scars on his left cheek, base of chin and on the left forearm.

On 17 July 1906 George enlisted for a period of twelve years service as an Ordinary Seaman and was promoted to Able Seaman on 26 February 1910. He served in a number of ships and shore establishments - HMS *Sutlej, Vivid I, Hibernia, Victory I, Hannibal, Vanguard, Anromeda, Sirius, Cumberland* and *Argyll.*

When war broke out he was serving on the Majestic Class pre-Dreadnought battleship, HMS *Illustrious.* She was launched in 1896 and was armed with four 12", twelve 6" and sixteen 12pdr guns. The battleship displaced 15,000 tons, had a top speed of 16½ knots and a crew of 760. In 1912 she was attached to the 3rd Fleet at Devonport.

A postcard of the battleship HMS Illustrious. (Author's Collection)

With the outbreak of hostilities *Illustrious* was recommissioned from the reserve fleet and was based in turn at Lough Swilly, the Tyne and Humber as a guard ship.

George had attended his father's funeral in Portadown on 3 October 1915 and was returning to duty when he died suddenly in mysterious circumstances. The circumstances of his death remained unclear until the report of an inquest in an English newspaper. It transpired that Able Seaman Grimason had been bitten (or stung) by an insect on or before 8 October and had suffered an acute allergic reaction which had rendered him unconscious and which was quickly followed by his death.

George's brother John (see entry **38 Private John Grimason**) was killed in action on 13 May 1915 in Belgium.

Samuel George Dillon Private 14130 10th Battalion, Royal Irish Fusiliers

Born	Portadown
Parents	Son of James and Mary Dillon of 60 Brighton Avenue, East Orange, New Jersey, USA
Residence	Bridge Street
Enlisted	September 1914, Portadown
Died	Died 7 January 1916, Belfast
Age	18
Buried	Seagoe Cemetery, Portadown
Commemorated	Portadown War Memorial (8)

James and Mary Dillon had nine children Edward, Prudence, Mary, David, Samuel, Bertha, Frederick, Harold and Lily. The family resided at 94 Bridge Street before emigrating to the United States (Samuel and Lily remained in Portadown). Samuel was employed by Mr. D. Chapman, Market Street, before enlisting.

He contacted a chill, which developed into pneumonia. Private Dillon was admitted to the military hospital in Belfast where he succumbed to his illness.

An immense assemblage of people gathered in Bridge Street on Sunday afternoon to attend the funeral of Private Samuel G. Dillon, 9th Battalion R.I.F., whose death took place on the previous Friday....The coffin was covered with the Union Jack, upon which were laid deceased's cap and belt, etc, and the scene as the hearse passed between the ranks of the soldiers (who fell in behind) was a most impressive one.

Portadown Express
14 January 1916

Grave of Private Samuel George Dillon. (Author's Collection)

Grave of Private Patrick Burns. (Author's Collection)

Patrick Burns
Private 5635,
Royal Irish Fusiliers

Parents — Son of Mary Burns of 50 Henry Street, Portadown.

Residence — Henry Street

Died — Died of wounds 20 January 1916, London

Age — 24

Buried — Drumcree Roman Catholic Churchyard, Portadown

Commemorated — Portadown War Memorial (118)

Private Burns wrote to his mother Mary from the trenches

Just a few lines to let you know I am well, and for so far have escaped unhurt, although I have been in some great "scraps" since coming here. The Germans are very good fighters, but can't stick it. They made an attack on us one night, and although they were in the majority as regards numbers, we managed to give them more than they bargained for. We lost a lot of men in this battle, but believe me the German losses were even greater...I have been in the trenches since I came out, and believe me they are no nice place to be in. We are standing in about two feet of water and mud, but with all these hardships, you would never hear a grumble, and everyone seems so happy.

Portadown News
6 March 1915

Private Burns received serious wounds to the head and was evacuated to St. Thomas' Hospital, London where he succumbed to his wounds nine months later. His mother received a letter from a number of his comrades

Just a line on behalf of Patrick's comrades who sympathise with you in your sad bereavement. We regret his loss very much for he was always a bright and cheery lad. When he was wounded we done our utmost for him until he went to hospital. We were always looking forward to his recovery, and we can assure you that it was a great shock to us when we read of his death. But we hope you will bear up in your troubles, for he died for his King and country - Believe us.

Yours Sincerely
Corporal J. McQuillan
Private T. Hewitt
Private Toppin

Portadown News
15 April 1916

Thomas Conlon
Private 22639, 10th Battalion, Royal Irish Fusiliers

Born	Benburb
Parents	Son of Robert Conlon of Ballyworkan
Residence	Jervis Street
Enlisted	Portadown
Died	Died 17 February 1916, Belfast
Age	17
Buried	Loughgall Old Churchyard, Loughgall
Commemorated	Portadown War Memorial (133)

Grave of Private Thomas Conlon. (Author's Collection)

St. Mark's Parish Church War Memorial

Thomas was a regular attender at St. Mark's Parish Sunday School. He underwent training at Lurgan and then at Newtownards.

At Newtownards he contacted a chill, which developed into pneumonia. Thomas was admitted to the military hospital at Victoria Barracks, Belfast where he succumbed to the illness.

George Toner
Private 19804, 5th Battalion, Royal Irish Fusiliers

Parents Son of John and Alice Toner of Derrykeeran
Residence Bann Street
Enlisted Portadown
Died Died 8 April 1916, United Kingdom
Age 45
Buried Drumcree Roman Catholic Churchyard, Portadown
Commemorated Portadown War Memorial (7)

George was the husband of Elizabeth Toner and they resided at 7 Bann Street, Portadown.

Grave of Private George Toner. (Author's Collection)

Moore Hill
Private 14299, 9th Battalion, Royal Irish Fusiliers

Born Portadown
Parents Son of William J. and Mary Hill of 5 Carleton Street, Portadown
Residence Carleton Street
Enlisted September 1914, Belfast
Died Died 10 May 1916, Edinburgh, Scotland
Age 19

Buried: Drumcree Church of Ireland Churchyard, Portadown

Commemorated: Portadown War Memorial (40)
St. Mark's Parish Church War Memorial

Moore's father William was employed as a coachman. His mother Mary was from County Westmeath. The couple had children Robert, Moore, William Arthur, Ethel and Eva. Moore was educated at Portadown Technical School.

He served in 'D' Company. Private Hill was taken ill in the trenches and evacuated to Edinburgh Military Hospital where he succumbed to his illness.

The sad news has reached Mrs Hill, Carleton Street, of the death of one of her sons, Moore Hill, of 9th R.I.F., who has succumbed to sickness contracted in the trenches. All who know her and who know her son, who was a most promising young man, feels deep sympathy for her.

Portadown Express
12 May 1916

Moore's brother Robert (see entry **39 Private Robert Hill**) died on 17 July 1916 at a hospital in England from wounds received at the Battle of the Somme.

Grave of Private Moore Hill and his brother Private Robert Hill. (Author's Collection)

Robert Hill
Private 16431, 9th Battalion, Royal Irish Fusiliers

Born: Portadown

Parents: Son of William J. and Mary Hill of 5 Carleton Street, Portadown

Residence: Carleton Street

Enlisted: Clandeboye

Died: Died of wounds 17 July 1916, Norfolk War Hospital, England

Age 22

Buried Drumcree Church of Ireland Churchyard, Portadown

Commemorated

Portadown War Memorial (39)
St. Mark's Parish Church War Memorial

Private Hill served in 'B' Company. He was wounded in action at the Battle of the Somme and was evacuated to a hospital in England for treatment. Robert's mother travelled over to see her wounded son.

Robert's brother Moore (see entry **40 Private Moore Hill**) died on 10 May 1916 in Edinburgh.

Within the space of two months Mary Hill lost her husband and two sons. She later married a Mr. Lindsay and resided at 27 Cumberland Street, Belfast

Albert Milton Boyle
Private 303, North Irish Horse

Parents Son of James and Margaret Boyle of Drumcree

Residence Drumcree

Died Died 27 October 1916, United Kingdom

Age 29

Buried Drumcree Church of Ireland Churchyard, Portadown

Commemorated

Portadown War Memorial (296)
Drumcree Parish Church War Memorial

Grave of Private Albert Milton Boyle. (Author's Collection)

Albert's father James was a farmer and had children William, Andrew, Clara, Thomas, Albert, Samuel and Martha. He died on 5 December 1910.

Private Boyle was a regular soldier and took part in the Retreat from Mons in August 1914. In a letter to the Reverend James Archer, rector of Seagoe, Trooper I. Walker wrote

I and Walter Vaughan were the only ones out of Seagoe Parish who were with the N.I.H. on the retirement from Mons. Milton Boyle of Drumcree Parish and William Morton of Ardmore Parish were also with us. So there were only four from Portadown serving with the N.I.H. I am glad to say we are all safe and sound yet.

Portadown News
13 March 1915

Private Boyle was considered as 'no longer fit for service' and was discharged on 9 September 1915.

Jackson Stothers
Private 14706, 10th Battalion, Royal Irish Fusiliers

Born	Portadown
Parents	Son of Ellen Stothers of 12 Bright Street, Portadown
Residence	Bright Street
Enlisted	Portadown
Died	Died 7 January 1917, Dublin
Buried	Grangegorman Military Cemetery, Dublin
Commemorated	Portadown War Memorial (20) Seagoe Parish Church War Memorial

Jackson served with the 9th Battalion, Royal Irish Fusiliers and returned from the front suffering from shell shock. On his return he was stationed at Portobello Barracks, Dublin with the 10th Battalion, Royal Irish Fusiliers.

On 8 December 1916 Jackson was last seen leaving the barracks and nothing was heard of him until his body was recovered from the Grand Canal at Portobello Bridge almost one month later. An inquest was held and the jury found that his death was as a result of drowning.

Jackson's brother Joseph (see entry **21 Private Joseph Stothers**) was killed in action on 1 July 1916 at the Battle of the Somme and his brother Maxwell (see entry **22 Private Maxwell Stothers**) died as a result on an accident on 7 October 1916.

William John Thompson
Driver M2/264326,
MT Repair Depot (Camberwell), Army Service Corps

Born	Portadown
Residence	Annagh
Enlisted	Glasgow
Died	Died 24 February 1917, United Kingdom

Buried Glasgow (Lambhill) Cemetery
Commemorated
Portadown War Memorial (251)
St. Mark's Parish Church War Memorial

William was the husband of Agnes Thompson of 8 Cheapside Street, Anderston, Glasgow.

Richard Currie
Private 11990, 3rd Battalion, Royal Irish Fusiliers

Born Drumcree
Residence Water Street
Enlisted 1 September 1914, Portadown
Died Died 8 April 1918, Portadown
Buried Drumcree Church of Ireland Churchyard, Portadown
Commemorated
Portadown War Memorial (228)
Drumcree Parish Church War Memorial
St. Mark's Parish Church War Memorial

Richard was the husband of Elizabeth Currie and the couple had a son Richard George who was born on 24 December 1911. He was a footballer and played for Portadown Football Club.

On enlistment in the 5th Battalion, Royal Irish Fusiliers, his particulars were given as follows: occupation - labourer, height - 5' 7", complexion - fresh, eyes - blue, hair - brown and age – 22 years.

From enlistment until 11 July 1915 he was on home service and was promoted unpaid Lance-Corporal on 10 April. On 1 May he was promoted paid Lance-Corporal. From 12 July until 3 September Richard served 54 days with the Mediterranean Expeditionary Force reverting to Private on 28 July. Private Currie took part in the Gallipoli campaign where he was wounded in the left thigh and hand.

On return to England he was sent to the Royal Irish Fusiliers depot before being posted first to the 3rd Battalion on 22 October and then the 6th Battalion. From March until September 1916 he served with the Mediterranean Expeditionary Force this time at Salonika.

While at Salonika Private Currie developed a cough and was sent to Malta for treatment where he remained until 29 September 1916. He was transferred to a Military Hospital in England suffering from bronchitis complicated by pleural effusion. On 2 November he was discharged from hospital and rejoined the 3rd Battalion, Royal Irish Fusiliers based at Londonderry.

On 4 December Private Currie was once again in hospital suffering from severe lung and respiratory problems. He was examined and found to be unfit for further military service and was discharged on medical grounds on 23 January 1917 aged 24.

On discharge Private Currie's military character was described as "very good" and under a paragraph entitled "Character awarded in accordance with King's Regulations" he was described as "A very good man, served his country well and suffered in Malta as a consequence".

His disability was found to have been as a result of active service, exposure at Gallipoli, was believed to have been the cause. It eventually developed into tuberculosis.

Private Currie was totally incapacitated and the discharge board recommended that future employers should be asked to give him "preference for such posts as light porter, messenger, lodge keeper at a gentleman's place or doorman".

Private Currie was unable to resume employment and after a spell in a sanatorium died on 8 April 1918 at his home in Portadown. His wife and son emigrated to Canada after the end of the Great War and resided at 748 St. Matthew's Avenue, Winnipeg, Manitoba.

Joseph Vennard
Private 18564, 9th Battalion, Royal Irish Fusiliers

Parents	Son of Thomas and Eliza Jane Vennard of 7 Park Road, Portadown
Residence	Park Road
Died	Died of wounds 14 June 1918, Portadown
Age	22
Buried	Milltown Church of Ireland Churchyard
Commemorated	Portadown War Memorial (201) St. Mark's Parish Church War Memorial

Joseph was a member of the Bann Lily Lodge of the British Order of Ancient Free Gardeners and Parkmount Temperance Flute Band.

Private Vennard was seriously injured on 31 May 1916 and his mother received a letter from the Reverand F. J. Halahan, rector of Drumcree, who was serving at the front.

He was injured in the hand and in the head by a shell, which burst close to where he was standing. He was immediately attended by the doctor, then sent onto the Field Ambulance. I went to see him next morning, but he had been sent to the Casualty Clearing Station before I arrived. I was speaking to the doctor, however, and while his injury is serious he hopes that he will recover in due course. I am very sorry that he was wounded, as indeed were we all, as he is one of our best bandsmen, and a very good quiet lad. I hope that you will soon receive good news from him.

Portadown Express
16 June 1916

Grave of Private Joseph Vennard. (Author's Collection)

Bertram Holland
Sapper 45122, 3rd Field Company, Canadian Engineers

Born	12 August 1890, Levaghery, Portadown
Parents	Son of George and Elizabeth Holland of Bridge Street, Portadown
Residence	Levaghery
Enlisted	24 September 1914, Valcartier, Canada
Died	Died 23 July 1918, Purfleet, England
Age	27
Buried	Knocknamuckley Church of Ireland Churchyard, Portadown
Commemorated	Portadown War Memorial (311) Seagoe Parish Church War Memorial

Bertram's father George was a carpenter by trade and had children Hester, Herbert, Lillie, Ernest, Bertram, Mabel and Clara. Bertram was a regular attender at Seagoe and Levaghery Sunday Schools and was also a member of Edenderry Men's Bible Class. He emigrated to Toronto, Canada around 1910 and worshipped at St. James' Cathedral.

On enlistment Bertram's particulars were given as follows: occupation - mechanical engineer, height - 5'7½", complexion - ruddy, eyes - brown, hair - dark.

Bertram sailed for England on 4 October 1914 on the SS *Zealand*. On 24 April 1915 he embarked for France and saw service at Messines and Vimy Ridge.

On 10 January 1918 he was admitted to No. 11 Canadian Field Ambulance suffering from trench fever. Over the next two months Sapper Holland was treated in a succession of hospitals including No. 18 Casualty Clearing Station, one in Boulogne and in Edmonton Military Hospital in England. In the middle of February he was admitted to Canadian Convalescent Hospital at Wokingham and was discharged to duty on 1 March.

On 15 July Sapper Holland was admitted to Purfleet Military Hospital where he was diagnosed as suffering from influenza. Further investigations showed him to be also suffering from an abdominal abscess, meningitis and TB. He died on 23 July 1918.

His brother Ernest also served with the Canadians during the Great War.

James Neill
Private 617046, 195th P.O.W. Company, Labour Corps

Born	Portadown
Parents	Son of Edward and Mary Neill
Residence	Fowlers Entry
Enlisted	Liverpool
Died	Killed in action 10 October 1918, RMS *Leinster*, Irish Sea
Age	46
Buried	Seagoe Cemetery, Portadown
Commemorated	Portadown War Memorial (100) St. Mark's Parish Church War Memorial

James had 22 years service in the Royal Irish Fusiliers and had served during the South African War 1899-1902. He was the husband of Elizabeth Neill and the couple had three children.

He emigrated to the USA and was living in Philadelphia when war was declared. He returned home and rejoined the 1st Battalion, Royal Irish Fusiliers with the serial number 18132. Private Neill saw action on the Western Front. Private Neill transferred to the 195th P.O.W. Company, Labour Corps. He was returning to his unit

on the RMS *Leinster* when she was torpedoed and sunk. The RMS *Leinster* was one of four ships known as the 'Provinces' as they were named *Munster, Ulster, Connaught and Leinster*. The RMS *Leinster* was launched in 1896 and displaced 2641 tons. She carried mail and passengers between Ireland and Britain.

On 10 October 1918 the RMS *Leinster*, with 700 passengers, service personnel and crew, left Kingstown for Holyhead. On board were 500 service personnel, travelling for a variety of reasons including coming off and going on leave. When approximately 16 miles offshore she came into the sights of Robert Ramm in command of German U-boat UB 123. He fired three torpedoes, the first missed, the second exploded forward of the bridge and the third hit the boiler room. The ship sank within 15 minutes with the loss of 500 lives, including 328 service personnel, one of whom was Private James Neill.

Over the next few days many bodies were recovered and brought ashore to the Dublin City Morgue and St. Michael's Hospital to be identified. On 14 October the bodies of 145 military personnel were buried in Grangegorman Military Cemetery, Dublin.

Private James Neill's body was recovered, identified and claimed by his relatives and he was brought home to Portadown for burial.

Thomas Henry Flavelle
Trooper 30404, Duke of Lancaster's Own Yeomanry

Born	Portadown
Parents	Son of Joseph and Mary Ann Flavelle of 76 Obins Street, Portadown
Residence	Obins Street
Enlisted	Armagh
Died	Died 6 November 1918, Tralee
Age	20
Buried	Drumcree Church of Ireland Churchyard, Portadown
Commemorated	Portadown War Memorial (184)

Thomas' father Joseph was employed as a painter. He and his wife Mary Ann had children Mary, William, James, Joseph, Luke, Elizabeth and Thomas Henry.

Private Thomas Flavelle, Obin St., who joined the colours about two months ago, died on Wednesday in Tralee from pneumonia following an attack of influenza.

Portadown News
9 November 1918

There is a Private T. Flavelle, 9th Battalion, Royal Irish Fusiliers commemorated on St. Mark's Parish Church War Memorial. However, it is unclear if this is the same person.

William Murphy
Private 5591, 3rd Battalion, Royal Irish Fusiliers

Born	1893, Drumcree
Parents	Son of John and Hannah Murphy of 28 Coronation Street, Portadown
Residence	Coronation Street
Enlisted	27 February 1911
Died	Died 20 November 1918, Portadown
Age	25
Buried	Drumcree Roman Catholic Churchyard, Portadown
Commemorated	Portadown War Memorial (70)

William's parents had ten children John, Henry, Patrick, William, Joseph, Gerald, Mary, Cathleen, Annie and Josephine. The family resided at Junction Row, Portadown before moving to 28 Coronation Street.

On enlistment in the 3rd Battalion, Royal Irish Fusiliers William's particulars were given as follows: occupation-weaver, height-5' 7$^1/_4$", eyes -blue, hair - brown.

He was mobilised on 5 August 1914 and in September 1915 was posted to the 6th Battalion for service overseas at Gallipoli and later in Serbia. On 31 December 1915 Private Murphy was hospitalised with jaundice at Calkali, Serbia and was evacuated to Malta. He was embarked on the Hospital Ship *Formosa* and arrived in England on 10 February 1916.

On 6 March he was admitted to Rock Spa Auxiliary Military Hospital, Llandrindod suffering from rheumatism of the shoulders, knees and ankles. Private Murphy was discharged from hospital and posted, on home service, to the 3rd Battalion, Royal Irish Fusiliers.

He was admitted to hospital in Londonderry on 2 August suffering from neurasthenia - a mental disorder triggered by stress or anxiety. William was transferred to a Cork hospital on 19 October and was discharged on 27 November 1916.

Private Murphy was discharged the service on medical grounds with 50% disability, on 14 June 1918. His condition was recorded as cardiac rheumatism brought about by contracting a severe chill during a snowstorm while on active service in Serbia.

On discharge Private Murphy's military character was described as "very good" and under a paragraph entitled "Character awarded in accordance with King's Regulations" he was described as "A very good man, served his country well and suffered in health as a consequence". Due to the nature of his illness, William was unable to return to employment as a weaver. A single man, he was granted a weekly allowance of 27 shillings and six pence for four weeks and thirteen shillings and 9 pence thereafter.

He died at home on 20 November 1918.

Thomas Fletcher Espie
Lieutenant, 5th Battalion, Royal Irish Fusiliers

Born 2 June 1895, Portadown
Parents Son of James George and Blanche Espie of Tavanagh Terrace, Portadown
Residence Church Street
Died Died 6 February 1919, Portadown
Age 24
Buried Seagoe Cemetery, Portadown
Commemorated
Portadown War Memorial (63)
Armagh Road Presbyterian Church War Memorial
First Presbyterian Church War Memorial, Edenderry
Lurgan College War Memorial

Thomas' father James George was from Londonderry. He was a schoolteacher and later principal of Academy National School, Portadown. His mother Blanche was from County Dublin and was also a schoolteacher. The couple had children Thomas Fletcher, George, Harry, Lillian, who died in infancy in 1897 aged four months and Samuel.

Thomas was educated at Academy National School and Lurgan College. Messrs Wm. Cowdy and Son, handkerchief manufacturers, Edward Street, Portadown, employed him in the linen industry. He was a member of the Ulster Volunteer Force and Portadown Rowing Club.

On the outbreak of war he enlisted in the 9th Battalion, Royal Irish Fusiliers.

On the outbreak of war he joined the Forces, training with the Ulster Division at Clandeboye. He went to France with his regiment in 1915, returning in October

1916 to go to Cadet School in Christ's College, Cambridge. In March 1917 he obtained a commission in the 9th Royal Irish Fusiliers, and in August of the same year proceeded to Salonika. From there he was transferred to Egypt and later went with the 5th Royal Irish Fusiliers to Palestine. He was in training in the 3rd Flying School, Cairo, for transference to the RAF when he contacted diphtheria. After spending about two months in hospital in Cairo he was "turned down" on returning to RAF owing to heart trouble contracted from diphtheria, and was then sent to rejoin the 5th Royal Irish Fusiliers in France. In September 1918 he was promoted to the rank of Lieutenant.

Portadown Express
14 February 1919

Family grave of Lieutenant Thomas Fletcher Espie. (Author's Collection)

Lieutenant Espie died of pneumonia following a bout of malaria at his parent's residence Tavanagh Terrace, Portadown.

William Victor Hall
Private 11968, 5th Battalion, Royal Irish Fusiliers

Born	Brooklyn, New York, USA
Parents	Son of William and Annie Hall of 14 Thomas Street, Portadown
Residence	Thomas Street
Enlisted	Portadown
Died	Died 22 February 1919, Portadown
Age	23
Buried	Drumcree Church of Ireland Churchyard, Portadown
Commemorated	Portadown War Memorial (120) St. Mark's Parish Church War Memorial

William took part in the Gallipoli campaign, saw action in Salonika and was present at the taking of Jerusalem. He later saw action in France.

Private Hall, who suffered from malaria, was on home leave when he contacted a chill, which developed into pneumonia. He died at his grandmother's residence in Henry Street, Portadown.

His sisters Annie and Deborah resided in New York, USA and sisters Margaret and Isabella resided in Holywood. He had a brother Thomas Arthur.

Randal Brown
Private 955, Canadian Army Medical Corps & Canadian Army Dental Clinic

Born	8 July 1891, Armagh
Parents	Son of James and Hessie Brown of Derrycorey
Residence	Derrycorey
Enlisted	31 March 1915, Toronto, Canada
Died	Died 25 February 1919, Basingstoke, England
Age	27
Buried	Basingstoke (Worting Road) Cemetery, Hampshire, England. Grave A. 14.
Commemorated	Portadown War Memorial (290) Drumcree Parish Church War Memorial

Randal was a member of the Ulster Volunteer Force.

On enlistment in No. 4 Canadian General Hospital Randal's particulars were given as follows: occupation - provision clerk, height - 5'3½", complexion - dark, eyes - blue, hair - black.

On 27 May 1915 he arrived in England and proceeded to the Duchess of Connaught Red Cross Hospital at Taplow, Buckinghamshire. In October he rejoined his unit and set sail for Alexandria from Devonport.

On 7 November 1915 Randal left Alexandria on the hospital ship *Carisbrooke Castle*, arriving in Salonika on 11 November. On 29 June 1916 Randal was admitted to hospital in Salonika suffering from dysentery. A month later he was transferred to the hospital ship *Essquibo* that was en route to a military hospital in Malta.

In June 1917 he was awarded his first Good Conduct Badge and returned to England via Taranto, Italy.

Private Brown served with the CAMC at Basingstoke from his return to England until October 1918 when he was attached to the Canadian Army Dental Corps London Area. In January 1919 he was granted 10 days leave and on 9 February he was admitted to hospital suffering from influenza. Private Brown's condition

progressively worsened and he died in No. 4 Canadian General Hospital, Basingstoke on 25 February 1919.

Phillip Ernest Fairley DCM Captain, 18th (County of London) Battalion, (London Irish Rifles)

Born	County Sligo
Parents	Son of Robert and Jane Fairley
Residence	Thomas Street
Enlisted	Portadown
Died	Died of wounds 2 April 1919, London
Age	30
Buried	Kilmore Church of Ireland Churchyard
Commemorated	Portadown War Memorial (221) St. Mark's Parish Church War Memorial

Phillip Ernest's father Robert was a musketry instructor in the Royal Irish Constabulary. His mother Jane was a schoolteacher. The couple had boys Phillip Ernest and Thomas, who were both born in County Sligo, and Jack. In 1901 the boys and their widowed mother resided at 48 West Street, Portadown.

Ernest, as he was known, opted for a career in the teaching profession and was pupil teacher in Enniskillen Model School. He taught at Water Street National School, Portadown and was appointed principal of Annaghmore National School. Ernest then accepted a teaching appointment under London County Council.

He was promoted to Sergeant-Major for gallantry in the field at the Battle of Loos 25 September 1915. Company Sergeant-Major Fairleigh was awarded the Distinguished Conduct Medal in 1916 "For conspicuous gallantry under heavy fire during the repair of trenches which had been blown in". He was later commissioned as Lieutenant and soon afterwards promoted to Captain.

He was severely wounded in the back and spent a considerable time in hospital and he died from his wounds on 2 April 1919. He was buried with full military honours from his mother's residence 89 Thomas Street.

Ernest Fairley was a member of Masonic Lodge No. 789, Tartaraghan.

His brother Thomas was principal of Church Street Primary School for many years and was also a member of Portadown Borough Council.

In the 1990s Ernest's details and surname, spelt as Fairley, were added to Portadown War Memorial at the request of a relative and now

his name appears twice firstly and originally as Fairleigh and secondly as Fairley.

James Woods
Rifleman 214, 9th Battalion, Royal Irish Rifles

Born	1882
Residence	Wilson Street
Enlisted	29 August 1916
Died	Died 13 January 1920, Lurgan Hospital
Age	37
Commemorated	Portadown War Memorial (244)

James was the husband of Jane Woods (nee McNally) and the couple had two children William James born 1908 and Edmund Patterson born 1915. The family resided at 74 West Street, Portadown. Jane Woods died on 27 December 1916. Messrs. McCammon and Sprott employed James as a pork curer.

On enlistment in the 20th Battalion, Royal Irish Rifles James' particulars were given as follows: occupation – labourer, height - 5' 7", eyes -blue, hair - brown, age - 35 years old.

On 5 January 1917 Rifleman Woods was posted to the 9th Battalion, Royal Irish Rifles and was sent to France and Flanders. He served at Ypres. He was hospitalised on 13 July suffering from nephritis and was evacuated to No. 110 Field Ambulance on 15 July. Four days later Rifleman Woods was transferred to No. 7 General Hospital at St. Omer and on 23 July was evacuated to England on the hospital ship St. David. On arrival in England he was sent to Birmingham War Hospital, Rednal where he spent the next ten weeks under going treatment.

Rifleman James Woods writes thanking the committee who administer Lady Carson's Ulster Divisional Fund for their great kindness to him while in hospital in England, and referring in appreciative terms to the good work, which they are doing for the wounded soldiers. He said he had not been long in hospital when he received a postcard inviting him to ask for any article he most required. He told the committee he was in need of a watch, and received a very useful timepiece by return of post.

Portadown News
11 August 1917

Rifleman Woods was discharged the service on medical grounds with 50% disability on 6 March 1918. His condition was recorded as nephritis brought about by exposure on active service.

On discharge Rifleman Woods' military character was described as "very good" and under a paragraph entitled "Character awarded in

accordance with King's Regulations" he was described as "A very good man, served his country well and suffered in health as a consequence".

He was granted a weekly allowance of 27 shillings and six pence for four weeks and thirteen shillings and 9 pence thereafter with an allowance for his two children of nine shillings and two pence and then four shillings and seven pence thereafter.

James Woods died on 13 January 1920 from chronic nephritis at Lurgan Hospital.

Thomas Francis Whalley
Private 5811, 1st Battalion, Royal Irish Fusiliers

Residence	Kilmoriarty
Enlisted	5 August 1912
Died	Died 24 February 1920, Portadown
Buried	Drumcree Church of Ireland Churchyard, Portadown
Commemorated	Portadown War Memorial (308)

Private Whalley enlisted in the 2nd Battalion, Royal Irish Fusiliers before transferring to the 1st Battalion. He arrived in France on 1 February 1915 and was discharged the service due to sickness on 27 August 1918 aged 24.

Thomas was a member of Kilmoriarty LOL 31.

Private T. Whaley, Kilmoriarty, Portadown, has been wounded in action, and is now in hospital in England.

Portadown News
27 March 1915

His sister Emily was the wife of James Magee (see entry **307 Private James Magee**) who was killed in action on 1 July 1916 at the Battle of the Somme.

Robert Johnston
Rifleman 1085, 17th Battalion, Royal Irish Rifles

Residence	West Street
Enlisted	8 June 1915, Newcastle, Co. Down
Died	Died 20 March 1920, Portadown
Buried	Seagoe Cemetery, Portadown
Commemorated	Portadown War Memorial (234)

Robert married Charlotte Hill in 1896 at St. Mark's Parish Church, Portadown. The couple had four children - Alice born 1901, Minnie born 1908, Elizabeth born 1911 and Flossie born 1912. He was a member of Johnston's Royal Standard LOL 99.

On enlistment Robert's particulars were given as follows: occupation - labourer, height - 5' $2\frac{1}{2}$", age - $38\frac{1}{2}$ years old, residence 4 Fowler's Entry, Portadown.

From enlistment until 29 June 1915 Rifleman Johnston served at home before being posted to France on 30 June. He served in France until 27 March 1918 when, during the Kaiser's offensive, he was wounded and captured and sent to Germany as a prisoner of war.

After the Armistice Rifleman Johnston was repatriated on 20 December and was discharged the service on Christmas Eve 1918 owing to wounds received in action and the effects of his captivity at the hands of the Germans. When discharged he was suffering 50% disability and was granted a weekly allowance of thirteen shillings and 9 pence.

James H. Chambers
Lance-Corporal 14052, 9th Battalion, Royal Irish Fusiliers

Parents — Son of William and Mary J. Chambers of 50 Carleton Street, Portadown
Residence — Carleton Street
Died — Died of wounds 29 July 1920, Portadown
Age — 26
Buried — Knocknamuckley Church of Ireland Churchyard, Portadown
Commemorated — Portadown War Memorial (36)

James' sister Anna died on 2 July 1914.

Lance-Corporal Chambers served in 'B' Company and was wounded in action at the Battle of the Somme on 1 July 1916.

Grave of Private Joseph H. Chambers. (Author's Collection)

On Sunday afternoon the remains of the late Br. James Chambers were interred in Knocknamuckley burying ground. Deceased has been identified with the Orange and Black Institutions the members of which attended in very large numbers to pay their last tribute of respect. The members of St. Mark's Bible Class walked in front of the hearse. The coffin was borne for a considerable length by the members of Edenderry Temperance and Benefit LOL 322. There were numerous beautiful wreaths. Deceased served with the 9th Batt., R.I.F. in France and Flanders and was severely wounded.

Portadown News
7 August 1920

Thomas Leonard
Private 17421, 1st Battalion, Royal Irish Fusiliers

Parents	Son of Susan Leonard of 3 Dawson's Court, Portadown
Residence	Dawson's Court
Enlisted	29 December 1914
Died	Died 7 February 1922, Portadown
Buried	Drumcree Church of Ireland Churchyard, Portadown
Commemorated	Portadown War Memorial (89)

Thomas was the husband of Catherine Leonard and they had three children. The family resided at 3 Dawson's Court, Portadown.

Private Leonard enlisted on 29 December 1914 and arrived in France on 10 March 1915. He was wounded in action in 1915 and was discharged the service on 18 April 1916 due to sickness. He died through illness contracted while on active service.

He had a sister Minnie and brother-in-law James Brownlee who resided at 11 Meadow Lane, Portadown.

William Linton
Private 516968, Labour Corps

Residence	Annagh
Died	Died 22 February 1923, Portadown
Buried	Christ Church Cemetery, Bessbrook
Commemorated	Portadown War Memorial (249)

William was the husband of Margaret Linton and they had two children. The family resided at 45 Annagh Hill, Portadown. He was a member of Johnston's Royal Standard LOL 99.

William had previously served in the Royal Irish Fusiliers as a Private with the serial number 5443. Private Linton was sent to France on 7 November 1914. He later transferred to the Labour Corps.

Billy as he was familiarly known served with the Fusiliers, and mid shot and shell had a cheery word for his comrades, which often had a wonderful effect during the dark hours of Flanders and France battlefields. Since his return from the army to civil life he suffered from throat trouble, possibly contracted during his army life, and this eventually was his undoing. During the latter period of his life he had joined the Salvation Army in which he displayed great interest.

Portadown News
3 March 1923

Richard John Pentland
Private 14615, 9th Battalion, Royal Irish Fusiliers

Parents	Son of Richard Pentland
Residence	Hanover Street
Enlisted	19 September 1914
Died	Died 30 March 1923, Portadown
Age	33
Buried	Seagoe Cemetery, Portadown
Commemorated	Portadown War Memorial (116)

Richard was the husband of Sarah Jane Allen daughter of James Allen of Annaghmore and the couple resided at 34 Hanover Street, Portadown. They had sons Alec, Billy and Richard. He was a member of Johnston's Royal Standard LOL 99.

Private Pentland arrived in France on 4 October 1915 and took part in

Family grave of Private Richard John Pentland. (Author's Collection)

the Battle of the Somme on 1 July 1916 suffering a wound to the right arm. He was later seriously wounded in the right lung at the Battle of Langemarck on 16 August 1917. Private Pentland was discharged the service on 24 July 1918 aged 28 years owing to wounds received in action.

Samuel Joseph Corkin
Lance-Corporal 23876, 9th Battalion, Royal Irish Fusiliers

Residence Jervis Street
Enlisted 24 January 1916
Commemorated Portadown War Memorial (134)

Samuel was employed as a dresser by Messrs. Spence, Bryson & Co. Ltd before enlisting.

He was wounded in action in the arm, leg and chin on 10 August 1916 while serving in France. Lt.-Colonel Stewart Blacker to his wife Eva

11 August 1916
2 men of a ration carrying party, McCommick and Corken (sic), both of 'B' Coy., wounded by M.G.

Seagoe Parish Magazine
1923

Pte. Sam Corkin, 9th Batt. R.I.F. (Ulster) Division paid a visit to his home in town on Tuesday last. He was on his way from England to the Royal Victoria Hospital, Belfast for special treatment for his right leg, which was fractured by an explosive bullet in August. He also received a slight wound on the chin. He is looking bright and cheery notwithstanding all he has suffered, and we wish him a speedy recovery.

Portadown Express
13 October 1916

Lance-Corporal Corkin was discharged the service on 14 November 1916 owing to wounds received in action. It has so far not been possible to obtain details of his death.

THEY ALSO SERVED IN THE GREAT WAR

It has so far been impossible to accurately identify a small number of servicemen who are commemorated on Portadown War Memorial. Their details are given below in the order that they appear on Portadown War Memorial. If anyone has further details please contact the author.

Henry Gallery DCM
Rifleman, Royal Irish Rifles

Residence Castle Street
Commemorated Portadown War Memorial (47)

Private Harry Gallery, Royal Irish Rifles, Portadown, has been killed in action at the front. His sister, Mrs Faloon, resides in Castle Street.

Portadown News
30 October 1915

It has so far been impossible to ascertain full service details of Rifleman Henry Gallery DCM.

Edward Hollywood
Private, Royal Inniskilling Fusiliers,

Residence Castle Street
Commemorated
Portadown War Memorial (48)
St. Marks Parish Church War Memorial

Private E. Holywood, formerly of Castle Avenue, Portadown, has died in hospital. He served with the Royal Inniskilling Fusiliers.

Portadown News
8 July 1916

Private E. Holywood is listed as having died of wounds in the Roll of Honour, which appeared in the Portadown News 11 November 1916 and those thereafter. These were published in the Portadown News at various times during and after the Great War. These Rolls of Honour detailed Portadown men who were killed, died of wounds or sickness, were wounded, taken prisoner or listed as missing.

It has so far been impossible to ascertain full service details of Private Edward Hollywood, Royal Inniskilling Fusiliers.

James Faloon
Private, Royal Irish Fusiliers

Residence Curran Street
Commemorated
Portadown War Memorial (48)

On Saturday intimation reached Portadown that Private James Faloon, Curran Street, had fallen in action.

Portadown News
30 December 1916

Private J. Faloon is listed as having been wounded in action in the Roll of Honour, which appeared in the Portadown News 28 December 1918.

It has so far been impossible to ascertain full service details of Private James Faloon, Royal Irish Fusiliers.

John Halligan
Gunner, Royal Garrison Artillery

Residence Curran Street
Commemorated
Portadown War Memorial (80)

Mrs Halligan, Curran Street, Portadown, has received official notification that her son, Gunner John Halligan, Royal Garrison Artillery, has been killed in action. Prior to joining the army he was employed in the Portadown Post Office.

Portadown
News 11 May 1918

Gunner John Halligan is listed as having been killed in action in the Roll of Honour, which appeared in the Portadown News 28 December 1918.

It has so far been impossible to ascertain full service details of Gunner John Halligan, Royal Garrison Artillery.

Harry Logan
Second Officer, Royal Naval Volunteer Reserve

Parents Son of David Logan
Residence Hanover Street
Commemorated
Portadown War Memorial (115)
First Presbyterian Church War Memorial,

Mr. Harry Logan, son of David Logan, is reported missing. The report is not confirmed and it is hoped that Mr. Logan may yet turn up. He is serving on the Royal Navy, and is one of the officers of his H.M.S.______.

Portadown News
31 March 1917

Lieutenant H. Logan is listed as missing in the Roll of Honour, which appeared in the Portadown News 11 November 1916, and those thereafter.

It has so far been impossible to ascertain full service details of Second Officer Harry Logan Royal Naval Volunteer.

Thomas H. Best
Private,
9th Royal Irish Fusiliers

Residence Montague Street
Commemorated
Portadown War Memorial (170)
St. Mark's Parish Church War Memorial

Private Best, 9th RIF, has arrived at his home in Edgarstown from an English hospital. He received some bullet wounds in his right arm on 1st July. He is one of the lucky ones.

Portadown News
11 August 1916

Private Thomas Best is listed as having been wounded in action in the Roll of Honour, which appeared in the Portadown News 28 December 1918.

It has so far been impossible to ascertain full service details of Private Thomas H. Best, Royal Irish Fusiliers.

James Metcalfe
Private, Labour Corps

Residence Montague Street
Commemorated
Portadown War Memorial (174)

James was the husband of Elizabeth Metcalfe and the couple resided at 53 Montague Street, Portadown. They had no children.

Mr. Joseph Metcalf, Tandragee Road, Gilford, has received intimation that his brother Private James Metcalf (sic), has been drowned in France.

Portadown Express
7 March 1919

It has so far been impossible to ascertain full service details of Private James Metcalfe, Labour Corps.

William J. Allen
Private, Royal Irish Fusiliers

Residence Queen Street
Commemorated
Portadown War Memorial (206)

Private William Allen is listed as having been wounded in action in the Roll of Honour, which appeared in the Portadown News 28 December 1918.

It has so far been impossible to ascertain full service details of Private William J. Allen, Royal Irish Fusiliers.

William J. Joyce
Driver, Army Service Corps

Residence West Street
Commemorated
Portadown War Memorial (236)

It has so far been impossible to ascertain full service details of Driver William J. Joyce, Army Service Corps

William Adamson
Private, Royal Irish Fusiliers

Residence Ballymacrandle
Commemorated
Portadown War Memorial (260)

Private W. Adamson is listed as having been wounded in action in the Roll of Honour, which appeared in the Portadown News 28 December 1918.

It has so far been impossible to ascertain full service details of Private William Adamson, Royal Irish Fusiliers.

John McCormick
Private, Royal Irish Fusiliers

Residence Breagh (Seagoe Parish)
Commemorated
Portadown War Memorial (271)

Private J. McCormick, Portadown is officially reported wounded.

Portadown News
4 November1916

McCormick, Private J. R.I.F., wounded.

Portadown Express
10 November1916

Private J. McCormick is listed as having been wounded in action in the Roll of Honour, which appeared in the Portadown News 11 November 1916 and those thereafter.

It has so far been impossible to ascertain full service details of Private John McCormick, Royal Irish Fusiliers.

James Cassidy
Private, Royal Irish Fusiliers

Residence Castle Street
Commemorated Portadown War Memorial (291)

Private James Cassidy is listed as having been wounded in action in the Roll of Honour, which appeared in the Portadown News 28 December 1918.

It has so far been impossible to ascertain full service details of Private James Cassidy, Royal Irish Fusiliers.

Joseph Flannagan
Private, Royal Irish Fusiliers

Residence Timulkenny
Commemorated Portadown War Memorial (321)

Mr. Flanagan, caretaker of the Free Library, has two sons with the Canadian contingent. One of them, Richard is with the Medical Corps, and the other, Joseph, is at present at Salisbury Plain. The latter belongs to Princess Patricia's Canadian Light Infantry, and arrived a few weeks ago with a draft of 500 to reinforce that regiment, which has been at the front since before Christmas.

Portadown Express
5 March 1915

It is not clear if this is the same person commemorated on Portadown War Memorial.

Private Flannigan is listed as having been wounded in action in the Roll of Honour, which appeared in the Portadown News 28 December 1918.

It has so far been impossible to ascertain full service details of Private Joseph Flannagan, Royal Irish Fusiliers.

Chapter 10
World War Two

World War Two was essentially two separate wars fought on opposite sides of the globe. One was fought in Europe, North Africa and the Atlantic against Nazi Germany and Fascist Italy from 1939-45 and the other was fought in Asia and the Pacific against the Empire of Japan from 1941-45.

The War Against Nazi Germany (1939-45)

On 1 September 1939 Hitler invaded Poland using Blitzkrieg or Lightning War tactics. Two days later on 3 September Britain and France declared war on Germany - World War Two had begun.

In 1940 in a succession of Blitzkrieg attacks the armed forces of the Third Reich subdued Denmark, Norway, Holland, Belgium, Luxembourg and France. Their plan to invade the United Kingdom was thwarted by the Luftwaffe's defeat by the Royal Air Force in the Battle of Britain. Hitler then turned his territorial ambitions eastwards attacking the Soviet Union on 22 June 1941.

German victories continued until late October 1942 when Rommel and the Africa Corps were defeated at El Alamein in Egypt. This defeat was followed by the destruction of the German 6th Army at Stalingrad in February 1943.

On 6 June 1944 came Operation Overlord - the invasion of Normandy. German forces were now engaged in a titanic struggle on two major fronts - caught between the Russian Red Army on the Eastern Front and the British, Canadian and American forces in the west. Final surrender came on 8 May 1945 Victory in Europe Day.

The Battle of the Atlantic (1939-45)

The war at sea lasted six long, gruelling and unremitting years. It was the longest campaign of World War Two lasting from 3 September 1939 with the sinking of the passenger liner SS *Athena* to 7 May 1945 when U2336 sank the cargo vessel *Anondale Park*. Between these dates German U-boats sank a heavy toll of Allied shipping which almost brought Britain to defeat.

Total Royal Naval casualties in all theatres of war amounted to 51,000 killed or lost at sea. In addition 32,000 merchant seamen, 2,500 Royal Naval Patrol Service, 1900 Fleet Air Arm personnel, 10,000 RAF Coastal Command personnel and 1300 (T124) merchant seamen serving under Royal Navy command lost their lives.

James Whitla
Able Seaman D/J 26083, Royal Navy, HMS *Courageous*

Born	7 January 1897, Portadown
Parents	Son of William Henry Whitla of 37 Mary Street, Portadown
Residence	Mary Street
Enlisted	25 July 1913
Died	Lost at sea 17 September 1939, HMS *Courageous*, S. W. Approaches
Age	42
Buried	No Known Grave
Commemorated	Plymouth Naval Memorial. Panel 33, Column 3. Portadown War Memorial (WW2-67) Thomas Street Methodist Church War Memorial

James enlisted as a Boy Sailor on 25 July 1913 and was based for his initial training at HMS *Impregnable* at Devonport. On enlistment his particulars were given as follows; occupation - messenger, height - 5'4$^{3}/_{4}$", complexion - fresh, eyes - grey, hair - brown. During the next year and a half he underwent training on the two-funnelled copper clad cruiser, HMS *Crescent*, at the shore base, HMS *Vivid* and on the battleship HMS *Ajax*.

He was serving aboard *Ajax* when war was declared and on 7 January 1915 he signed on for a period of 12 years and was promoted Ordinary Seaman. *Ajax* was a battleship displacing 23,400 tons, armed with ten 13$^{1}/_{2}$" guns and with a top speed of 21 knots. Ordinary Seaman Whitla was on board the battleship when she took part in the Battle of Jutland on 31 May 1916.

Able Seaman James Whitla. (Jack Whitla)

Promoted Able Seaman on 22 June 1916 James returned to HMS *Vivid* and was based there until he volunteered for special duties with secret 'Q' ships in June 1917. These were merchant ships armed with hidden guns, which roamed the seas in an effort to lure unsuspecting U-boats to the surface where they could be attacked.

Able Seaman Whitla served on three 'Q' Ships the first of which was HMS *Chagford*, which he joined on 18 June 1917. *Chagford* was an ex-Admiralty collier displacing 2,000 tons. For her new role she was equipped with one four-inch gun, two 12-pounder guns, a howitzer, machine guns and torpedo tubes.

On 2 August she sailed from Lough Swilly for an anti U-boat patrol in the Atlantic Ocean off Tory Island. On 5 August *Chagford* was torpedoed three times by U44, although the 'Q' ship managed to fire at the U-boat, the submarine escaped. The *Chagford* sank on 7 August after a failed towing attempt.

After a spell at HMS *Vivid* Able Seaman Whitla was posted to the 'Q' ship HMS *Heather*, a flower class sloop displacing 1,250 tons armed with two four inch, two 12-pounder and one three pounder guns. He served onboard until 31 December 1917 before being transferred to his third 'Q' ship HMS *Stockforce* commanded by Lieutenant Harold Auten, RNR.

She was a small, newly built, vessel displacing 730 tons but was heavily armed with two four inch, two 12-pounder and one three-pounder guns and two torpedo tubes.

Able Seaman Whitla's service in 'Q' ships ended in June 1918 when he was transferred to the Auxiliary Patrol Service depot ship HMS *Colleen* based at Queenstown. A couple of weeks later saw him return to HMS *Vivid* where he was stationed for one month before transfer to HMS *Defiance*, the Torpedo and Gunnery School, based at Plymouth. He remained at the shore base until 28 October 1918.

From October 1918 until May 1919 Able Seaman Whitla was stationed at various shore establishments and after a short spell onboard the battleship HMS *Warspite* he was again stationed at shore establishments until May 1925.

On 12 May 1925 Able Seaman Whitla was posted to the Iron Duke Class battleship HMS *Emperor of India*. She was launched in 1913 and displaced 26,000 tons, was armed with ten 13½" guns and had a top speed of 21 knots. She carried

HEROES ALL OF THEM. R.I.P. GONE BUT NOT FORGOTTEN.

Capt. W. T. Makeig-Jones.

IN SORROWFUL AND PROUD REMEMBRANCE OF THE GALLANT 518 OFFICERS AND MEN OF THE ROYAL NAVY, ROYAL MARINES, ROYAL AIR FORCE, FLEET AIR ARM, ROYAL FLEET RESERVE, AND PENSIONERS OF H.M.S. COURAGEOUS WHO WERE DROWNED BY THE SINKING OF THEIR SHIP BY A GERMAN SUBMARINE ON SUNDAY SEPTEMBER 17TH 1939.

Memorial card for the aircraft carrier HMS Courageous. (Jack Whitla)

a crew of 925. Able Seaman Whitla spent two and a half years onboard the battleship from May 1925 until December 1927.

James was an electrician and for a time was employed in Shillington's Saw Mill in Portadown. He was the husband of English woman Anne Whitla and the couple had a son, Rodney. The family settled in Plymouth.

Able Seaman Whitla served on the converted aircraft carrier HMS *Courageous* and in 1937, when the ship visited Belfast, he paid a visit to his family in Portadown.

On 17 September 1939 *Courageous* was patrolling in the South Western Approaches when she was torpedoed and sunk by U29, commanded by KL Otto Schuhart. The aircraft carrier sank within twenty minutes with the loss of 518 of her crew. Able Seaman Whitla was one of those lost.

The Whitla family had a fine military tradition of service in the armed forces. During the Great War James' father, William Henry, and brother John, served in the Army. His brother William Henry served in the Royal Flying Corps and lost his

leg in an accident at a railway station.

During World War Two William Henry served as an Air Raid Warden in the ARP and his brother Hugh served in the Signal Section of the Royal Artillery.

Able Seaman James Whitla was the first serviceman from Portadown to lose his life during World War Two. Although he was commemorated on Thomas Street Methodist Church War Memorial his name was not included on the World War Two section of Portadown War Memorial.

In June 2001 at the request of his nephew, Jack Whitla of Fitzroy Street, Portadown, the name of Able Seaman James Whitla was added to Portadown War Memorial. The Reverend Tom Taylor in the presence of the Royal British Legion, Jack Whitla and other relatives, conducted a dedication ceremony.

Henry Kane
Signalman D/JX 165720, Royal Navy, (Royal Fleet Reserve), HMS *Cape Howe*

Born 19 May 1897, Red Row, Portadown
Parents Son of William Henry and Margaret Kane of Joseph Street, Portadown
Residence Watson Street
Enlisted 27 July 1912
Died Lost at sea 21 June 1940, HMS *Cape Howe*, S. W. Approaches
Age 43
Buried No Known Grave
Commemorated
Plymouth Naval Memorial. Panel 39, Column 2.
Portadown War Memorial (WW2-27)
Seagoe Parish Church War Memorial
Thomas Street Methodist Church War Memorial

Henry's father William Henry was employed as a weaver. William married Margaret McKee, daughter of James McKee, a sawyer, on 4 March 1892 at Thomas Street Methodist Church. The couple had four children Johanna born 1893, James born 1895, Henry born 1897, and Minnie born 1900. Margaret died in 1903 and William Henry married his cousin, Sarah Ann Holland, daughter of David Holland of Carn, on 3 November 1906 in Seagoe Parish Church.

William Henry served in the Royal Munster Fusiliers in Burma in 1882-1887 and the Royal Garrison

Regiment in Malta during the Boer War. He died in 1907 eleven days after the birth of his son David.

His son Henry enlisted as a Boy Sailor on 27 July 1912 and was based for his initial training at HMS *Impregnable* at Devonport. On enlistment his particulars were given as follows: occupation - van boy, height - 5' 6", complexion - fresh, eyes - grey, hair - light brown. From enlistment until the outbreak of hostilities in August 1914 Harry served on the cruiser HMS *Gibraltar*, the shore station HMS *Vivid* and the torpedo gunboat HMS *Gossamer*.

In October 1914 he was posted to HMS *Rinaldo*, a sloop displacing 980 tons, armed with four 4" guns and with a top speed of 13 knots. On 27 October the ship was operating in support of the military off the Belgian coast and was heavily shelled by German artillery. Eight of the crew, including Boy First Class Kane, were wounded. He was then posted to the destroyer HMS *Attack* and took part in the Battle of Jutland on 31 May 1916. His next ship was the 765 ton destroyer HMS *Phoenix*.

Henry married Sarah McCann, a winder and daughter of James McCann of Edenderry in Lurgan Registry Office on 1 March 1917. The couple had two children, James Henry born 1919 and Vera born 1927.

After the wedding Signalman Kane was posted to the Mediterranean Sea arriving at Mudros in August 1917. For the next year HMS *Phoenix* was deployed on a number of operations including convoy duty and anti-submarine patrols. On 14 May 1918 the Austrian U-boat U27 whilst patrolling the Straits of Otranto between Italy and Albania torpedoed her. Signalman Kane went onboard an Italian trawler, which took the crippled destroyer on tow, to relay messages and was later commended for his actions. However, HMS *Phoenix* sank soon afterwards with the loss of two of the crew.

Signalman Henry Kane. (Author's Collection)

The 'Q' ship HMS Cape Howe. (Author's Collection)

When he was demobbed in 1920 Portadown Gas Company employed him, firstly in the manufacture of gas, and later as a lamplighter.

Harry remained in the Royal Fleet Reserve throughout the inter war years attending annual camps and training courses in England. Harry was a member of Edenderry LOL 322 and RBP 744. He was also Chairman of Edenderry Arch Committee and just before he left for service in the destroyer HMS *Eclipse* was presented with an inscribed watch.

He was called up in August 1939 as the political situation in Europe worsened. On 9 August at the Weymouth Naval Review Signalman Kane was one of those inspected and spoken to by His Majesty King George VI.

In March 1940 Signalman Kane was posted to the 'Q' ship HMS *Cape Howe* at the special request of his former Captain of HMS *Eclipse* Lt.-Commander Eric Langton Woodhall. 'Q' ships had been deployed during the Great War and nine ships were converted for similar service during World War Two.

On 21 June 1940 when on anti U-boat patrol in the South Western Approaches HMS *Cape Howe* was torpedoed and sunk by the U28. All the crew managed to get into the lifeboats and rafts and awaited rescue. Nothing more was heard of the crew until a lifeboat was rescued on 23 June and a raft on 27 June. All other crew members including Signalman Kane were lost at sea.

Harry's watch however was returned to his widow Sarah in 1941. He had given it to fellow Ulsterman and crewmate, Seaman Robert Ayre from Belfast who was one of those rescued. Seaman Ayre had given the watch to his mother who was bombed out of her house in April 1941 and evacuated to Portadown.

Harry's brother James was wounded serving with the Royal Irish Rifles and Machine Gun Corps during the Great War. With the outbreak of World War Two he volunteered for service in the Royal Marine Police. His half brother David served with the 3rd Searchlight Regiment, Royal Artillery and was evacuated from Dunkirk. He later served on Gibraltar.

Harry's son James enlisted in the Royal Air Force in 1938 was promoted to Corporal and served throughout World War Two as an Instrument Repairer. During the Normandy landings he served on the south coast of England servicing Typhoon ground attack aircraft, which played a leading roll in the defeat of the German panzers.

Henry's nephew George McCann (see entry **WW2-37 Private George McCann**) was killed in action on 17 April 1945 in Germany.

Henry's niece Minnie McCann was the wife of William Bleeks, (see entry **WW2-5 Leading Aircraftman William Bleeks**) who was accidentally killed on 20 June 1942 in England while serving with the Royal Air Force

William Edward Callaghan Sergeant (Wireless Op./Air Gunner) 623929, 220 Squadron, Royal Air Force

Parents	Son of Edward and Evelyn Callaghan of 15 Wilmar Gardens, Annagh, Portadown
Residence	Wilmar Gardens
Died	Lost on air operations 27 December 1940, Cornwall, England
Age	19
Buried	No Known Grave
Commemorated	Runnymede Memorial, Surrey, England. Panel 12. Portadown War Memorial (WW2-7) St. Mark's Parish Church War Memorial

William was posted to 220 Squadron of Coastal Command. Coastal Command played a vital part in the war against the U-boats in the Battle of the Atlantic providing

much needed air cover for convoys and mounting attacks on U-boats.

The squadron was reformed on 17 August 1936 at Bircham Newton as a reconnaissance unit equipped with Ansons. After the outbreak of war the squadron began anti-shipping/U-boat patrols with newly equipped Hudsons. From 6 November 1940 to 28 April 1941 the squadron was based at St. Eval, Cornwall.

Sergeant Callaghan was a Wireless Operator/Air Gunner on a Hudson Mark II, serial number T9372 NR-G, piloted by Squadron Leader Rogenhagen. The other two members of the crew were Sgt. Lane and Sgt. Jack Lawrence Rees.

The aircraft took off from St. Eval on 27 December 1940 on a routine anti-submarine patrol. The Hudson ran out of fuel on the return leg of the patrol and the crew abandoned the aircraft by parachute about three miles south east of Trevose Head, Cornwall. Two of the crew Squadron Leader Rogenhagen, who suffered a broken arm and leg, and Sgt. Lane, were recovered. Sgt. William Callaghan and Sgt. Rees were considered to have landed in the sea. Their bodies were not recovered. Sgt. Rees is commemorated on the Runnymede Memorial, Panel 18.

At 2129 hours the crewless Hudson crashed near Towan Head, Newquay, Cornwall.

William James Graham Hunter
Stoker LT/KX 108031,
Royal Naval Patrol Service,
HM Trawler *Bervie Braes*

Parents	Son of James Hunter
Residence	Florence Court
Died	Killed in action 1 February 1941, HMT *Bervie Braes*, Off Falmouth
Buried	Falmouth Cemetery, Cornwall, England
Commemorated	Portadown War Memorial (WW2-24) Seagoe Parish Church War Memorial

William, a painter from 63 Walmer Street, Belfast, married Emma Webb, daughter of James Webb, a weaver of Edenderry, on 25 December 1925 at Seagoe Parish Church. The couple resided at 12 Florence Court, Portadown and had four children Robert born 1927, Rita Carol born 1935, William James Graham born 1938 and George Boris born 1940.

Stoker Hunter was serving on board HM Trawler *Bervie Braes*, built in 1917 and requisitioned for minesweeping service in World War

Two. The trawler displaced 200 tons, was 115 feet long, armed with two 12-pounder guns and had a complement of 20.

On 26 January 1941 a mine off Falmouth damaged *Bervie Braes*. On 1 February, a week later, Stoker Hunter's body was recovered from the sea on the south coast of England. His widow Emma died on 12 February 1942 aged 41 in Lurgan Hospital.

Matthew Thomas Archer
Petty Officer D/JX 193627, Royal Navy, (HMS *President III*), SS *Empire Impala*

Died	Lost at Sea 11 March 1943, SS *Empire Impala*, Atlantic Ocean
Age	30
Buried	No Known Grave
Commemorated	Plymouth Naval Memorial. Panel 78 Column 2. Portadown War Memorial (WW2-1)

HMS *President III* was a shore base at Bristol and was used as the accounting headquarters for all naval personnel allocated for service as Defensively Equipped Merchant Ship (DEMS) gunners. All British merchant ships were armed with guns with which to defend themselves against U-boat, surface raider, disguised raider or aircraft attack. Royal Navy personnel manned these guns.

Petty Officer Archer was posted, as a member of the DEMS gun crew, aboard the SS *Empire Impala*. The ship displaced 6,000 tons and was owned by the Ministry of War Transport. She had a crew of 43 and six gunners to man the DEMS gun. Petty Officer Archer was a member of this gun crew.

She left New York on 23 February 1943 and joined Convoy SC 121 sailing from Sydney, Halifax, Canada and bound for the UK. The convoy comprised 59 merchant ships and was escorted by the cutter *Spencer*, the destroyer *Greer* and four corvettes *Dauphin, Dianthus, Rosthern* and *Trillium*.

Wolf pack Westmark, operating in mid Atlantic with 17 U-boats, and the nine U-boats of Wolf pack Ostmark were directed onto the convoy, which was sighted on 6 March 1943.

On 11 March 1943 the *Empire Impala* was steaming to the aid of survivors from the 2,800-ton cargo liner *Egyptian*, torpedoed by U230, when she was torpedoed and sunk by U591 under the command of Hans-Jurgen Zetzsche.

James Craig
Stoker First Class D/KX 162389, Royal Navy, HMS *Kite*

Parents	Son of William Craig of 52 Montague Street, Portadown
Residence	Montague Street
Died	Lost at Sea 21 August 1944, HMS *Kite*, Norwegian Sea
Buried	No Known Grave
Commemorated	Plymouth Naval Memorial. Panel 89 Column 3. Portadown War Memorial (WW2-10)

James was nicknamed 'Nipper' and played for Greenview, a local football club.

Stoker First Class Craig was serving aboard the 1,350-ton sloop HMS *Kite*. In August 1944 she was part of the escort for the Arctic Convoy JW 59 comprising 28 ships bound for the Soviet Union.

On the evening of 20 August HMS *Keppel*, another escort vessel, made contact with a U-boat and together with *Kite* attacked her throughout the night with hedgehogs and depth charges. Early the next morning *Kite* was forced to slow down as her foxer cables had become entangled (foxers were towed to 'fox' torpedoes). At 0644 when approximately 220 miles south west of Bear Island in the Norwegian Sea, two torpedoes fired by U344 commanded by KL Ulrich Pietsch hit her. HMS *Kite* sank within minutes taking 185 of her crew, including Stoker First Class Craig, down with her. Nine crew members survived.

The next day, 22 August the U344 was herself sunk with the loss of all hands, by aircraft from the escort carrier HMS *Vindex*.

A postcard of Plymouth Naval Memorial. (Author's Collection)

Dunkirk (1940)

On 10 May 1940 German panzers invaded Belgium, Holland, Luxembourg and France. By 20 May enemy advance units reached the English Channel at Abbeville thus encircling the British Expeditionary Force. The BEF was forced to withdraw in the direction of the channel ports and by the end of May 1940 defended a small perimeter around Dunkirk.

Across the channel the Royal Navy hastily mounted a rescue operation codenamed Operation Dynamo. From 27 May until 4 June almost 340,000 British, Belgian and French troops were rescued from Dunkirk.

British casualties amounted to 3,500 killed, 13,500 wounded, and 40,000 prisoners.

Alexander Wright
Rifleman 7009511, 2nd Battalion, Royal Ulster Rifles

Parents	Son of Alexander and Martha Wright of 33 Alexandra Gardens, Portadown
Residence	Watson's Lane
Died	Killed in action/Died of wounds/Died 28 May 1940, France
Age	33
Buried	Le Clion Sur Mer Cemetery, Loire Atlantique, France. Collective Grave 4.
Commemorated	Portadown War Memorial (WW2-65)

Alexander's father, Alexander served as a Sergeant with the 8th Battalion, Royal Irish Rifles during the Great War and was awarded the Military Medal. He died on 19 October 1924.

Alexander was the husband of Lily Wright and the couple had four children. The family resided at 1 Watson's Lane, Portadown. His daughter Marlene resided at 33 Alexandra Gardens, Portadown. He was a member of the British Legion.

Rifleman Wright had served in India and was in the Army Reserve.

The 2nd Battalion, Royal Ulster Rifles formed part of the 9th Infantry Brigade attached to the 3rd Infantry Division in the battle for France. On 14 May 1940 they were in and around the Belgian city of Louvain when the Germans attacked. The battalion held their ground for five days before withdrawing in the direction of the Channel ports.

Mrs. Lily Wright 1 Watson's Lane, Portadown, has received official intimation that the body of her husband, Rifleman Alexander Wright, Royal Ulster Rifles, was washed ashore near St. Nazaire in July last

and was buried at Clion-sur-mer, Loire Inferieure.

Portadown Times
29 November 1940

He had brothers Willie; Archie, who resided at Red Row; Bertie, who played football for Portadown and Glentoran and Jack who resided in Devonport and who served with the Royal Navy during World War Two. His brother Freddie also played football for Portadown.

John Turbitt
Bombardier 6974101, 12 Bty, 3rd (Ulster) Searchlight Regiment, Royal Artillery

Residence	Meadow Lane
Died	Killed in action 30 May-22 June 1940, Dunkirk, France
Buried	Dunkirk Town Cemetery, Nord, France. Grave 1. 1. 1.
Commemorated	Portadown War Memorial (WW2-57) St. Mark's Parish Church War Memorial

John was the husband of Annie Turbitt and they had two daughters Ruth and Joy. The family resided at 7 Meadow Lane, Portadown.

He had previously served in the Seaforth Highlanders in India and Palestine. John was employed by Henry's Cable Company in Belfast and rejoined the army on the outbreak of war.

The 3rd Searchlight Regiment, Royal Artillery was formed in Belfast and was sent to France in December 1939. In March 1940 the unit received the title Ulster.

Bombardier Turbitt was reported missing after the evacuation of Dunkirk and was buried on 22 June 1940.

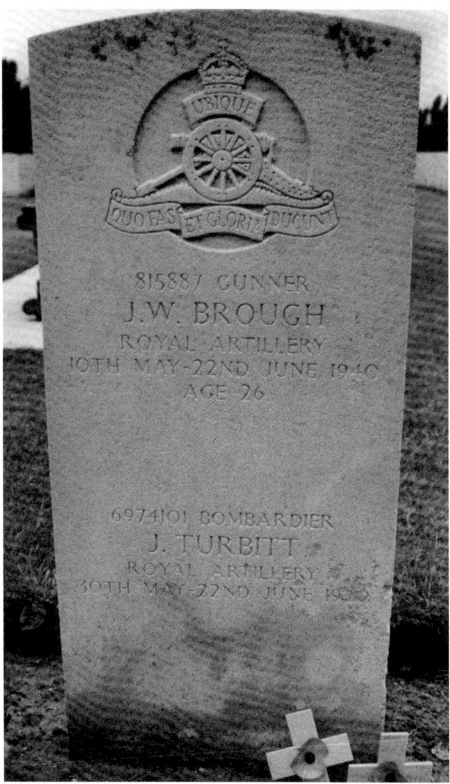

Grave of Bombardier John Turbitt. (Author's Collection)

Samuel Webb
Driver T/7013121, Royal Army Service Corps

Parents	Son of Edward and Susanna Webb of 45 Mourneview Street, Portadown.
Residence	Mourneview Street
Died	Killed in action 31 May - 2 June 1940, Dunkirk, France
Age	25
Buried	No Known Grave
Commemorated	Dunkirk Memorial, Nord France. Column 139. Portadown War Memorial (WW2-59)

Dunkirk Memorial. (Author's Collection)

Samuel was a former employee of the late Mr. Edward Anderson, Grocer, Church Street, Portadown. He was a former member of Portadown Pipe Band and Portadown Cycling Club.

Samuel had been in the army about four years before he was killed.

The Blitz (1940-41)

From July until October 1940 the Luftwaffe and the RAF battled it out for dominance of the skies in what became known as the Battle of Britain. Day after day German bombers, protected by fighters, attacked airfields, radar sites, command and control centres and aircraft factories in an attempt to systematically destroy the Royal Air Force. The pilots of Fighter Command inflicted such casualties that the Luftwaffe was forced to change tactics and began bombing at night. They turned their attention to bombing London and other major cities including Belfast.

The German invasion of the Soviet Union in June 1941 saw the reduction of bombing raids over the United Kingdom, as many Luftwaffe

units were withdrawn to support the invasion. Casualties from 1939-1941 amounted to over 44,500 killed.

George Hunniford
Sergeant (Radar Op./Observer) 950488, 219 Squadron, Royal Air Force (VR)

Parents	Son of George and Rebecca Hunniford of 30 Margretta Park, Portadown
Residence	Margretta Park
Died	Killed on air operations 15 December 1941, Fontwell, England
Age	22
Buried	Seagoe Church of Ireland Churchyard, Portadown
Commemorated	Portadown War Memorial (WW2-23) Portadown College War Memorial Seagoe Parish Church War Memorial Thomas Street Methodist Church War Memorial

George was an only son. His father George was principal of Thomas Street Public Elementary School. He was educated at Portadown College and was a member of the school rugby 1st XV 1936-37. George was formerly in the employ of the local branch of the Belfast Savings Bank before enlisting in the Royal Air Force.

George was posted to 219 Squadron of Fighter Command. The squadron was reformed on 4 October 1939 at Catterick and equipped with Blenheim fighters for shipping protection duties. Later the squadron was exclusively involved in night defence. In October 1940 the squadron moved south to protect London during the Blitz, being equipped with Beaufighters.

Sergeant Hunniford was a Radar Operator/Observer on Beaufighter Mark IF serial number R2154 piloted by Sergeant John P. Ranger. The aircraft took off from Tangmere on 15 December 1941 on a routine patrol. At 1940 the Beaufighter flew into high ground while attempting to land in the dark and crashed near Fontwell three miles northeast of Tangmere. Sergeant Hunniford and Sergeant Ranger were both killed.

Sergeant John P. Ranger lies buried at Brookwood Military Cemetery, Woking, Surrey. Sergeant Hunniford's funeral took place on 23 December 1941.

George had a sister Nancy and brother-in-law Douglas Stoops, who also resided in Margretta Park.

North Africa and the Mediterranean (1940-43)

From 1940 until 1943 British, Commonwealth, Italian and German forces were engaged in a seesaw battle covering thousands of miles of the North African desert and the waters of the Mediterranean Sea.

In August 1942 General Bernard Montgomery took charge of the British forces and made preparations for a major assault on the over extended Axis armies. The assault came on 23 October 1942 with the Battle of El Alamein. The battle raged for two weeks and resulted in the almost annihilation of Italian forces and the retreat of the Africa Corps.

In November 1942 came the Allied landings in French North Africa codenamed Operation Torch. By 1943 the Axis forces had been pushed into Tunisia where General von Armin surrendered on 12 May 1943, thus ending the war in the desert.

David Dawson Todd
Sergeant 530811,
Royal Air Force

Born	1912, Portadown
Parents	Son of Robert and Ann Todd of 72 Hanover Street, Portadown
Residence	Hanover Street
Enlisted	1937
Died	Lost on air operations 30 August 1941, Mediterranean Sea
Age	29
Buried	No Known Grave
Commemorated	Malta Memorial, Panel 2 Column 1. Portadown War Memorial (WW2-55)

David's father Robert enlisted in the 1st Battalion, Royal Irish Fusiliers in 1898 at Gough Barracks, Armagh. He served during the South African War and was awarded the Queen's South Africa Medal with clasps South Africa 1901, Transvaal, Orange Free State and Cape Colony. He served as a Private with serial number 6742 during the Great War. Robert served alongside his brother Francis William who was killed in action on 22 October 1914.

After 22 years service in the army Robert became a carter by trade and had stables in Meadow Lane, Portadown. He and his wife Ann had children Frank, David Dawson, Harriet and Agnes.

David Dawson was a keen local footballer and played for Spurs Football Club. The side were winners of the Maloco Cup in 1935 when they defeated Lismore United

2-1 in the final. David was also a member of Thomas Street Silver Band. It is believed he worked in the office of Spence Bryson and Company before leaving to enlist in the Royal Air Force.

David married Emily Somme Black, daughter of Isaac Black. He had served as a Private with serial number 9-15858 in the 9th Battalion, Royal Irish Fusiliers during the Great War. He took part in the attack of the 36th (Ulster) Division on 1 July 1916 and was very seriously wounded. On 1 July 1918 his daughter Emily was born and was given the middle name Somme after the battle in which her father was injured. The couple had two sons Robert, known as Bobby, born in 1939 and Hadden born in 1940.

David had reached the rank of Corporal when he received a wound to his left eye on 13 June 1940 as a result of war service. He was treated at St. Giles Hospital, Camberwell where his close friend Abbie Rusk, only recently evacuated from Dunkirk, visited him. Corporal Todd trained as an Air Gunner and was promoted to Sergeant. He was stationed in North Africa from where he sent the family a 'Greetings from Egypt' postcard.

Sergeant David Dawson Todd was journeying back to his unit when his aircraft was shot down in the Mediterranean. The aircraft, a twin engine Wellington, serial number W5559, took off from Portreath, Cornwall on a ferry flight to the Middle East via Gibraltar. On board were Pilot Sgt. W.F. Butler, Sgt. Thomas Preston Butterfield, Sgt. Maurice Henry Cope, Sgt. Donald Robert Arthur Garrick and Sgt. David Dawson Todd. Somewhere over the Mediterranean Sea the aircraft was attacked and shot down by two Italian CR42 fighters with the loss of all on board. They are all commemorated on the Malta Memorial.

Sergeant David Dawson Todd. (Bobby Todd)

David's son Bobby enlisted as a 15 year old boy soldier in the Royal Army Service Corps. He was stationed in Germany and saw service in Kenya, Uganda and Swaziland during the early 1960s when locally raised regiments mutinied. In 1964 he was posted to Aden and served in the Radfan on active service against terrorists. After 12 years service Bobby was discharged in 1966 and was placed on the Special Reserve for three years. In 1970 he was recruited into the Ulster Defence Regiment in which he served for 22 years.

David's son Hadden enlisted in the Royal Air Force in 1955 and was posted to Malaya where he was injured and was subsequently discharged on medical grounds.

David's uncle Francis William Todd (see entry **210 Private Francis William Todd**) was killed in action on 22 October 1914 in France.

Albert Hamilton
Able Seaman D/SSX 26639, Royal Navy, HMS *Neptune*

Parents	Son of Samuel and Anne Hamilton of 10 Water Street, Portadown
Residence	Water Street
Enlisted	July 1938
Died	Lost at Sea 19 December 1941, HMS *Neptune*, Mediterranean Sea
Age	25
Buried	No Known Grave
Commemorated	Plymouth Naval Memorial. Panel 47 Column 1 Portadown War Memorial (WW2-21) St. Mark's Parish Church War Memorial

Albert's father Samuel served during the Great War and died in 1928. He and his wife Annie had a daughter and a son Albert. Albert was educated at Park Road Public Elementary School and was a former employee of Messrs Spence Bryson and Co. before joining the Royal Navy.

Able Seaman Albert Hamilton. (Portadown Times)

Able Seaman Hamilton served in the 5,200 ton cruiser HMS *Neptune*. On 18 December 1941 she sailed from Malta as part of Force K, which comprised two other cruisers, HMS *Penelope* and HMS *Aurora*, and four destroyers. Their mission was to sink Axis supply ships transporting men, munitions, oil and equipment to General Rommel's German and Italian forces in North Africa.

In the early hours of 19 December 1941 *Neptune* struck a mine in an uncharted minefield when approximately 15 miles off Tripoli. Soon afterwards two more mines were detonated by the cruiser, which soon lay crippled in the water. *Aurora* also strayed into the minefield and was damaged and *Penelope* suffered superficial damage when a mine exploded nearby.

The destroyer HMS *Kandahar* mounted a rescue attempt but she too struck a mine and had to be sunk later by HMS *Jaguar*. As the crippled *Neptune* drifted without power she struck a forth mine and within minutes capsized and sank taking with her 764 officers and crew. Only one crewmember, Able Seaman John Walton, who was rescued by the Italians, survived.

Albert's mother Anne was engaged on war work in England when she was notified of her son's death in action.

William John Stanfield Gunner 880709, 107th (South Notts Hussars) Regiment, Royal Horse Artillery

Born	4 May 1920, Portadown
Parents	Son of Thomas Edward and Mary Jane Stanfield of Levaghery
Residence	Levaghery
Died	Killed in action 27 May 1942, North Africa
Age	22
Buried	No Known Grave
Commemorated	
	Alamein Memorial, Egypt. Column 14. Portadown War Memorial (WW2-53) Seagoe Parish Church War Memorial

William's father Thomas Edward was employed as a weaver. He married Mary Jane Weir, a stitcher and daughter of Robert Weir of Edenderry, on 4 November 1911 at Seagoe Parish Church. The couple had nine children Mabel Agatha born 1912, Olive born 1914, Thomas Edward born 1917, Gladys born

1918, William John born 1920, Frances Helen born 1922, Robert Weir born 1924, Roy born 1926 and Ruth Phyllis born 1928.

Thomas Edward served as a Lance-Corporal in the 1st Battalion, Royal Irish Fusiliers during the Great War and was wounded at Arras. After the war he returned to employment as a weaver and later became a cabinetmaker. His wife Mary Jane died on 26 June 1940 aged 41.

Gunner Stanfield took part in the campaign in France 1940 and was evacuated from Dunkirk.

The 107th (South Notts Hussars) Regiment was mobilised in Nottingham in September 1939 and was sent to Palestine in 1940. It saw service in various parts of North Africa including Egypt and Tobruk and in March 1942 formed part of the 22nd Armoured Brigade.

British and Commonwealth forces were defending positions between Gazala on the coast and Bir Hacheim in the south when on 26/27 May 1942 Rommel launched an offensive. It began with feint attacks by the Italians along the coast while his panzers were unleashed in an outflanking move to the south. The British eventually fell back with the 107th (South Notts Hussars) Regiment being almost annihilated in the process. Tobruk fell to the Germans on 21 June 1942. The British halted their withdrawal at El Alamein.

Seagoe Parish Church War Memorial. (Author's Collection)

Patrick Grimley
Private 3853199,
115th Provost Company,
Corps of Military Police

Parents	Son of Patrick and Bella Grimley of Portadown
Died	Lost at sea 14 November 1942, SS *Scillin*, Mediterranean Sea
Age	35
Buried	No Known Grave
Commemorated	Alamein Memorial, Egypt. Column 83. Portadown War Memorial (WW2-19)

The SS *Scillin* was an Italian vessel displacing 1,500 tons. In November 1942 around 800 British and Commonwealth prisoners of war were crowded on board for onward transportation to Sicily.

On 14 November with the ship north-west of the port of Mahdia, Tunisia she was torpedoed and sunk by the British Submarine HMS *Sahib* commanded by Lieutenant John Bromage. The Lieutenant had no knowledge that the ship was carrying British prisoners and it was only when 27 of the PoWs were rescued that this was realised. Also saved were 35 members of the crew. At a subsequent court of inquiry Lieutenant John Bromage was exonerated from any wrong doing in the sinking of the SS *Scillin*.

George Lyttle (see entry **WW2-35 Signalman George A. Lyttle**) was also lost at sea on the SS *Scillin*.

George A. Lyttle
Signalman 3712389, 4 L. of C. Sigs, Royal Corps of Signals

Parents	Son of Alfred and Mary Ann Lyttle of 3 Craigwell Avenue, Portadown
Residence	Craigwell Avenue
Died	Lost at sea 14 November 1942, SS *Scillin*, Mediterranean Sea
Age	22
Buried	No Known Grave
Commemorated	Alamein Memorial, Egypt. Column 52. Portadown War Memorial (WW2-35)

George was employed by Portadown Foundry Ltd. before he enlisted.

Signalman Lyttle was captured by the Italians at Bengazhi, North Africa and sent to a temporary prisoner of war camp. He was transported on the SS *Scillin*, the same ship as Private Patrick Grimley (see entry **WW2-19 Private Patrick Grimley**), which was torpedoed by HMS *Sahib* with heavy loss of life.

Albert Tinman
Corporal 6983317, 6th Battalion, Royal Inniskilling Fusiliers

Parents	Son of Robert and Fanny Tinman of 16 North Street, Portadown
Residence	North Street
Died	Died of wounds 7 April 1943, Tunisia, North Africa
Age	27
Buried	Medjez-El-Bab War Cemetery, Tunisia. Grave 12. H. 17.
Commemorated	Portadown War Memorial (54) St. Mark's Parish Church War Memorial

Albert was an only son. He was employed in Tavanagh Weaving Co. Ltd. before the outbreak of war. He was a member of Corcrain Flute Band. Albert had a sister who resided at 32 Henry Street, Portadown.

The 6th Battalion, Royal Inniskilling Fusiliers formed part of the 38th (Irish) Brigade attached to the 78th (Battleaxe) Infantry Division during the Tunisian campaign.

On 5/6 April 1943 the Battalion took part in battles 20 miles south west of Tunis in the Djebel el Mahdi Mountains.

Italy (1943-1945)

The invasion of Sicily took place on 10 July 1943 under the codename Operation Husky and after heavy fighting fell to the Allies on 16 August 1943. British casualties amounted to 5,000 killed or missing and 7,500 wounded. American loses were 2,500 killed or missing and 6,000 wounded. The Italians lost 2,000 killed, 5,000 wounded and almost 150,000 prisoners. German loses amounted to 5,000 killed and 6,000 prisoners.

After the Italian surrender of 8 September 1943 the Allies landed at Salerno and Taranto. The country was a defender's paradise with the landscape of mountains and rivers forming natural defensive features and it took the Allies 20 months of arduous fighting to slowly advance up through Italy.

German forces surrendered in Italy on 2 May 1945. The Italian campaign cost the Allies over 300,000 killed, wounded or missing.

Robert James Irwin
Fusilier 7014337, 2nd Battalion, Royal Inniskilling Fusiliers

Parents	Son of Jacob and Margaret Irwin of Toronto, Canada
Residence	Mary Street
Enlisted	July 1939
Died	Killed in action 11 July 1943, Sicily
Age	21
Buried	No Known Grave
Commemorated	Cassino Memorial, Italy. Panel 6. Portadown War Memorial (WW2-25) St. Mark's Parish Church War Memorial

Robert resided with his uncle (also called Robert) and grandmother at 7 Mary Street, Portadown until he enlisted in July 1939. He had a sister who resided in Derrycrew, Loughgall.

The 2nd Battalion, Royal Inniskilling Fusiliers formed part of the 13th Infantry Brigade of the

5th Infantry Division during the Sicily campaign. The battalion landed at Cassibile south of Syracuse and was engaged in driving the Axis forces from Salarino on 11 July 1943.

David McClatchey
Rifleman 7902391, 2nd Battalion, The London Irish Rifles, Royal Ulster Rifles

Parents	Son of Edward and Isabel McClatchey of 22 Queen Street, Portadown
Residence	Mons Villas
Died	Died of wounds 10 August 1943, Sicily/Italy
Age	30
Buried	No Known Grave
Commemorated	Cassino Memorial, Italy. Panel 11. Portadown War Memorial (WW2-38) St. Mark's Parish Church War Memorial

David was in the hairdressing business before enlisting. He was the husband of Carol McClatchey and they resided at 2 Mons Villas, Armagh Road, Portadown.

The 2nd Battalion, The London Irish Rifles, Royal Ulster Rifles formed part of the 38th (Irish) Brigade of the 78th (Battleaxe) Infantry Division during the Sicily campaign.

Rifleman McClatchey was wounded in the head during the invasion of Sicily and captured by the Germans. He was removed to an enemy hospital where he died whilst undergoing surgery. It is not clear if this hospital was located on Sicily or the Italian mainland.

Albert Lyttle MM
Corporal 7015490,
6th Battalion,
Royal Inniskilling Fusiliers

Parents	Son of Mrs A. Lyttle of 10 Queen Street, Portadown
Residence	James Street
Enlisted	1939
Died	Killed in action 8 April 1944, Italy
Age	23
Buried	Cassino War Cemetery, Italy. Grave III. B. 22.
Commemorated	Portadown War Memorial (WW2-34) St. Mark's Parish Church War Memorial

Albert was the husband of Margaret Lyttle and they had two children Ronnie and Olive. The family resided at 6 James Street, Portadown.

ANOTHER PORTADOWN M.M.

Young Soldier's Award.

SICILIAN CAMPAIGN.

Portadown men continue to win award for valour in the various theatres of war, in the air and at sea. In the latest list of awards to men of Ulster Regiments is contained the name of Acting Corporal Albert Lyttle, formerly of 10, Queen Street, Portadown, now serving with the Royal Inniskilling Fusiliers in Italy.

A/Corp. ALBERT LYTTLE

This 22 year old soldier has been awarded the Military Medal. He is a member of a family which has an excellent military record. He joined up in 1939 and was formerly with the Royal Ulster Rifles and Royal Irish Fusiliers. He served in North Africa and was one of the first into Sicily. Latest news to hand is that he is serving with the Inniskillings in Italy.

Newspaper cutting of award of Military Medal to Corporal Albert Lyttle. (Portadown News)

He enlisted in 1939 and saw service with the Royal Ulster Rifles and the Royal Irish Fusiliers. He took part in the North African campaign and saw action at Centuripe during the invasion of Sicily July-August 1943. The 6th Battalion, Royal Inniskilling Fusiliers formed part of the 38th (Irish) Brigade of the 78th (Battleaxe) Infantry Division during the Italian campaign.

Corporal Albert Lyttle was awarded the Military Medal for bravery in the field for his part in the Sangro battles in November 1943.

On 23 November 1943 during an attack by the Inniskillings on River Li Colli a platoon of 'C' Coy. was being held up by an enemy post occupying a house. Corporal Lyttle, with complete disregard for his personnel safety made his way to the house himself, and then rushed at it firing his gun from the hip. He succeeded in killing one and wounding two of the enemy, thus causing the post to surrender.

By this rigorous and decisive action the further advance of his platoon was able to continue and valuable lives were saved. This N.C.O. has shown outstanding powers of leadership and initiative, both during the Italian and the Sicilian campaigns.

Portadown News
30 January 1945

His widow Margaret was presented with the award on behalf of her late husband. Corporal Lyttle had three brothers Billy, Ernie and Tommy. Tommy served in the Royal Artillery as a Lance-Bombardier during World War Two.

His brother-in-law James Tweedie (see entry **WW2-34 Trooper James Taylor Tweedie**) husband of his sister Annie was killed in action on 6 September 1944 also in Italy.

James Ernest Ivor Clulow
Sergeant 7902378, North Irish Horse, Royal Armoured Corps

Parents	Son of Joseph and Eleanor Clulow of Portadown
Residence	David Street
Died	Died of wounds 4 August 1944, Italy
Age	28
Buried	Arezzo War Cemetery, Italy. Grave I. D. 12.
Commemorated	Portadown War Memorial (WW2-9) St. Mark's Parish Church War Memorial

James was employed in Atkinson's factory before enlisting. He was a member of Portadown Pipe Band. His mother remarried a Mr. Graham after the death of her first husband and they resided at 25 David Street, Portadown.

At the end of July to the beginning of August 1944 the North Irish Horse was involved in fighting between Arezzo and Florence, which was defended by elements of the 104th Panzer Grenadier Regiment. On 4 August 1944 the Regimental Headquarters was shelled by the enemy wounding nine men, two of whom subsequently died from their injuries.

Sergeant Clulow's mother received a letter from Major A. R. Booth

He was with me for the first two years in Enniskillen and Portrush and I know what a sterling character he was. He was always cheerful and willing and was a reliable chap and the type that will be badly missed.

Portadown News
2 September 1944

He had a sister Ruby and his brother Joseph served in the Royal Maritime Artillery during World War Two.

James' father Joseph (see entry **231 Private Joseph Clulow**) was killed in action on 16 August 1917 at the Battle of Langemarck in Belgium.

Francis Berry
Private 7013410, 1st Battalion, Argyll and Sutherland Highlanders

Parents	Son of Francis and Sarah Berry
Residence	John Street
Enlisted	1 September 1939
Died	Killed in action 1 September 1944, Italy
Age	25
Buried	Florence War Cemetery, Italy. Grave II. C. 4.
Commemorated	Portadown War Memorial (WW2-2)

Francis was employed by Messrs Hamilton Robb Ltd. before enlisting in the Royal Ulster Rifles. He was the husband of Sarah Berry and they had three sons. The family resided at 50 John Street, Portadown.

He was recalled to the colours on 1 September 1939 and later saw action in North Africa and Sicily. He wrote a letter to thank the people of Portadown for the receipt of a parcel

I have pleasure in thanking the people of Portadown for their kind generosity in sending the parcel, which I received when at home.

I would like you to know how some of the Portadown boys here are doing. First on the list is Edmund McAdam of John Street. He is in the same Division as myself, as is also Bertie McAteer, of Fowler's Entry. We are all doing fine and hope to be able to go out to Shamrock Park again and cheer the Ports to victory. There are a few more lads from the town in the Eighth Army with us, and they all send their best wishes to you all. Hoping you will convey this message on behalf of all the lads of the town serving in the Eighth Army through your news columns.

Portadown News
5 June 1943

During the advance to the Gothic Line the 1st Battalion, Argyll and Sutherland Highlanders was engaged in heavy fighting in the villages of Doccio and San Brigida near the River Arno. On 1 September 1944, as the battalion entered the village of Doccia, it came under heavy German artillery fire, the first salvo of which, inflicted heavy casualties on the Company HQ. As the remnants of the company reformed they came under machine-gun and mortar fire.

Francis' cousin John also served during World War Two and was wounded at Dunkirk.

John O'Neill
Private 3327269, 1st Battalion, Argyll and Sutherland Highlanders

Died	Killed in action 4 September 1944, Italy

Age 33
Buried Florence War Cemetery, Italy. Grave II. C. 2.
Commemorated Portadown War Memorial (WW2-43)

John was the husband of Elizabeth O'Neill. He was a member of Portadown Homing Pigeon Society.

On 2 September 1944 'B' and 'D' Companies were ordered to attack the 2000 feet high Mount Abetino. There was fierce resistance from the German defenders. The Argylls and the 3/8th Punjabis fought for six days to take the mountain, which fell into British hands on 8 September. The cost to the Argylls was two officers killed in action, two missing in action and two wounded in action; nine other ranks killed in action, 41 missing in action and 31 wounded in action.

James Taylor Tweedie
Trooper 7902799, North Irish Horse, Royal Armoured Corps

Parents Son of Joseph and Elizabeth Tweedie of 15 Coronation Street, Portadown.
Residence Queen Street
Enlisted December 1939
Died Died of wounds 6 September 1944, Italy
Age 37
Buried Gradara War Cemetery, Italy. Grave I. B. 17.
Commemorated Portadown War Memorial (WW2-58) St. Mark's Parish Church War Memorial

James' parents had eight children John, Joseph, Carson, James Taylor, Emily, Susan, Dorcas and Ruby.

Ballyworkan LOL 19 Lambeg drum in memory of Trooper James Taylor Tweedie. His great great granddaughter, Madison Clasper-Parr, aged nine, on right. (Portadown Times)

James Taylor was the husband of Annie Tweedie (nee Lyttle) and the couple had a daughter Wendy. The family resided at 10 Queen Street, Portadown. James was a member of Ballyworkan LOL 19.

His brother John left Portadown to take up employment on important war work in England and was accidentally killed on 9 April 1941 aged 20.

The North Irish Horse was part of 46th Division and was involved in the fighting to break through the defences of the Gothic Line between Pesaro and Rimini on the northern Adriatic coast of Italy. From 6-11 September 1944 the regiment was taken out of the line for rest and maintenance. 128th Infantry Brigade made mention of the regiment

A special tribute must be paid to squadrons of the N.I.H. Day after day their Churchills forced positions and supported our infantry over appalling tank country.

North Irish Horse
Battle Report 1946

Trooper Tweedie's widow received an air gram from Lord O'Neill, commanding officer of the North Irish Horse.

I remember well when Mr. Montgomery brought your husband along from Fivemiletown to join the Regiment. Ever since he has been a most loyal, painstaking and hard working member of the North Irish Horse. His death will be mourned by many in the Regiment, and since he was with me on many occasions when I commanded 'A' Squadron I feel his loss very much.

Portadown News
30 September 1944

His brother-in-law Albert Lyttle (see entry **WW2-34 Corporal Albert Lyttle MM**) was killed in action on 8 April 1944 in Italy.

Alfred Hall
Fusilier 7046077, 1st Battalion, Royal Irish Fusiliers

Parents	Son of William and Mary Hall of 4 David Street, Portadown
Residence	David Street
Died	Killed in action 8 October 1944, Italy
Age	21
Buried	Santerno Valley War Cemetery, Italy. Grave I. L. 15.
Commemorated	Portadown War Memorial (WW2-20)

Alfred's parents had children Willie, Thomas, Danny, George, Larry and Trish.

The 1st Battalion, Royal Irish Fusiliers formed part of the 38th (Irish) Brigade of the 78th (Battleaxe) Infantry Division during the Italian campaign.

Fusilier Alfred Hall. (Dan Murphy)

On 5/6 October 1944 the battalion relieved a regiment of the US 88th Infantry Division north of the Castel del Rio on the River Santerno. On 7/8 October the battalion attacked Axis positions north of the River Sauterne on Point 382.

Fusilier Hall, a Bren gunner, was taking part in a night patrol with eleven of his colleagues when he was killed. His actions saved the lives of the rest of the patrol.

His brother Thomas served in the Royal Inniskilling Fusiliers during World War Two. He was evacuated from Dunkirk, and later served in Madagascar, India and Burma where he was wounded. His brother Robert enlisted in the Royal Ulster Rifles before the war and was stationed in Palestine and later served on the North West Frontier of India. He was wounded in action during the Normandy campaign.

Fusilier Alfred Hall was a close friend of William Murphy (see entry **WW2-42 Private William James Murphy**) who was killed in action on 21 October 1944. Both servicemen are buried in Santerno Valley War Cemetery, Italy.

William James Murphy Private 14437714, 2nd Battalion, The London Irish Rifles, Royal Ulster Rifles

Born	23 February 1924, Navan, Co. Meath
Parents	Son of William James and Marion Murphy of 31 Union Street, Portadown and of Navan, Co. Meath
Residence	Union Street
Enlisted	21 July 1943
Died	Killed in action 21 October 1944, Italy
Age	20
Buried	Santerno Valley War Cemetery, Italy. Grave I. G. 13.

Commemorated
Portadown War Memorial (WW2-42)

William's father William James enlisted in the Royal Irish Fusiliers on 16 July 1913. He served as Sergeant 7808443 during the Great War and was awarded the French Croix de Guerre with Swords for bravery in the field. After demobilisation William James was employed as a timekeeper for the Great Northern Railway at Navan railway station. It was there that he met his wife Marion who resided in the town's Railway Street.

The couple had children William James, Paddy, Dan, Rita, Stella, Mary, Hugo, Peter and Josephine. Josephine was born on 28 September 1937 the same day as the family returned to Portadown.

William James was educated at the Christian Brothers School in Navan. After leaving school he was employed by a number of local firms including Logan's rope works and Messrs. Grew before he enlisted.

On enlistment his particulars were given as follows: occupation - labourer, height 5'6", complexion - fresh, eyes - brown, hair - dark brown. Private Murphy underwent training in reaction to a gas attack in September 1943 and in rifle shooting and light machine gun fire in October. He completed a motor transport course as a driver on 24 January 1944.

Private Murphy, together with his unit, was posted to Cairo, Egypt to get acclimatised for future action in the Italian campaign.

The family have lovingly kept all of William's letters. On 20 May William wrote to his parents

Dear Mum and Dad
...Well I am somewhere in Italy now but can't tell you where. It's very warm just now and I am well sunburned. The crossing on the ship was very good.

Letter to parents
20 May 1944

In another undated letter he wrote

Well I have joined my Battalion 2nd London Irish Rifles. We have been up the line last week we are out for a rest now. But it is not as bad as you might think.

Letter to parents undated

The 2nd Battalion, The London Irish Rifles, Royal Ulster Rifles formed part of the 38th (Irish) Brigade of the 78th (Battleaxe) Infantry Division during the Italian campaign. William served in 'H' Company.

In June 1944 William was able to visit Rome but just too late to have an audience with Pope Pius XII. William, together with comrades

Private William James Murphy. (Dan Murphy)

from his unit, was invited to the Irish College in Rome where the nuns gave them an ample supply of cigarettes and soap. William met a young nun from Kells in County Meath near to where he was born.

Private William Murphy was killed in action during an attack on the slopes of Point 387 in the Battle for the Po Valley, Northern Italy

H Company fought hand to hand up the slopes of Point 387 but lost heavily in a counter-attack. All officers except commanding officer Major William Craig were killed and the platoons had to give up the ground gained.

London Irish at War

Major William Craig, William's commanding officer, wrote to the late soldier's father

Dear Mr. Murphy
...Your son was a first class soldier, and a very popular member of this company. I had known him for a considerable time and always found him a young man of very high character. He was a courageous fighter, always willing and cheerful even in difficult and dangerous conditions. At the time of his death he was advancing with the rest of us, when he came under fire from a German machine gun. He must have died at once.

Letter to Mr. William Murphy
9 December 1944

The family also received a letter from Father Daniel Kelliher MC, who was the Roman Catholic Padre to the 38th (Irish) Brigade

...I am so sorry I wasn't with him when he was killed, but the Battalion had confession and Holy Communion shortly before the battle and I know your dear son was ready to meet his God. I have since offered the Holy Mass for him and will continue to remember him and you all.

Letter from Father Daniel Kelliher MC

Father Kelliher was awarded the Military Cross for helping wounded soldiers during the Battle of

Cassino. A native of Co. Kerry he was killed in a traffic accident in Germany after the war.

Private William James Murphy was a close friend of Alfred Hall (see entry **WW2-20 Fusilier Alfred Hall**) who was killed in action on 8 October 1944. Both servicemen are buried in Santerno Valley War Cemetery, Italy.

William's brother Dan served as an SDLP Councillor on Craigavon Borough Council from 1977-85. He died, aged 77, in 2006 after a short illness.

Robert Lynas
Corporal 530316,
Royal Air Force

Parents	Son of James and Margaret Lynas of Clonroot
Residence	Clonroot
Died	Died 14 May 1945, Italy
Age	20
Buried	Naples War Cemetery, Italy. Grave IV. H. 13.
Commemorated	Portadown War Memorial (WW2-33)

Robert's father James served during the South African War and the Great War. His brother Mr. S. Lynas also served during the Great War and resided at 60 Cavour Street, Belfast.

Robert had nine years service in the Royal Air Force. He died as a result of a shooting incident.

The RAF Bomber Offensive (1940-45)

Royal Air Force Bomber Command was the only means available with which Britain could directly hit back at the enemy and from the outset of war the RAF mounted daylight raids on targets in Germany initially without much success. With heavy losses incurred during daylight raids Bomber Command switched to bombing mainly by night.

The total number of aircrew that served in Bomber Command was 125,000 of which 55,500 lost their lives from all causes. A further 10,000 became prisoners of war.

Thomas Dawson
Pilot Officer 42339,
144 Squadron, Royal Air Force

Parents	Son of William Joseph and Sarah Dawson of Rosnaree, Eden Crescent, Portadown
Residence	Eden Crescent
Enlisted	May 1939
Died	Lost on air operations 1 November 1940, Germany

Age 20
Buried No Known Grave
Commemorated
Runnymede Memorial, Surrey, England. Panel 7.
Portadown War Memorial (WW2-14)
Portadown College War Memorial

Thomas was educated at Portadown College. He entered the Royal Air Force in May 1939, receiving his commission two months later. Thomas was posted to 144 Squadron of Bomber Command. The squadron was reformed on 11 January 1937 at Bicester and just before the outbreak of war was equipped with Hamdens.

Pilot Officer Dawson was pilot on a Hamden Mark I serial number X2915 the other crew members were Sgt. Ernest Arthur Barker, Sgt. Ronald Leslie Hayes and Sgt. Joseph Cutler. The aircraft took off from Hemswell at 2335 hours on 31 October 1940 on a bombing mission to Berlin. After a routine message nothing more was heard from the aircraft and it was presumed lost on 1 November.

Thomas' father received a letter from Squadron Leader G. F. Lerrwill

The aircraft on the operational flight took off and crossed our coast in the normal manner and from that point we have heard nothing at all. His trip was, however, scheduled to cover a considerable distance over land, and there should be quite a good prospect of his having been forced down in enemy territory and taken prisoner.

Portadown Times
15 November 1940

Family grave of Pilot Officer Thomas Dawson. (Author's Collection)

The Hampden was lost without trace and all four crewmembers are commemorated on the Runnymede Memorial.

William Terence Chambers Seale Squadron leader 37694, 7 Squadron, Royal Air Force

Parents	Son of William Pilkington and Dorothy Margaret Seale
Enlisted	1936
Died	Killed on air operations, 30 June 1941, Germany
Buried	Becklingen War Cemetery, Soltau, Germany. Grave 12. H. 1.
Commemorated	Portadown War Memorial (WW2-50) Portadown College War Memorial St. Mark's Parish Church War Memorial

William Pilkington Seale was a native of Kilkenny and entered service with the Belfast Bank serving in Portadown, Downpatrick and Tandragee. In 1921 he was appointed manager of the Belfast Bank, Portadown Branch and resided at Belfast Bank House. He was elected President of Portadown Rotary Club in 1941.

He was a member of the Select Vestry of St. Mark's Parish Church and had been churchwarden and honorary treasurer of the parish. William Pilkington was a member of Abercorn Masonic Lodge No. 219, Past King of Abercorn Royal Arch Chapter No. 219 and Past Preceptor of Tandragee High Knights Templar No. 105. He also took a keen interest in golf and was a member of Portadown and Tandragee Golf Clubs. He had five children William, Dorothy, Moira, Theophillis and Dr. W. B. Seale who later practised medicine in Uganda.

William Terence Chambers was the eldest son and was educated at Portadown College where he played rugby for the school. He was a member of the 1st XV team from 1933-35.

He entered the RAF in 1936 and rose rapidly in the service and shortly before the outbreak of war was appointed a flying instructor.

Flight Lieutenant Seale was posted to 7 Squadron of Bomber Command. The squadron was reformed on 1 August 1940 at Leeming with Stirling four engine bombers. He married Betty Forge of Beverley, Yorkshire in November 1940 at Herwell, Berkshire.

In January 1941 William was 'mentioned in despatches' and in March he was promoted to the rank of Squadron Leader.

Squadron Leader Seale was pilot on a Stirling Mark I serial number N6001 MG the other crew members were Sgt. Harold Thorpe Archer, Sgt. Maurice George Brown, Sgt. Laurence Whittle; F/S Bernard William Grocock and F/S Roland Ernest Walls all of the RAF and Sgt. Richard Lyndon Barrett of the RAAF.

The aircraft took off from Oakington at 2257 hours on 29 June 1941 on a bombing mission to Hamburg. When the aircraft was over Germany Helmut Lent Stafflekapitan of 6./NJG1 shot it down. The Stirling crashed at Wesermunde-Bremerhaven with the loss of all seven crewmembers. All are buried in Becklingen War Cemetery.

Helmut Lent was one of the top German night fighter aces with 110 victories and was one of just two awarded the Knights Cross with Oak leaves, Swords and Diamonds. He died on 7 October 1944 from wounds received in action with the Americans.

His brother Theophillis (see entry **WW2-49 Lieutenant Theophillis John Seale**) died on 1 June 1944 in England during the preparations for D-Day.

Henry Howard Maginn
Sergeant (Air Gunner) 637636, 15 Squadron, Royal Air Force

Parents	Son of William and Adelaide Maginn of 43 Ormonde Street, Portadown
Residence	Ormonde Street
Died	Killed on air operations 11 September 1942, England
Age	29
Buried	Seagoe Church of Ireland Churchyard, Portadown
Commemorated	Portadown War Memorial (WW2-41) St. Mark's Parish Church War Memorial

Henry's father William was employed as a bread man. He married Adelaide Walsh, whose family ran a boarding house in Thomas Street, Portadown. The couple had nine children Norman, Henry Howard, Robert, Herbert, Victor, Basil, Annie, Ethel and Martha.

John Gibson and Co. Grocers of Woodhouse Street, Portadown, employed Henry for 11 years. He married Emma Cull of Watson Street, Portadown in 1933 at St. Mark's Parish Church. The couple

had two children, Howard born 1937, and Audrey born 1942.

He was goalkeeper for Gilford Crusaders, Ulster Rangers and All Sports. He was also a former member of Portadown Cycling Club. Henry studied at St. Mark's Bible class and was a member of the White Ribboners temperance movement.

Sergeant Henry Howard Maginn. (Audrey Nolan)

Henry was a member of Dr. Kane's Crimson Star LOL 417, and he had been secretary and lecturer of the lodge for many years. He was also a member of Brackagh RBP 265 and the Apprentice Boys of Derry.

Shortly before the outbreak of World War Two Henry enlisted in the Royal Air Force and was posted to 15 Squadron of Bomber Command. The squadron was reformed on 1 June 1934 at Abingdon with Harts, Wellingtons and then Stirlings.

Sergeant Maginn was a rear gunner on Stirling Mark I serial number BF347 LS-J the other crew members were F/S H. E. Bannister, Sgt H. E. Williams, P/O C. W. Higgins, Sgt. W. E. Pittendrigh, Sgt. N. A. Prime and Sgt. S. Mansfield

The aircraft took off from Bourn at 2105 hours on 10 September 1942 on a bombing mission to Dusseldorf. The raid was successfully completed but as the aircraft attempted an emergency landing at West Malling airfield in Kent at 0255 hours on 11 September it crashed. There were no survivors.

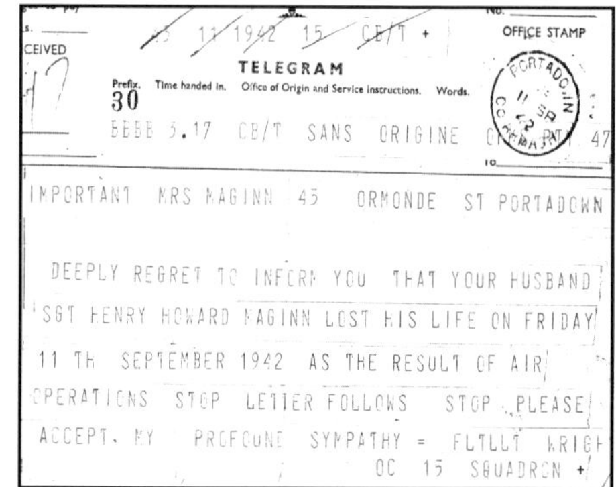

TELEGRAM

OFFICE STAMP

Prefix. 30 Time handed in. Office of Origin and Service Instructions. Words.

BBBB 3.17 CB/T SANS ORIGINE

IMPORTANT MRS MAGINN 45 ORMONDE ST PORTADOWN

DEEPLY REGRET TO INFORM YOU THAT YOUR HUSBAND SGT HENRY HOWARD MAGINN LOST HIS LIFE ON FRIDAY 11 TH SEPTEMBER 1942 AS THE RESULT OF AIR OPERATIONS STOP LETTER FOLLOWS STOP PLEASE ACCEPT MY PROFOUND SYMPATHY = FLTLLT WRIGH[T] OC 15 SQUADRON +

Telegram informing Mrs Maginn of the death of her husband. (Audrey Nolan)

Two of Henry's brothers Norman and Robert served in the Royal Artillery and Royal Army Service Corps and his sister Ethel served in the Auxiliary Territorial Service during World War Two. His father William worked in the munitions industry and his mother, Adelaide, was also employed in the war effort in the NAAFI.

After the war Henry's widow Emma married Leslie Montgomery and they had a son Leslie born in 1948.

Grave of Sergeant Henry Howard Maginn. (Author's Collection)

Valentine Robertson Wilson Sergeant (Navigator) 1389001, 115 Squadron, Royal Air Force (VR)

Parents	Son of Valentine and Nellie Wilson of Oakfield, Ballyworkan
Residence	Ballyworkan
Died	Killed on air operations 11 April 1943, France
Age	28
Buried	Le Thour Communal Cemetery, France. Joint Grave 4-5.
Commemorated	Portadown War Memorial (WW2-62) St. Mark's Parish Church War Memorial

Valentine Robertson's father Valentine was a solicitor by profession. He took a keen interest in the affairs of Portadown and was appointed under sheriff for County Armagh. He served for three years from 1908-11 on Portadown Urban Council. Valentine was closely involved in St Mark's Parish Church and served on the Select Vestry and the General Synod of the Church of Ireland. He was also Deputy Sherrif of County Armagh.

He married Nellie Robertson, daughter of D.W. Robertson of 8

Bedford Terrace, Edinburgh on 12 August 1914 at Darlings Regent Hotel, Edinburgh. They had two sons Valentine Robertson and Ronald McIlroy. Nellie died on 8 July 1927 and Valentine later married Christine Stewart, daughter of Dr. William Stewart J.P. of Alton Place, Portadown. Valentine died on 22 February 1934.

His eldest son Valentine Robertson enlisted in the RAF and was posted to 115 Squadron of Bomber Command. The squadron was reformed on 15 June 1937 at Marham with Hendons and later with Wellington two engine bombers. It was re-equipped with Stirlings in April 1941.

Sergeant Navigator V R Wilson
RAF. VR. (Bomber Command)
Killed in action 10th April 1943

The medals of Sergeant Valentine Robertson Wilson are on display in Portadown Royal British Legion. (Portadown RBL)

Sergeant Wilson was pilot on a Stirling Mark I serial number N6001 MG the other crew members were Sgt. Harold Thorpe Archer, Sgt. Maurice George Brown, Sgt. Laurence Whittle, F/S Bernard William Grocock and F/S Roland Ernest Walls all of the RAF and Sgt. Richard Lyndon Barrett of the RAAF.

The aircraft took off from East Wretham at 0050 hours On 11 April on a bombing mission to Frankfurt. It later crashed at Le Thour in the Ardennes at 0229 hours with the loss of all seven crewmembers. All are buried in Le Thour Communal Cemetery. A total of 23 aircraft failed to return from the raid.

Valentine's younger son Ronald followed in his father's footsteps and became a solicitor being initially employed by Mr. H. Murray Gibson, Portadown and then in his late father's firm of solicitors.

On 15 August 1940 he received a commission from a cadet training college as a Second-Lieutenant in the 1st Battalion, Royal Ulster Rifles. He took part in the airborne assault on D-Day 6 June 1944. He was soon promoted to the rank of Major. Major Wilson was wounded in action during the assault across the River Rhine in March 1945 when his glider was hit by anti-aircraft fire.

After the war he was appointed Crown solicitor for County Armagh and later became chief executive of

Craigavon Development Commission. Major Wilson was also President of the Portadown Branch of the Royal British Legion.

George Joseph Wilson
Sergeant (Wireless Operator/Air Gunner) 1383005, 460 (RAAF) Squadron, Royal Air Force (VR)

Parents	Son of Spear and Catherine Caroline Wilson of 34 Portmore Street Portadown
Residence	Portmore Street
Died	Killed on air operations 16 April 1943, Germany
Age	23
Buried	Durnbach War Cemetery, Bayern, Germany. Grave 7. C. 3.
Commemorated	Portadown War Memorial (WW2-60)

George's father Spear was born in Belfast and joined the Royal Ulster Constabulary on its formation. He served in Portadown and Armagh and settled in Portadown. He married Catherine Caroline McIlvenna and they had six children Jack, George, Agnes, Carol, Spiers and Sheila.

George joined the Metropolitan Police when he was 18 years old and served during the Blitz of 1940-41. He enlisted in the Royal Air Force and qualified as a Wireless Operator on 2 September 1942. The next day L.A.C Wilson was sent to No. 8 Air Gunnery School at Evanton for four weeks intensive training as an Air Gunner, qualifying on 3 October 1942.

He spent the next few months, from November 1942 until February 1943, at 28 Operational Training Unit undertaking numerous training flights known as circuits and landings. It also involved cross country flying, practice bombing runs all in Wellington two engine bombers and various lectures and courses on gunnery, photography and escape and evasion techniques.

In March 1943 Sergeant Wilson was posted to 1656 Conversion Unit at Lindholme where the crews were trained on Halifax and Lancaster four engine bombers. By this time Sergeant Wilson had clocked up 86 hours daytime flying hours and 46 night time flying hours.

On 6 April 1943 Sergeant Wilson was posted to 460 (Royal Australian Air Force) Squadron of Bomber Command. The squadron was formed on 15 November 1941 at Molesworth and was originally equipped with Wellingtons before converting to Halifaxes and then Lancasters.

He was one of a crew of seven in a Lancaster Mark I serial number W4331 UV-R. The other crewmembers were F/S Ian Gordon Miller, Sgt Norman Percy Richmond, Sgt. Maurice Capon, Sgt. Ronald Alfred Hall, Sgt. Ronald Francis Beaumont and Sgt. Duncan Curtis. This crew had taken part in three previous bombing missions to Duisburg on 9/10 April, Frankfurt on 10/11 April and Stuttgart on 14/15 April.

The aircraft took off from Breighton at 2106 hours on 16 June 1943 on a bombing mission to the Skoda Armament Works at Pilsen.

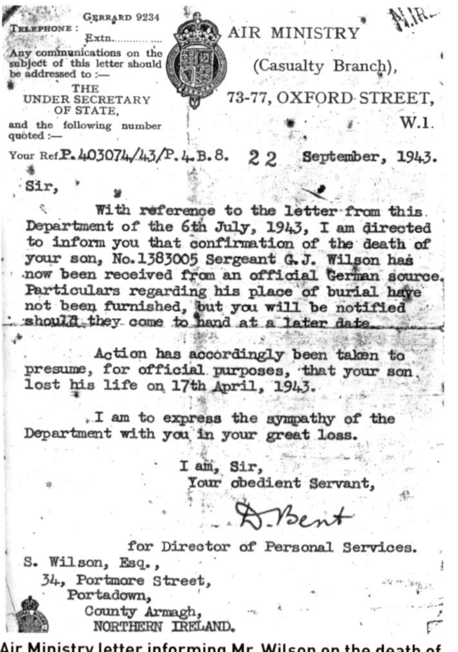

TELEPHONE: GERRARD 9234
Extn.............

Any communications on the subject of this letter should be addressed to:—
THE UNDER SECRETARY OF STATE,
and the following number quoted:—

AIR MINISTRY
(Casualty Branch),
73-77, OXFORD STREET,
W.1.

Your Ref. P.403074/43/P.4.B.8. 22 September, 1943.

Sir,

With reference to the letter from this Department of the 6th July, 1943, I am directed to inform you that confirmation of the death of your son, No.1383005 Sergeant G.J. Wilson has now been received from an official German source. Particulars regarding his place of burial have not been furnished, but you will be notified should they come to hand at a later date.

Action has accordingly been taken to presume, for official purposes, that your son lost his life on 17th April, 1943.

I am to express the sympathy of the Department with you in your great loss.

I am, Sir,
Your obedient Servant,

D. Bent

for Director of Personal Services.

S. Wilson, Esq.,
34, Portmore Street,
Portadown,
County Armagh,
NORTHERN IRELAND.

Air Ministry letter informing Mr. Wilson on the death of his son Sergeant George Joseph Wilson. (Spiers Wilson)

The aircraft crashed into a lake at Ludwigshafen-Oggersheim with the loss of all of the crew. The crew were buried locally and after the war were reinterred in Durnbach War Cemetery. A total of 36 aircraft failed to return from the raid.

In 1999 the local angling club drained the lake in order to dredge out the silt and discovered some wreckage including part of an aero engine and undercarriage from Sergeant Wilson's Lancaster W4331 UV-R, which had crashed into the lake on 17 June 1943.

George's brother Jack, a carpenter, enlisted in the Royal Air Force in 1936 and served as a Flight Sergeant. He served in Egypt, Palestine, Iraq and North Africa and was wounded in action when dropping supplies over Italy. After the war he joined the Ulster Special Constabulary and then served in the Ulster Defence Regiment.

His sisters Agnes and Carol helped the war effort by serving in the NAAFI. His brother Spiers followed his father into the Royal Ulster Constabulary in which he served for 33 years. In 1995 he was awarded an M.B.E.

There is a Sgt. J. Wilson RAF commemorated on St. Mark's Parish Church War Memorial but it is unclear if this refers to Sergeant George Joseph Wilson or Sergeant Samuel James Wilson.

Spiers Wilson at the grave of his brother Sergeant George Joseph Wilson. (Spiers Wilson)

Norman Nicholas England
Sergeant
(Wireless Operator/Air Gunner)
1130657,
44 (Rhodesia) Squadron,
Royal Air Force (VR)

Parents	Son of William Henry and Evelyn England of 181 West Street, Portadown
Residence	West Street
Died	Lost on air operations 22 June 1943, Germany
Age	24
Buried	No Known Grave
Commemorated	Runnymede Memorial, Panel 148. Portadown War Memorial (WW2-16) St. Mark's Parish Church War Memorial

Nicholas was posted to 44 (Rhodesia) Squadron of Bomber Command. He was one of a crew of seven in a Lancaster Mark I serial number W4331 UV-R. The other crewmembers were P/O Hugh Conn Thompson from Carnalea, Co. Down, P/O L. S. Welsh, Sgt. Louis Renton McGrath from Belfast, Sgt. S. D. Mindel, Sgt. L. A. Harrison, Sgt. N. Metcalfe and Sgt. J. H. Arlow.

The aircraft took off from Dunholme Lodge at 2350 hours on 21 June 1943 on a bombing mission to Krefeld. The town had a population of 170,000 and was a major production centre for high-grade steel used for aircraft engines and the armaments industry. Nothing more was heard from the aircraft and it was deemed lost without trace on 22 June 1943. All seven crew members are commemorated on the Runnymede Memorial.

Of 705 aircraft dispatched 561 bombed the town causing a major reduction in industrial output. A total of 36 aircraft failed to return from the raid.

Sergt. England joined the R. A. F. about 3 years ago, and his many operational flights embraced targets in Italy and Czechoslovakia, as well as in Germany. He was formerly employed in Canavan's Pharmacy, and before that with Mr. W. J. Anderson.

Portadown News
3 July 1943

David Gillis
Sergeant (Air Gunner) 1025077,
90 Squadron,
Royal Air Force (VR)

Parents	Son of J. Gillis of 31 Victoria Terrace, Portadown
Residence	Victoria Terrace
Died	Killed on air operations 22 June 1943, Germany
Age	24
Buried	Bergen General Cemetery, Netherlands. Grave 2. D. 19.
Commemorated	Portadown War Memorial (WW2-18) Thomas Street Methodist Church War Memorial

David was educated at Thomas Street Public Elementary School and Portadown Technical School. He was a Sergeant in 1st Portadown Company, Boys' Brigade and played football for Parkmount Football Club. Messrs. Hamilton Robb Ltd employed David. He was a member of Parkmount LOL 127.

David was trained in Canada under the Empire Air Training Scheme and met his wife there. His wife and baby daughter, whom he never saw, resided at Monkton, New Brunswick. On his return to England Sergeant Gillis was posted to 90 Squadron of Bomber Command.

Sergeant Gillis was one of a crew of seven in a Stirling Mark III serial number EE887 WP-T. The other crewmembers were P/O H. N. Peters RAAF, Sgt. E. Bradshaw, Sgt. D. J. Davies, Sgt. B. A. Abraham, Sgt. A. S. Andrews and Sgt. R. R. Law RCAF.

The aircraft took off from West Wickham at 2346 hours on 21 June 1943 on a bombing mission to Krefeld. The aircraft was shot down by a night fighter in the early hours of 22 June and crashed at Hoogwoud, North Holland with the loss of all of the crew. All are buried in Bergen General Cemetery.

Ernest Bramwell Blair
Sergeant 1796405, 578 Squadron, Royal Air Force (VR)

Parents Son of John and Martha Blair
Died Lost on air operations 15 February 1944, Germany
Buried No Known Grave
Commemorated
Runnymede Memorial, Surrey, England. Panel 225. Portadown War Memorial (WW2-4)

Ernest's father John died on 13 April 1938.

Ernest was posted to 578 Squadron of Bomber Command. He was one of a crew of seven in a Halifax Mark III serial number LW557 LK-Q. The other crew members were W/O J. B. Morgan RAAF, F/O L. J. Linbridge, F/O J. K. Kerr RCAF, Sgt. F. W. Hayman, Sgt. M. K. Piper and Sgt. W. J. Leiper RAAF.

The aircraft took off from Burn at 1749 hours on 15 February 1944 on a bombing mission to Berlin. The aircraft crashed due to engine failure near Tribohm, four miles NNE of Marlow with the loss of three of the crew.

W/O Morgan RAAF was buried in the War Cemetery in Berlin and, Sergeant Blair and Sergeant Piper are commemorated on the Runnymede Memorial. The other four crewmembers became prisoners of war.

Family grave of Sergeant Ernest Bramwell Blair. (Author's Collection)

Samuel Joseph Clayton
Sergeant (Wireless Operator/Air Gunner) 1545659, 218 Squadron, Royal Air Force (VR)

Born 1920, Portadown
Parents Son of William and Elizabeth Clayton of 2 Eden Avenue, Portadown
Residence Eden Avenue
Died Killed on air operations 2 May 1944, France
Age 24

Buried Poix de Picardie Churchyard, Somme, France. Grave A. 11.

Commemorated Portadown War Memorial (WW2-8)

William was employed as a bus driver and he and his wife Elizabeth had six children Samuel Joseph, Winifred, May, Billy, Margaret and Isaac, who died in infancy. The family worshipped at Edenderry Memorial Methodist Church.

Samuel was educated at Edenderry Primary School and Portadown Technical School. He was employed in a number of local firms after leaving school. Samuel was keenly interested in the Royal Air Force and achieved his boyhood dream when he was accepted for aircrew training. He was posted to 218 Squadron of Bomber Command.

He was one of a crew of eight in a Stirling Mark III serial number EF259 HA-G. The other crewmembers were F/O N. S. Eliot RAAF, F/O E. G. Hawkins, F/S G. A. Hassett, F/S K. J. Lynch RAAF, Sgt. H. F. Wilson, (attached from Training Command), Sgt. C. F. Weir and Sgt. J. R. Grantham.

The aircraft took off from Woolfox Lodge at 2217 hours on 1 May 1944 on a bombing mission to destroy the railway and stores depot at Chambly, France. The operation was part of a concerted Allied plan to disrupt German communications in the run up to the Normandy invasion.

Sergeant Samuel Joseph Clayton. (Sam Preston)

The aircraft came down at La Houssaye near Auneuil in the early hours of 2 May with the loss of four of the crew - F/O Hawkins, F/S Hassett, Sgt. Clayton and Sgt. Grantham. All are buried in Poix de Picardie Churchyard. The four surviving crewmembers all evaded capture.

Normandy (1944)

The D-Day landings on 6 June 1944 were the largest amphibious assault in history. Five Divisions, two US, two British and one Canadian landed on five beaches at Normandy - Utah, Omaha, Gold, Sword and Juno. In addition three airborne divisions were dropped to protect the flanks of the beachhead from enemy counter-attacks. By the end of the first day 130,000 troops had been landed and the Allies had gained a foothold on mainland Europe.

Over the next few weeks intense and bitter fighting took place as the Allies began preparations for their breakout from the beachhead. The focal point of the fighting was in and around the town of Caen, which was in the British and Canadian sector. They faced the bulk of the German forces in France including the 2nd SS Panzer, 9th SS Panzer, 10th SS Panzer, 12th SS Panzer, 21st Panzer and Panzer Lehr Divisions as well as independent tank units equipped with the feared Tiger tank.

Howard Lutton
Lance-Corporal 7013186, 1st (Army Air Corps) Special Air Service Regiment

Parents: Son of Charles Lutton of Margaret Street, Portadown
Enlisted: 1937
Died: Died of wounds 6 July 1944, France
Buried: Clichy Northern Cemetery, Hauts de Seine, France. Grave 16. 16. 14.
Commemorated: Portadown War Memorial (WW2-31)

Howard's father Charles served with the Royal Irish Fusiliers during the Great War. After the end of the war he, together with his daughter, Minnie, emigrated to Canada. She married and settled in St. Catherine's, Ontario while her father returned to Portadown. In addition to Minnie Charles had six sons William, George, Andy, Ronnie, Wesley and Howard and a daughter, Frances. Wesley became a Methodist minister.

The Lutton brothers gave years of military service for King and country. William enlisted in the Royal Ulster Rifles in 1930 and served for nearly 40 years both as a regular and later as a Territorial soldier. He saw service in Egypt, Palestine, Hong Kong, India where he took part in actions against the Pathan tribesmen on the North West Frontier. One of the family's most treasured possessions was a photograph, taken in the deserts of North Africa, of William standing

beside General Bernard Law Montgomery. He was awarded an M.B.E.

George enlisted in the Royal Artillery and saw service in France in 1940 and was evacuated from Dunkirk.

Andy enlisted in the Royal Ulster Rifles in 1943. He saw active service in Italy, France and Austria.

Howard enlisted in the Royal Ulster Rifles in 1937 and later transferred to the SAS. He was very proud of the fact that he served alongside fellow Ulsterman Lieutenant-Colonel Blair 'Paddy' Mayne, co-founder and legend of the Special Air Service Regiment.

Lance-Corporal Howard Lutton. (Andy Lutton)

Their role was to disrupt German communications and supply lines and generally to cause havoc behind enemy lines.

At 2334 on 4 July 1944 a Stirling, with 12 members of 'D' Squadron, SAS onboard, took off from Keevil in Wiltshire on an operation behind enemy lines. The 12 soldiers parachuted into a clearing in the Forest of Fontainebleau, where they were to be greeted by the local French Resistance. However, the operation was betrayed when the Gestapo arrested, interrogated and then shot one of the Maquisards who gave details of the drop. Instead of being greeted by members of the Resistance the group was met with a hail of gunfire from the Gestapo and SS lying in wait.

Four of the soldiers Captain Garstin, Lieutenant Weihe, Lance-Corporal Lutton and Trooper Barker, from Cookstown, were wounded and were taken to La Pitie Hospital in Paris. Lance-Corporal Lutton died of his wounds two days later. Five members of the group, Corporals Ginger Jones, Serge Vaculik and troopers Varey, Billy Young, from Randalstown and Joe Walker, from Moira, were captured and subjected to interrogation and torture. Three of the SAS soldiers, Troopers Morrison, Norman and Castellow, managed to escape and return to Allied lines.

Andy Lutton at the grave of his brother Lance-Corporal Howard Lutton. (Andy Lutton)

On 8 August 1944, after a month in captivity, seven of the prisoners were told that they were to be exchanged with German agents in Switzerland. They were informed that they would have to travel in civilian clothes. In the early hours of 9 August as the lorry and escort approached a wood at Beauvais near Noailles the men were ordered out and were told they were going to be shot. The prisoners made a bolt for freedom, with Corporals Jones and Vaculik, managing to make good their escape in the confusion. Captain Garstin and Troopers Barker, Walker, Varey and Young were shot and killed by the Gestapo.

John William Johnson Lance-Corporal 4915099, 7th Battalion, South Staffordshire Regiment

Died — Killed in action 8 July 1944, Normandy, France

Buried — Cambes en Plaine War Cemetery, Calvados, France. Grave B. 5.

Commemorated — Portadown War Memorial (WW2-26)

The 7th Battalion, South Staffordshire Regiment arrived in Normandy on 25 June 1944. It formed part of the 176th Brigade of the 59th (Staffordshire) Division during the Normandy campaign.

On 8 July three divisions, including the 59th, launched an attack, codenamed Operation Charnwood, on the city of Caen. After heavy fighting the Germans withdrew across the River Orne and the British and Canadians entered the city the next day.

Herbert Stewart Topley
Private 14421449,
8th Battalion, Royal Scots

Residence	Union Street
Died	Killed in action 16 July 1944, Normandy, France
Age	19
Buried	Banneville La Campagne War Cemetery, Calvados, France. Grave XII. B. 17.
Commemorated	Portadown War Memorial (WW2-56) Thomas Street Methodist Church War Memorial

Herbert was an only son and his mother resided at 1 Union Street, Portadown. He was employed at Tavanagh factory before he enlisted.

He joined the army along with his best friend Billy Thompson. The two friends underwent their basic training together at Ballymena. On completion Herbert was posted to the Royal Scots and Billy was posted to the London Irish serving in North Africa, Sicily and Italy.

The 8th Battalion, Royal Scots formed part of the 44th (Lowland) Brigade of the 15th (Scottish) Division during the Normandy campaign.

Henry Thompson at the grave of Private Herbert Stewart Topley. (Henry Thompson)

Ernest Smith
Private 69837, 6th Battalion, King's Own Scottish Borderers

Born	October 1922
Parents	Son of Robert and Martha Smith of 59 Montague Street, Portadown
Residence	Montague Street
Enlisted	August 1940
Died	Killed in action 9 August 1944, Normandy, France
Age	22
Buried	Bayeux War Cemetery, France. Grave 20. B.15.
Commemorated	Portadown War Memorial (WW2-52) St. Mark's Parish Church War Memorial

Ernest's father Robert was originally from Tartaraghan and was wounded whilst serving in the Royal Field Artillery during the Great War. He married Martha Forde, her brother Samuel James Forde, was killed on 22 February 1916 whilst serving with the 9th Battalion, Royal Irish Fusiliers. The couple had eight children.

During World War Two Robert served in the Dockside Police at Rosyth and in London where he was wounded during the Blitz. His daughter Gertrude, aged three, died as a result of a traffic accident near her home in Montague Street on 12 October 1942.

Private Ernest Smith. (Sammy Smith)

Ernest was educated at Tartaraghan School and enlisted in August 1940 in the Royal Inniskilling Fusiliers and was transferred to the Royal Irish Fusiliers. Later he was posted to the 6th Battalion, King's Own Scottish Borderers, which formed part of the 44th (Lowland) Brigade of the 15th (Scottish) Division during the Normandy campaign.

During the breakout of the Normandy beachhead the 6th Battalion, King's Own Scottish

Borderers was engaged in heavy fighting in the Caen area. From 8-10 August 1944 the battalion, together with the 6th Battalion, Royal Scots Fusiliers and tanks from the 4th Battalion, Grenadier Guards was involved in fierce fighting for the village of Estry 25 miles south west of Caen.

William Henry Wolsey
Lance-Corporal 7047419, 11th Battalion, Royal Scots Fusiliers

Parents	Son of William Henry and Elsie Wolsey of Carleton House, Portadown
Residence	Carleton House
Died	Killed in action 9 August 1944, Normandy, France
Age	21
Buried	Ranville War Cemetery, Calvados, France. Grave III. B. 1.
Commemorated	Portadown War Memorial (WW2-63) Portadown College War Memorial Royal Scots Fusiliers War Memorial, Edinburgh Castle St. Mark's Parish Church War Memorial

William's father W. H. Wolsey was proprietor and editor of the Portadown Times and a former Mayor of the Borough of Portadown.

Private William Henry Wolsey. (Brian Courtney)

William was educated at Portadown College where he excelled at sport being a member of the school rugby XV and cricket XI. William went on to play cricket for Portadown Cricket Club; his father and members of staff of the Portadown Times revived the club in the 1930s. Before leaving to join the army in 1941 William received presentations from his cricket team colleagues at a dinner held in a local café.

His brother George was on the reporting staff of the Belfast Newsletter and later held an important position with the BBC in London in their broadcasting news department. The Portadown News employed his sister Mollie and she later worked for the Inland Revenue.

Thomas Henry England
Lance-Sergeant 2718941,
3rd Battalion, Irish Guards

Parents	Son of John and Sarah England of Baltylum
Residence	Baltylum
Died	Killed in action 11 August 1944, Normandy, France
Age	24
Buried	St. Charles De Percy War Cemetery, Calvados, France. Grave III. D. 9.
Commemorated	Portadown War Memorial (WW2-17) St. Mark's Parish Church War Memorial

Thomas Henry, known as Harry, was a member of Corcrain Flute Band.

Guards Memorial, Horse Guards, London. (Author's Collection)

He served in the Norwegian campaign of 1940. His brother Samuel served in the Royal Artillery during World War Two.

The 3rd Battalion, Irish Guards formed part of the 32nd Infantry Brigade (Guards) attached to the Guards Armoured Division during the Normandy campaign.

Charles Joseph McVeigh
Sergeant 7013567, 2nd Battalion, Royal Ulster Rifles

Residence	Woodhouse Street
Died	Killed in action 12 August 1944, Normandy, France
Age	27
Buried	St. Charles De Percy War Cemetery, Calvados, France. Grave VI. C. 4.
Commemorated	Portadown War Memorial (WW2-40)

Charles was married and his wife resided in Larne. He took an interest in the sporting life of the community in Portadown.

Sergeant McVeigh served in Palestine before the war and took part in the French campaign of 1940 being evacuated from Dunkirk.

The 2nd Battalion, Royal Ulster Rifles formed part of the 9th Infantry Brigade attached to the 3rd Infantry Division during the Normandy campaign.

Arnhem (1944)

The airborne assault began on 17 September 1944 with a huge airborne operation involving 2,000 aircraft and gliders. Two German SS divisions, the 9th and 10th SS Panzer, were in the area to re-equip and regroup. The lightly armed airborne troops were ill equipped to face tanks and armoured vehicles and suffered heavy casualties. A small group fought their way to the road bridge at Arnhem but without artillery and armoured support were unable to hold their objective. The troops withdrew across the River Rhine on the night of 25 September after eight days of bitter fighting.

Of over 10,500 airborne troops of the 1st Airborne 1,500 were killed or died of wounds and 6,500 became prisoners of war. 2,400 made it back across the river to the Allied lines.

Ernest Lynas
Lance-Corporal 7043594, 156th Battalion, (Army Air Corps) Parachute Regt.

Residence	Hopefield Terrace
Died	Killed in action 25 September 1944, Arnhem, Netherlands
Age	26

Buried Arnhem Oosterbeek War Cemetery, Netherlands. Grave 28. B. 2.

Commemorated Portadown War Memorial (WW2-32)

Ernest was the husband of Violet Lynas and they resided at 14 Hopefield Terrace, Portadown.

The 156th Battalion took off from Saltby aerodrome on 18 September on their way to reinforce the landings at Oosterbeek situated to the west of Arnhem.

Lance-Corporal Ernest Lynas. (Portadown Times)

Of the 625 men of the 156th Battalion who landed at Arnhem almost 100 were killed or died of wounds, with 450 being posted as missing - many of whom became PoWs. A total of 68 men made it back across the River Rhine on the night of 25/26 September.

Ernest's widow Violet emigrated to Canada after the end of World War Two but returned shortly afterwards to Northern Ireland. She married Thomas Thompson from Lurgan and the couple had two daughters Janet and Heather.

Ernest had a brother Tom who also served during World War Two.

Germany (1944-45)

By October 1944 the Germans had managed to regroup behind the defences of the Siegfried Line after their defeat and subsequent retreat from France.

On 16 December came the 'Battle of the Bulge' the last ditch German offensive through the lightly defended Ardennes region of Belgium and Luxembourg. Initially the Allies were taken completely by surprise and the Germans made small gains, which formed a small bulge in the Allied lines hence the name given to the battle.

On 23/24 March 1945 the British, Canadian and American forces crossed the River Rhine in a combined airborne and amphibious assault supported by artillery and aircraft. The British and Canadians advanced through Holland and into northern Germany, the Americans advanced through central and southern Germany. Meanwhile the Russian Red Army advanced on Berlin where Hitler committed suicide on 30 April 1945.

On 4 May the German forces surrendered to Field Marshal Bernard Law Montgomery at Luneberg Heath followed a few days later by the unconditional surrender of all German forces.

George Robinson
Lance-Corporal 884882,
2nd (Army Air Corps) Special Air Service Regiment

Died: Killed in action 16 October 1944, Germany
Age: 24
Buried: Durnbach War Cemetery, Bayern, Germany. Grave 3. K. 3.
Commemorated: Portadown War Memorial (WW2-47) St. Mark's Parish Church War Memorial

Ian John Jamieson Picken
Lieutenant 162941, 10th Batt., Highland Light Infantry (City of Glasgow Regt.)

Parents: Son of James and Edith Picken of 43 Church Street, Portadown
Residence: Church Street
Died: Killed in action 24 March 1945, Germany
Age: 30
Buried: Reichswald Forest War Cemetery, Germany. Grave 58. B. 11.
Commemorated: Portadown War Memorial (WW2-45)

Ian's parents had three children. His father James died on 5 May 1933 when the family resided at 153 Raeberry Street, Glasgow and he was buried in Cathcart Cemetery.

Messrs. R. Corbett and Sons Ltd. employed Ian before the war. He was a member of Portadown Rugby Club.

He served with the Royal Artillery in the French campaign of 1940 and was evacuated from Dunkirk. In 1941 Ian obtained a commission in the Sherwood Foresters and later served with the Durham Light Infantry.

The 10th Battalion, Highland Light Infantry formed part of the 227 Infantry Brigade of the 15th (Scottish) Division during the advance into Germany.

George McCann
Private 14429060,
7/9th Battalion, Royal Scots
(The Royal Regiment)

Born	1 May 1926, Portadown
Parents	Son of James and Minnie McCann of 1 Florence Court, Portadown
Residence	Florence Court
Enlisted	14 April 1943, Omagh
Died	Killed in action 17 April 1945, Germany
Age	18
Buried	Becklingen War Cemetery, Germany. Grave 15. B. 14.
Commemorated	Portadown War Memorial (WW2-37) Seagoe Parish Church War Memorial

George's father James served as a Sergeant in the Royal Artillery during the Great War and rejoined the colours in 1939. He and his wife Minnie McCann had twelve children - Mary Jane born 1921, James born 1922, Thomas born 1924, George born 1926, Eunice born 1928, Harold born 1931, Doris born 1933, Cyril born 1935, Henry born 1937, Thelma born 1940, Ronald born 1943 and Vera born 1947.

George enlisted on 14 April 1943 at Omagh. On enlistment his particulars were given as follows: occupation - barman, height - 5'5 3/4", weight 12 stones, complexion - fresh, eyes - blue, hair - brown. George gave his date of birth as 1 May 1925, which would have made him almost 18 years old on enlistment. In actual fact his date of birth was 1 May 1926 which meant that he was two weeks short of his 17th birthday and therefore under age.

Although George enlisted for general service he indicated that, if possible, he would prefer to serve with the Royal Inniskilling Fusiliers and after basic training joined that regiment on 16 May 1943. On 18 August 1943 Fusilier McCann was transferred to the Royal Scots. He was on Home Service with that regiment until being posted to North West Europe on 8 January 1945.

The 7/9th Battalion, Royal Scots formed part of the 155 Infantry Brigade of the 52nd (Lowland) Division during the advance into

Germany. Private McCann was killed in action in the town of Soltau on 17 April 1945. His father James received a letter from Lt.-Col. J.G. Dawson 7/9 Royal Scots

May I, on behalf of all ranks of the Battalion, offer you our most heartfelt sympathy on the death in action of your son. He was killed on the evening of 17th April during an action at Soltau in Germany. His platoon had entered a German barracks and had quickly captured about 40 prisoners. They had begun searching them when a German from a far building fired a Panzer Faust, which exploded and killed your son and another man in his platoon, and wounded the platoon's commander. At the same time it killed three Germans and wounded two others. Your boy's death was instantaneous and I'm sure you would want to know that he did not suffer.

Again with all our very deepest sympathy to you and yours.

Yours Very Sincerely
J.G. Dawson, Lt.-Col. O/C
7/9 Royal Scots
Letter to James McCann
30 April 1945

A few weeks before his nineteenth birthday Private George McCann, The Royal Scots Regiment, of 1 Florence Court, Portadown, has been Killed in Action in Germany. He enlisted about two years ago in the Royal Inniskilling Fusiliers and was sent to the Continent shortly before Christmas (sic). His father, Sergt. James McCann, Royal Artillery, fought in the last war and rejoined the Colours in 1939. A brother of the deceased is Able Seaman James McCann, Junior, of the Royal Navy.

Portadown News
5 May 1945

Private George McCann. (Author's Collection)

George's brother, James, known as Patsy, served in the Royal Navy during World War Two. He joined the navy aged 20 and served as a stoker on HMS *Paisley*, taking part in a number of Russian convoys. Towards the end of the war he served in the Far East.

George's uncle Henry (see entry **WW2-27 Signalman Henry Kane**) was lost at sea on 21 June 1940

while serving on board HMS *Cape Howe.*

George's brother-in-law William (see entry **WW2-5 Leading Aircraftman William Bleeks**) was accidentally killed on 20 June 1942 in England while serving with the Royal Air Force.

The War Against the Empire of Japan (1941-45)

In the Far East the Japanese were engaged on a similar course of territorial expansion in China, Korea and the Pacific. On 7 December 1941 in an audacious airborne strike they attacked and destroyed much of the United States Pacific Fleet based at Pearl Harbour, Hawaii.

The Far Eastern campaign was marked by early Japanese victories. They quickly occupied Hong Kong, Malaya, Singapore, Borneo, the Netherlands East Indies, Thailand, Burma, the Philippine Islands and a host of small Pacific islands.

The Battle of Midway 3-6 June 1942 turned the tide of Japanese expansion and from this date onwards the Allies began to retake the Japanese held islands. It was a grim, brutal and merciless campaign, which was to have culminated with the invasion of the Japanese home islands in November 1945. In the event the invasion never materialised.

On 6 August 1945 the first atomic bomb was dropped on Hiroshima followed three days later with the attack on Nagasaki. On 15 August 1945 Emperor Hirohito broadcast the surrender of the Empire of Japan, which was signed on board the USS *Missouri* on 2 September.

Hong Kong (1941-42)

The Japanese invaded Hong Kong, British since 1841, on 8 December 1941. It took the invaders a week to secure Kowloon and the New Territories before they launched the final assault on the island of Hong Kong itself on 18 December, which fell on 25 December.

The defence of Hong Kong cost the lives of 1500 British and Commonwealth service personnel. The rest were made prisoners of war and almost 3,000 of these PoWs were to die from starvation, torture and inhuman treatment by their captors.

Samuel John Boyce Lance-Bombardier 1063039, 965 Defence Battery, Royal Artillery

Parents	Son of Isaiah Boyce of Bridge Street, Portadown
Residence	Bridge Street

Died	Lost at Sea 1 October 1942, *Lisbon Maru*, East China Sea
Age	40
Buried	No Known Grave
Commemorated	Sai Wan Memorial, Hong Kong, Column 3. Portadown War Memorial (WW2-6)

Samuel Boyce was attached to the 965 Defence Battery, Royal Artillery that was made up of 150 officers and men commanded by Major Basil Forrester. The Battery had a beach defence role with armament as follows 1 x 6" and 2 x 4.7" guns at Belcher's Battery sited to the west of the island and 6 x 18 pounder and 4 x 2 pounder guns sited around the Hong Kong coast at Braemer, Stanley View, Wanchai and Taikoo. These guns were systematically put out of action from 19-25 December 1941.

After the surrender Lance-Bombardier Boyce was made a prisoner of war. On 25 September 1942 1816 British and Commonwealth PoWs were crammed into the three holds of the Japanese transport ship *Lisbon Maru*. Royal Artillery personnel were allocated to hold No. 3. Also on board were Japanese troops returning to their homeland including a number of injured soldiers. The 7,000 ton ship was armed with 2 x 4" guns and had no markings to indicate that she was carrying PoWs. She sailed on 27 September for Japan.

At 4.00am on 1 October 1942 in the East China Sea south of Shanghai she was torpedoed by the United States submarine USS *Grouper* under the command of Lt/Cdr. Clarence Duke. He had no idea that the ship was carrying Allied PoWs. After the explosion the Japanese interpreter, Nimori, had the hatches battened down. The Senior British Officer, Lieutenant-Colonel Stewart, appealed to Nimori to open the hatches and allow the prisoners some water, he responded by having a bucket of urine passed into the hold.

During the night the Japanese troops were taken off by other transports but as the prisoners tried to come up on deck they were fired upon. Early in the morning of 2 October the *Lisbon Maru* began to sink with the Japanese still shooting at the prisoners as they tried to abandon ship. Japanese ships rescued some PoWs, others were taken onboard Chinese junks and some swam to nearby islands. Altogether 840 British and Commonwealth PoWs were lost in

the *Lisbon Maru.*

After the war Nimori was convicted of eight war crimes and sentenced to 15 years imprisonment.

News has reached Portadown of the death by enemy action in Far Eastern waters in October 1942, of L./Bdr. Samuel John Boyce, son of the late Mr. and Mrs. Isaiah Boyce, Bridge Street, Portadown. It is known that he was captured in Hong Kong and was on a Jap prison ship.

Portadown News
7 October 1944

Samuel had two sisters Mrs. David McMullen, 95 Bridge Street and Mrs. Charles Hegan, 40 Union Street, Portadown.

Singapore (1942)

It took the Japanese just two months to fight their way through the Malayan jungle to the Straits of Singapore. On 8/9 February 1942 they launched their final assault on the island. A week later in the biggest defeat in the history of the British armed forces General Percival surrendered 90,000 British, Australian, Indian and local troops. Many of these men were to die from starvation, ill treatment and disease in Japanese PoW camps and on the Burma railway. Approximately 7,500 British and Commonwealth troops lost their lives in the battles for Malaya and Singapore.

Singapore Memorial. (Norman Harrison)

Robert James Ludlow
Sergeant 1064310, 9th Coastal Regiment, Royal Artillery

Born	Portadown
Parents	Son of James and Elizabeth Ludlow
Residence	Henry Street
Died	Killed in action 13 February 1942, Singapore
Age	34
Buried	No Known Grave
Commemorated	Singapore Memorial, Column 5. Portadown War Memorial (WW2-30) St. Mark's Parish Church War Memorial

Robert's mother Elizabeth resided at 35 Henry Street, Portadown. He was the husband of Gladys Georgina Ludlow and they resided at 25 Milton Road, Exeter.

Sergeant Ludlow had 17 years service in the army. He was attached to the 9th Coastal Regiment, Royal Artillery that operated a number of batteries around the coast of Singapore. The main batteries were Johore with 3 x 15" guns, Beting Kusa 2 x 6", Tekong Besar 3 x 9.2", Sphink 2 x 6", Pengerang 2 x 6" and Chani 2 x 6". In addition there were smaller gun batteries with 6 and 12 pounder guns.

The regiment received orders on 29 November 1941 to man all the gun batteries. Just over a week later the Japanese landed at Kota Bahru on the eastern coast of Malaya and began the advance down the Malay peninsular, which took them to within sight of Singapore island at the beginning of February 1942.

On 5 February three batteries, Johore, Tekon Besar and Sphinx opened up on the Japanese for the first time and from this date until 12 February the batteries kept up an intermittent fire on the enemy. Targets included troop concentrations, tanks, a Japanese railway gun and enemy artillery positions.

On 9 February the Japanese launched their attack on Singapore Island with the batteries of 9th Coastal Regiment bombarding their positions. At 1300hours on 12 February Johore and Changi batteries were ordered to expend all their ammunition and all the defences in Changi Fire Command - forts, guns and magazines were wired for demolition, which was carried out at 2045 hours.

The next day, 13 February, all personnel were assembled on Balestier Recreation Ground to be formed into four infantry companies. It was on this date that

Sergeant Robert James Ludlow was killed in action. It is not clear if he was part of these infantry units or was based at another gun battery.

Robert's sister served in the Auxiliary Territorial Service during World War Two.

Irene Wright
Sister 209440,
Queen Alexandra's Imperial Military Nursing Service

Parents	Daughter of Eliza Jane and Albert Ernest Wright of Park Road, Portadown
Residence	Park Road
Died	Lost at sea 14 February 1942, SS *Kuala*, Pompong Island, Singapore
Age	29
Buried	No Known Grave
Commemorated	Singapore Memorial, Column 114. Portadown War Memorial (WW2-64) St. Mark's Parish Church War Memorial

Irene's father Albert Ernest served during the Great War and was employed in the family baking business situated at West Street, Portadown.

Irene was educated at Portadown Technical College, and played hockey for the school team. She chose nursing as her vocation and underwent training at Aintree, Liverpool. After the outbreak of war she volunteered for service in Queen Alexandra's Imperial Military Nursing Service.

Her cousin Eva also trained as a nurse and was stationed at a hospital at Croydon, Surrey during the Battle of Britain and the Blitz. Irene's brother, William, was a draughtsman at Harland and Wolff, Belfast before emigrating to Canada.

Edith Harrison locates the name of Sister Irene Wright on the Singapore Memorial. (Norman Harrison)

Before she took up her final posting Irene paid a last visit to her cousin, Eva, but was unable, for security reasons, to tell her where she was going. It was Singapore.

The Japanese landed at Kotu Bahru on 8 December 1941 and began their rapid advance, which took them to within sight of Singapore Island on 1 February 1942. As surrender looked inevitable preparations got underway to evacuate non-combatant women, children and civilian officials. Numerous ships and boats left from Singapore in a 'Dunkirk' style evacuation in the dying days of the fighting.

Sister Irene Wright was embarked on the *Kuala* an auxiliary anti submarine vessel built in 1911 and displacing 954 tons. The ship left Singapore at 6.00pm On 13 February. The next morning Japanese aircraft sank her off Pompong Island, 90 miles south of Singapore.

Although there were some survivors, Sister Irene Wright, was not one of them, she was lost at sea and is commemorated on the Singapore Memorial.

Sister Irene Wright is the only service woman commemorated on Portadown War Memorial.

India (1944-45)

As in the Great War, India provided large numbers of troops for the war effort. Of over two and a half million service personnel who enlisted 36,000 were killed, 64,000 were wounded and 80,000 became PoWs.

India was a major strategic base for the prosecution of the war against Japan. In 1944 a Japanese invasion of India was repulsed at the Battles of Kohima and Imphal.

Hampton Atkinson Dougan MC Lieutenant-Colonel 127133, Royal Army Medical Corps

Parents	Son of Dr. George and Mary Louisa Dougan of Millicent Terrace, Portadown
Residence	Millicent Terrace
Died	Died 20 October 1944, India
Age	29
Buried	Ranchi War Cemetery, India. Grave 4. C. 10.
Commemorated	Portadown War Memorial (WW2-15) St. Mark's Parish Church War Memorial

In the 1870s George Dougan set up a medical practice at Tartaraghan and settled in Portadown. He had three sons, Hampton, Fred and George who was born in 1881. All three sons became doctors.

Hampton lost his life in 1912 in Burma serving in the Indian Medical Service.

Fred was educated at Trinity

College, Dublin where he graduated as a medical doctor in 1914 just before the outbreak of war. He gained a commission in the Royal Army Medical Corps and reported for service in December 1914 in Manchester. He served on several fronts including the campaign in South West Africa.

George also attended Trinity College, Dublin where he excelled at sport particularly rowing. He was a member of Portadown Rowing Club. After graduation he followed his father into the family medical practice.

George was commander of 'F' Company of the Portadown Battalion, Ulster Volunteer Force. He married Mary Louisa McDonald of Cranagil in 1915. The couple had three boys Hampton Atkinson, John McDonald and George.

He gained a commission in the Royal Army Medical Corps in 1916 and served in Mesopotamia during the Great War. He was 'mentioned in despatches' for gallantry and devotion to duty. George Dougan was heavily involved in the affairs of the local community and in addition to running the family medical practice was appointed Coroner for North Armagh in 1939. He founded and was president of Portadown Rotary Club was a member of Portadown Golf Club and oversaw the running of the St. John Ambulance Brigade in Portadown. Like his father, Dr. Dougan was closely associated with St. Mark's Parish Church. He was appointed rector's churchwarden in 1923 and was a member of the Select Vestry, the Armagh Diocesan Synod and the General Synod.

Dr. Dougan was a member of the Urban Council and was elected to the Stormont Parliament as Unionist MP for Central Armagh in 1941. He became Worshipful District Master of Portadown District LOL 1 on the death of Major Graham David Shillington MP.

Lieutenant-Colonel Hampton Atkinson Dougan MC. (Portadown Times)

His eldest son Hampton Atkinson was named after his uncle, Major George Hampton Dougan, who died in Burma in 1912 while serving with the Indian Medical Service. Hampton was educated at Portadown College and at Campbell College. He studied medicine at Trinity College, Dublin where he was captain of the TCD Athletics Club. He secured first place in his final exams of the Royal College of Surgeons in Ireland in June 1939.

On 30 June 1939 his engagement to Nancy Warren, eldest daughter of J. J. Warren, of Temple Gardens, Landsdowne, Dublin, was announced in the Portadown Times. When war was declared Hampton gained a commission in the Royal Army Medical Corps.

Lieutenant Dougan was awarded the Military Cross for bravery in the field during the evacuation from Dunkirk. He was then posted to the 37th General Hospital West African Force and then served with the No. 1 West African Field Ambulance, India Command.

Gaining further successful promotions Major Dougan was posted to India and was further promoted to Lieutenant-Colonel. He died on active service from an illness received while engaged on research work.

Family grave of Lieutenant-Colonel Hampton Atkinson Dougan MC. (Author's Collection)

George's second son, John McDonald, was also educated at Portadown College and Campbell College and graduated as a medical doctor. He gained a commission in the Royal Army Medical Corps in December 1940.

Lieutenant John McDonald Dougan married Helen Joy Simpson, daughter of T. Godfrey Simpson, of the Old Malt House, Bourne End, Buckinghamshire, on 7 June 1941 at Cookham Parish Church.

In November 1941 he was posted to the Middle East with the Mountain Warfare Unit of the Mediterranean Expeditionary Force.

He too was awarded a Military Cross for bravery in the field. Captain John McDonald Dougan was the third member of the family to receive the award as in addition to his older brother, Lieutenant Colonel Hampton Atkinson Dougan, his uncle, Fred Dougan RAMC, had been awarded the Military Cross during the Great War. After the war John McDonald Dougan emigrated to Canada.

George Dougan, the youngest son, was born on 12 July 1920 and graduated, as did his two brothers, as a medical doctor. He joined the family medical practice. He followed his brothers into the forces and gained a commission in the Royal Artillery serving in the Eighth Army in North Africa.

William Joseph Smart
Warrant Officer 1021128,
205 Squadron,
Royal Air Force (VR)

Parents	Son of George Alexander and Mary Elizabeth Smart of 241 Bognor Terrace, Portadown
Residence	Bognor Terrace
Enlisted	14 September 1940
Died	Killed on training operations 26 July 1945, India
Age	26
Buried	Madras War Cemetery, Chennai, India. Collective Grave 9. A. I. 14.
Commemorated	Portadown War Memorial (WW2-51) St. Mark's Parish Church War Memorial

William's father George Alexander was from Crumlin in County Antrim and his mother Mary Elizabeth Laycock was from Newtown-hamilton. They had three boys Blacker, William and George. The family resided in Pomeroy for a time before coming to Portadown with George taking up employment with W.D. Irwin's. He was later employed as a lorry driver for the Northern Ireland Road Transport Board. The Smart's resided in Bognor Terrace then moved to Blacker's Mill, then Levaghery Garden's, before returning to Bognor Terrace in 1935.

William was employed at Denny's pork processing factory before he enlisted in the Royal Air Force. He was posted overseas in January 1942 and served in Africa and was then posted to the Far East and India.

Warrant Officer Smart was posted to Amarda Road Airfield in India

Airmen pay tribute to their dead comrades who lost their lives in an accidental collision between two RAF planes in India just before World War Two ended. Portadown man Warrant Officer William Smart was one of the 14 dead RAF crew members. He is now buried in the Commonwealth War Graves Commission cemetery in Madras. 26-38.

Original graves of both aircraft crews. (Blacker Smart)

where he underwent training with the Air Fighting Training Unit (AFTU), 228 Group, South East Asia Command. At the AFTU personnel underwent a two-week intensive training course in gunnery, navigation, bombing and formation flying in preparation for future operations against the Japanese.

On 26 July 1945 at 0915 six B-24 Liberators took off from Amarda Road Airfield on a navigational and formation flying exercise. Squadron Leader Felix Heynert, DFC, piloted liberator EW 225 with a crew of eight. Liberator EW 247, with a crew of six, including Warrant Officer Smart, was piloted by P/O Alfred Herbert. As the six aircraft climbed the weather worsened and they entered some dense cloud.

On coming out of the cloud aircraft number 1 (EW 225) and aircraft number 3 (EW 247) captained by P/O Herbert, were seen to be in close proximity, and number 3 was then seen to pull up and collide with number 1. The tail unit of number 1 was torn off, causing the aircraft to crash. Once the crash occurred neither pilot had any chance to execute a reasonable force landing, nor was

there sufficient time for any member of the crew to a make a parachute descent.

Accident Report MOD Air, Historical Branch 16 June 1995

The 14 members of both crews were buried 20 miles north of Contai, Orissa. In 1953 the bodies were removed and reburied in Madras War Cemetery.

Warrant Officer William Joseph Smart. (Blacker Smart)

The Home Front (1939-45)

Many Portadown soldiers and airmen served on the Home Front providing support and supplies to the British forces. Some were killed in training accidents or died of natural causes. Others were killed in road traffic accidents, which increased considerably because of the blackout conditions prevailing around the United Kingdom during the war years.

Wilfred Wright
Aircraftman 2nd Class 538668, 103 Squadron, Royal Air Force

Born 6 February 1920

Parents Son of James and Esther Wright of 12 Burnbrae Avenue, Portadown

Residence Burnbrae Avenue

Died Died 4 January 1940, Warmwell, England

Age 19

Buried Drumcree Church of Ireland Churchyard, Portadown

Commemorated

Portadown War Memorial (WW2-66)

Thomas Street Methodist Church War Memorial

Wilfred was employed in Tavanagh Weaving Factory where his father was foreman tenter. His father was a member of the Orange and Black Institutions as well as Portadown Rechabites, Portadown Bowling Club and Portadown Football Club.

Wilfred was a former member of the 1st Portadown Company (Thomas Street) Boys Brigade and a member of the Portadown Rechabites.

William had three years service with the Royal Air Force and was posted to 103 Squadron. The squadron was reformed in 1936 at Andover, which was equipped with Hawker Hind aircraft and later reequipped with Fairy Battles. Aircraftman 2nd Class Wright died following a sudden illness.

He had brothers Dick, Jim and Eric and his brother Earl served with the RAF during World War Two.

Aircraftman Wilfred Wright. (Portadown Times)

Grave of Aircraftman Wilfred Wright. (Author's Collection)

Samuel John Kerr
Aircraftman 2nd Class 976712, Royal Air Force (VR)

Parents	Son of Samuel and Alice Kerr of 7 Watson Street, Portadown
Residence	Watson Street
Enlisted	December 1939
Died	Died 26 November 1940, England
Age	20
Buried	Seagoe Cemetery, Portadown

Commemorated
Portadown War Memorial (WW2-28)
St. Mark's Parish Church War Memorial

Samuel's father Samuel served in the Royal Garrison Artillery during the Great War. Samuel was employed by the Great Northern Railway and was a member of Edenderry Recreation Club.

He enlisted in the RAF in December 1939 and became an assistant cook. Aircraftman 2nd Class Kerr died as a result of an accident. His mother Alice received a letter from Samuel's Wing Commander

It was a most unfortunate accident. He was playing with a fellow-airman when he slipped and fell, sustaining injuries to his neck, which proved fatal.

Your son was extremely popular among his fellow men and his Flight Commander was always most satisfied with your son's behaviour. He passed a conduct sheet of which you may well be proud. In these times of strain and stress, there is at least the consolation that your son died in the uniform of one of the fighting services while serving his king and country in our effort to bring lasting peace to the world.

Portadown Times
6 December 1940

Samuel had a brother Cecil and sister Vera.

Grave of Aircraftman Samuel John Kerr. (Author's Collection)

Norman Prentice
Driver T/58593,
Royal Army Service Corps

Residence Woodhouse Street
Died Died 15 February 1941, Warrington, England
Age 29
Buried Lylo Roman Catholic Churchyard, Portadown
Commemorated
Portadown War Memorial (WW2-46)

Norman was the husband of Vera Prentice and they had four children.

The family resided at 33 Woodhouse Street, Portadown. He was employed as a lorry driver for Mr. T. H. McCann, fruit exporters, of Ballyhegan House, Loughgall before enlisting.

Driver Prentice met his death while motorcycling. Two months previously his father had predeceased him. It appears that on 14 February 1941 he failed to negotiate a bend on the main road near Warrington and crashed into railings. Driver Prentice died the following day in Warrington Infirmary. He had been in the army about 18 months.

Grave of Driver Norman Prentice. (Author's Collection)

The remains were interred in Lylo burying ground on Thursday. There was a large attendance at the funeral. A military party walked alongside the hearse bearing the coffin, which was covered with a Union Jack.

Portadown News
22 February 1941

William John Craig
Fusilier 6984364,
70th Battalion,
Royal Inniskilling Fusiliers

Parents	Son of John and Mary Craig of 42 Mourneview Street, Portadown
Residence	Mourneview Street
Died	Died 21 May 1941, Northern Ireland
Age	19
Buried	Seagoe Cemetery, Portadown
Commemorated	Portadown War Memorial (WW2-11) St. Mark's Parish Church War Memorial

Fusilier Craig served in 'C' Company.

A verdict of accidental death was returned on Wednesday by Dr. Lowe, Belfast Coroner, at the inquest on Fusilier W. J. Craig (19) of Mourneview St., Portadown who died in a military hospital on May 21 following a gunshot wound to the head.

Evidence was given that the safety catch of a rifle carried by a companion of Craig was loose, and could easily have been knocked forward accidentally.

The Coroner told Craig's companion that no one could attach the slightest blame to him.

Portadown Times
30 May 1941

William had four brothers James, Carl, William and Harry. Harry served as a Gunner in the Royal Artillery during World War Two.

Grave of Fusilier William John Craig. (Author's Collection)

William James Bleeks
Leading Aircraftman 1035372, Motor Transport Section, Royal Air Force (VR)

Parents	Son of Robert and Elizabeth Anna Bleeks of Hawthorne Cottage, Stewartstown
Residence	Watson's Lane
Died	Died 20 June 1942, England
Age	24
Buried	Seagoe Cemetery, Portadown
Commemorated	Portadown War Memorial (WW2-5) Seagoe Parish Church War Memorial

William had been six years on the staff of the Imperial Hotel, Portadown before enlisting in the Royal Air Force shortly before the outbreak of World War Two. He married Mary Jane McCann, a weaver and daughter of James McCann of Florence Court, Portadown on 25 May 1939 at Seagoe Parish Church. The couple had two children Roberta May born 1940 and William James born 1942. The family resided at 5 Watson's Lane, Portadown.

Leading Aircraftman Bleeks died as a result of an accident.

His brother-in-law George McCann (see entry **WW2-37 Private George McCann**) was killed in action on 17 April 1945 in Germany.

Leading Aircraftman William James Bleeks. (Vera Brady)

Grave of William James Bleeks. (Author's Collection)

Samuel James Wilson Sergeant (Wireless Op./Air Gunner) 1026302, 27 OTU, Royal Air Force (VR)

Parents	Son of Albert and Mamie Wilson of Shillington Street, Portadown
Residence	Shillington Street
Enlisted	March 1940
Died	Killed on training operations, 19 July 1942, Wales
Age	22
Buried	Seagoe Church of Ireland Churchyard, Portadown
Commemorated	Portadown War Memorial (WW2-61)

Samuel's father Albert was from Lisnisky and was the market caretaker in Portadown. He had a keen interest in music and at one time was conductor of three bands Lurgan Amateur, Parkmount Temperance and Richhill Conservative Flute Bands. Albert and Mamie Wilson had six children Norman, Albert, Samuel, Mamie, Vera and Edna.

Samuel was educated at Portadown Technical School and was a former member of St. Mark's Boys' Brigade. He was a member of Parkmount Temperance Flute Band, of which his father was

conductor, and the Night Lights Dance Band of which his brother was leader. He took part in troop entertainment before enlisting in the Royal Air Force.

Sergeant Samuel James Wilson. (Portadown Times)

Sergeant Wilson was attached to 27 Operational Training Unit (OTU) and was one of a crew of five on a Wellington 1c serial number DV 800, the other crew members were Sgt. E.H. Longbottom, RAAF, the pilot, Sgt. R.T. Bannister, RAAF, Sgt. R.I. Bowen, RAFVR and Sgt. Traylen, RAFVR.

The aircraft took off from RAF Lichfield on the morning of 19 July 1942. It was on a routine four-hour cross-country flight to the Isle of Man and back, crossing the Welsh coast at Llandudno, and returning to RAF Lichfield. Practice bombing was also to be carried out at Cannock Chase.

At 1206 the last radio message was received from the aircraft, which was posted as missing. On 21 July a local man noticed an area of scorched earth on the mountainside, which on closer inspection turned out to include aircraft wreckage. The police and RAF were notified and a search party was mounted. The bodies of the five missing crewmembers were recovered on 27 July 1942.

The accident report on Wellington DV800 stated

Weather conditions were good over the Irish Sea but cloud hid the high ground of North Wales. It seems that the pilot entered this cloud, became lost, and began a descent in order to break cloud and pinpoint his position. The cloud base over Carneddau range at this time was about 2000 feet; the ridge between Carnddau Llywelyn and Dafydd however is considerably higher than that. The aircraft struck the ridge at about 2,500 feet and burnt fiercely, killing all on board.

RAF Lichfield
OTU Accident Report
19 July 1942

There is a Sgt. J. Wilson RAF commemorated on St. Mark's Parish Church War Memorial but it is unclear if this refers to Sergeant Samuel James Wilson or Sergeant George Joseph Wilson.

Hugh Roney
Bombardier 1453086, 43rd (5th Duke of Wellington's) Searchlight Regiment, Royal Artillery

Born	17 July 1906, Portadown
Parents	Son of James William and Mary Isabella Roney of Portadown
Residence	Eden Avenue
Died	Died 26 July 1942, England
Age	36
Buried	Seagoe Church of Ireland Churchyard, Portadown
Commemorated	Portadown War Memorial (WW2-48) Seagoe Parish Church War Memorial

Hugh's father James William was a mechanic by trade. He and his wife Mary Isabella had six children Hugh born 1906, James William born 1910, Norman born 1912, Myrtle born 1915, Anne Isabella born 1918 and Henry Lewis born 1928

Messrs. Hamilton Robb Ltd employed Hugh as a mechanic. He was the husband of Phoebe Roney (nee Mullen) and they had two children Jean born 1936 and James born 1938. The family resided at 9 Eden Avenue, Portadown.

The 43rd Searchlight Regiment formed part of the 31st Anti Aircraft Brigade and was based in West Yorkshire.

Grave of Bombardier Hugh Roney. (Author's Collection)

George Pentland
Gunner 956614, Royal Artillery

Born	17 July 1915, Portadown
Parents	Son of Robert and Jane Pentland of 29 Carrickblacker Road, Portadown
Residence	Carrickblacker Road
Enlisted	February 1940
Died	Died 20 September 1942, England
Age	27
Buried	Seagoe Cemetery, Portadown
Commemorated	Portadown War Memorial (WW2-44) Seagoe Parish Church War Memorial

George was a former member of Seagoe Church Lads' Brigade. He was an accomplished musician and was a member of Battlehill, Derrycarne and Seagoe Pipe Bands. He was also a member of Dr. Kane's Crimson Star LOL 417.

He married Rhoda Gilmore, a weaver and daughter of Samuel Gilmore of 26 Carrickblacker Road, Portadown, on 10 March 1941 in Seagoe Parish Church. They had a daughter. He had brothers William Robert and Ben.

Gunner Pentland died as a result of an accident.

Gunner George Pentland. (Portadown Times)

Grave of Gunner George Pentland. (Author's Collection)

Theophillis John Seale
Lieutenant 268965, attached 1st Airborne Battalion, Royal Ulster Rifles

Born	Tandragee
Parents	Son of William Pilkington and Dorothy Margaret Seale of Portadown
Died	Died of wounds 1 June 1944, England
Age	23
Buried	Oxford (Botley) Cemetery, Oxfordshire, England.
Commemorated	Portadown War Memorial (WW2-49) Portadown College War Memorial St. Mark's Parish Church War Memorial

Theophillis was educated at Portadown College where he was a keen and versatile sportsman. He was captain of the school 1st XV rugby team 1937-38. After leaving school he was employed by the Belfast Banking Company Ltd, Enniskillen Branch.

In 1940 he joined the Royal Ulster Rifles and undertook initial training at Ballymena. In 1942 he was commissioned into the Royal Irish Fusiliers being attached to the 1st Airborne Battalion of the Royal Ulster Rifles. He was heavy weight boxing champion of the battalion in 1942.

During the last week of May 1944 the 1st Battalion moved to their final transit camp at RAF Broadwell in Oxfordshire where final preparations were undertaken for the airborne assault on Hitler's Europe. The 1st Airborne Battalion of the Royal Ulster Rifles formed part of 6th Air Landing Brigade.

On 1 June 1944 Lieutenant Seale and his senior platoon NCO, Sergeant Dwyer, were in a tent making final adjustments to their weapons and kit in preparation for their imminent departure for Normandy. Sergeant Dwyer was priming anti-tank grenades when one of them exploded killing him instantly and seriously wounding several other soldiers, including Lieutenant Seale, who was rushed to hospital, but died later the same day.

His brother William (see entry **WW2-50 Squadron Leader William Terence Chambers Seale**) was lost on air operations on 30 June 1941.

John Harrison
Lance-Corporal 1573121,
Pioneer Corps

Parents — Son of James and Sarah Harrison of Portadown.
Died — Died 7 June 1945, United Kingdom
Age — 35
Buried — Drumcree Roman Catholic Churchyard, Portadown
Commemorated — Portadown War Memorial (WW2-22)

John was the husband of Margaret Harrison of Portadown.

Grave of Lance-Corporal John Harrison. (Author's Collection)

Ernest Stewart Currie
Driver T/107789,
Royal Army Service Corps

Parents — Son of Moses and Margaret Currie of Portadown
Died — Died 18 June 1945, United Kingdom
Age — 29
Buried — Seagoe Cemetery, Portadown
Commemorated — Portadown War Memorial (WW2-13) St. Mark's Parish Church War Memorial

Ernest was the husband of Muriel Enza Currie of Portadown.

Grave of Driver Ernest Stewart Currie. (Author's Collection)

They Also Served In WW2 (1939-45)

It has so far been impossible to accurately identify five servicemen who are commemorated on the World War Two Section of Portadown War Memorial. Information has been included where possible. Their details are given below in the order that they appear on the memorial. If anyone has further details please contact the author.

Richard Alexander Black
Lance-Corporal,
Royal Ulster Rifles

Commemorated

Portadown War
Memorial (WW2-3)

There is one soldier with the name Richard A. Black listed in the CWGC and Soldiers Died WW2 Registers although it is not clear if this is the same person commemorated on Portadown War Memorial.

Details are Lance-Corporal 7011400 Richard A. Black, Corps of Military Police (South Staffordshire Regt.). He was born in Armagh. He lost his life between 25 April 1941 - 2 May 1941 in the Battle for Crete and is buried in Suda Bay War Cemetery.

It has so far been impossible to ascertain full service details of Lance-Corporal Richard Alexander Black, Royal Ulster Rifles.

Robert Crossan
Fusilier, Royal Irish Fusiliers

Commemorated

Portadown War
Memorial (WW2-12)

There is one soldier with the name Robert Crossan listed in the CWGC and Soldiers Died WW2 Registers although it is not clear if this is the same person commemorated on Portadown War Memorial.

Details are Fusilier 3781429 Robert Crossan, Royal Inniskilling Fusiliers. He was the husband of Clara Augusta Crossan of Morecombe, Lancashire. He was born in Londonderry and resided in Lancashire. He died on 10 April 1944 in Delhi, India, aged 31 and is buried in Delhi War Cemetery.

It has so far been impossible to ascertain full service details of Fusilier Robert Crossan, Royal Irish Fusiliers.

John Joseph Liggett
Private, Pioneer Corps

Commemorated

Portadown War
Memorial (WW2-29)

There is no one listed under the name John Joseph Liggett in the CWGC and Soldiers Died WW2 Registers.

There is a John Joseph Liggett who was born on 8 March 1888 in Drumenagh the son of Joseph and Susanna Liggett. The family resided at 6 Florence Court, Portadown. He served as a Gunner with serial number 37286 in the Royal Artillery during the Great War and re-enlisted in Belfast on 15 December 1939. He was discharged through ill health in 1940-41. He was the husband of Julia Liggett. John Joseph Liggett died on 19 May 1941 aged 52.

Although it is likely that this is the same person commemorated on Portadown War Memorial there is insufficient documentary evidence to enable a positive identification.

It has so far been impossible to ascertain full service details of Private John Joseph Liggett, Pioneer Corps.

Arthur McCann
Private, Border Regiment

Commemorated

Portadown War Memorial (WW2-36)

There is one soldier with the name Arthur McCann listed in the CWGC and Soldiers Died WW2 Registers although it is not clear if this is the same person commemorated on Portadown War Memorial.

Details are Gunner 32455327 Arthur McCann, 7 Battery, 5th H.A.A. Regiment, Royal Artillery. He was the son of Peter and Alice McCann and was born in Armagh.

Gunner McCann was killed in action on 19 December 1941 in Hong Kong aged 27. He has no known grave and is commemorated on the Sai Wan Memorial, Hong Kong.

It has so far been impossible to ascertain full service details of Private Arthur McCann, Border Regiment.

Joseph McConachie
Fusilier, Royal Irish Fusiliers

Commemorated

Portadown War Memorial (WW2-39)

There is no one listed under the name Joseph McConachie in the CWGC and Soldiers Died WW2 Registers.

It has so far been impossible to ascertain full service details of Fusilier Joseph McConachie, Royal Irish Fusiliers.

Appendix One
Wreaths Laid at Portadown War Memorial 13 November 1925

The complete list of wreaths laid at Portadown War Memorial on 13 November 1925 was as follows

Services

Royal Ulster Constabulary
(Captain Andrews)
Ulster Special Constabulary
(Captain Phelps and J. Clarke)
Survivors of No. 7 Platoon,
9th Battalion, Royal Irish Fusiliers
Royal Irish Fusiliers
Royal Ulster Rifles

Churches

St. Mark's Parish Church
St Patrick's Roman Catholic Church
(Mr. John Greenaway)
Portadown Methodist Circuit

Organisations

Portadown Ex-Servicemen
(Mr. William J. Whiteside)
Urban District Council
(Mr. W.J. Johnston J.P.)
Loyal Orange Lodge 56
Corcrain Flute Band
(Messrs. J. Kennedy and J. Wright)
Parkmount Flute Band
Ancient Order of Hibernians
First Portadown Boy Scouts
St. Mark's Girl Guides
1st Portadown Company
Boys' Brigade
Girls' and Boys' Life Brigade,
Thomas Street Church
(Miss Forsythe and Mr. Gray)

Schools

Edgarstown No. 1 Primary School
Thomas Street Primary School
(Miss O. McKinley)

Factories and Businesses

Passenger Goods and Locomotive
Department GNR, Portadown
(Messrs. Barbour, Frazer, Hughes,
Calliston and Dawson)
Parkside Weaving Factory
(Mrs Lappin and Mrs McLoughlin)
Bannview Weaving Company Ltd.
(Mr. John Muldoon)
Messrs Hamilton Robb
(Miss Teresa Lappin)
Post Office Staff
(Messrs. J. Galbraith, J. Lappin
and M.C. Day)
Spence Bryson & Co. Ltd.
(Mr. W.J. Hull and Michael Garvey)
Portadown Weaving Co. Ltd.
(Mr. William Mitchell)
Castleisland Weaving Co. Ltd.
(Mr. Alex Foster)
Tavanagh Weaving Co. Ltd.
(Mrs McWilliams)

Henry Logan & Sons
(Mr. Thomas Fulton)

Individuals

Mr Thomas McCourt
Mrs Mary. J. Wright
Mrs Holland
Mrs S. Russell
Mrs E. Brown
Miss M. Fulton
Miss M. Weir
Mrs Moore and family
Miss E. Flannagan
Mr & Mrs Monteith
Mrs E.J. Patton
Miss M. Hughes
Mrs M. Green and family
Mrs Vallely and family
Mrs Annie Anderson
Mrs H. McCardle
Mr. James Brown
Mrs S. Sinnamon
Mr & Mrs Hugh Gracey
Mrs M. A. Greenaway
Mr & Mrs Dalzell
Mr. James Sheppard
Mrs M. Faloon
Mr. Alex Orr
Mr Robert Todd
Mr. John Jenkinson
Miss Rachel Taylor
Miss T. Flannagan
Mrs E. Cordy
Mr. M. Hewitt
Mrs M. Lewis
Mrs M. Brown and family
Mrs A. Neill
Mr & Mrs Fulton
Mrs May Woods
Mr. James Tedford
Mrs and Master Kenneth Brew
Mrs L. Currie
Mr W. J. Hull
Mr William McMullen
Miss E. England
Miss Sarah Quinn
Mrs Mortimer and family
Mr & Mrs Espie
Mrs G. Forker
Major D. G. & Mrs Shillington
Mrs M. Forker
Mrs Jones
Mrs Vennard
Mr. & Mrs David Logan
Mrs A. Brownlee
Mr & Mrs Thomas Gardiner
Mr J. Sharpe
Mrs Clulow
Mrs E. Doak
Mr & Mrs Malcolmson
Miss J. Grimley
Mrs Abraham
Mrs M. Marshall
Mrs Marshall
Mother & Sisters
Mr David Rowan
Mr James Rowan
Mrs Greenaway and family
Mr & Mrs Bailie
Mrs Sprott and family
Mrs J. May
Mrs Wright
Mr. Thomas Hughes
Miss Magee
Miss L. Robb
Mrs Haack
Miss M. Teggart
Mr & Mrs James Joyce
Mr T. J. Montgomery and family

Portadown War Memorial
Regiments as per War Memorial

Irish Regiments	**(239)**
Royal Irish Fusiliers	195
Royal Irish Rifles	25
Royal Inniskilling Fusiliers	7
Irish Guards	3
Royal Irish Regiment	3
North Irish Horse	2
Royal Dublin Fusiliers	2
Royal Munster Fusiliers	2
Empire Forces	**(26)**
Canadian Forces	19
Australian Forces	6
South African Forces	1
Composite Regiments	**(23)**
Royal Army Service Corps	5
Machine Gun Corps	4
Royal Engineers	4
Royal Army Medical Corps	3
Royal Field Artillery	3
Labour Corps	2
Royal Garrison Artillery	2
English Regiments	**(15)**
South Lancashire Regiment	5
4th Hussars	1
Cheshire Regiment	1
Durham Light Infantry	1
Kings Royal Rifle Corps	1
Lancaster Yeomanry	1

Portadown War Memorial
Correct Regiments as per Research (incl. 13 unidentified - units as per War Memorial)

Irish Regiments	**(235)**
Royal Irish Fusiliers	185
Royal Irish Rifles	29
Royal Inniskilling Fusiliers	7
Irish Guards	3
Royal Irish Regiment	5
North Irish Horse	2
Royal Dublin Fusiliers	2
Royal Munster Fusiliers	2
Empire Forces	**(27)**
Canadian Forces	20
Australian Forces	6
South African Forces	1
Composite Regiments	**(24)**
Army Service Corps	5
Machine Gun Corps	5
Royal Engineers	3
Royal Army Medical Corps	3
Royal Field Artillery	4
Labour Corps	2
Royal Garrison Artillery	2
English Regiments	**(17)**
South Lancashire Regiment	5
4th Hussars	1
Cheshire Regiment	1
Durham Light Infantry	1
Kings Royal Rifle Corps	2
Lancaster Yeomanry	1

Lancashire Fusiliers	1
London Irish	1
Royal Berkshire Regiment	1
Sherwood Foresters	1
South Staffordshire Regiment	1

Scottish Regiments	**(12)**
Argyll & Sutherland Highlanders	3
Highland Light Infantry	3
Scottish Rifles	2
Cameron Highlanders	1
Gordon Highlanders	1
Royal Scots	1
Seaforth Highlanders	1

Naval and Air Forces	**(5)**
Royal Navy	2
Royal Marine Light Infantry	1
Royal Naval Volunteer Reserve	1
Royal Air Force	1

Allied Forces	**(1)**
French Red Cross	1

Supreme Sacrifice **321**

Lancashire Fusiliers	1
London Irish	1
Royal Berkshire Regiment	1
Sherwood Foresters	1
South Staffordshire Regiment	1
Royal Lancaster Regiment	1

Scottish Regiments	**(12)**
Argyll & Sutherland Highlanders	3
Highland Light Infantry	3
Scottish Rifles	2
Cameron Highlanders	1
Gordon Highlanders	1
Royal Scots	1
Seaforth Highlanders	1

Naval and Air Forces	**(5)**
Royal Navy	2
Royal Marine Light Infantry	1
Royal Naval Volunteer Reserve	1
Royal Flying Corps	1

Allied Forces	**(1)**
French Red Cross	1

Supreme Sacrifice **321**

Appendix Three
Great War Casualties
Portadown War Memorial

Deaths By Year

1914	16
1915	48
1916	126
1917	47
1918	58
1919-25	13
Unidentified	13
Supreme Sacrifice	**321**

* * *

Deaths By Service

Army	315
Royal Navy	4
Royal Flying Corps	1
French Red Cross	1
Supreme Sacrifice	**321**

Deaths By Theatre of Operations

Western Front	238
Gallipoli	13
Salonika	8
Egypt & Palestine	6
Mesopotamia	3
South Africa	2
Malta	1
India	1
Burma	1
Home Front	35
Unidentified	13
Supreme Sacrifice	**321**

Appendix Four
World War Two Casualties
Portadown War Memorial

Deaths By Year

1939	1
1940	8
1941	7
1942	11
1943	8
1944	21
1945	6
Unidentified	5
Supreme Sacrifice	**67**

* * *

Deaths By Service

Army	43
Royal Navy	6
Royal Air Force	18
Supreme Sacrifice	**67**

Deaths By Theatre of Operations

Battle of the Atlantic	6
Dunkirk	3
The Blitz	1
North Africa & Med.	6
Italy	10
RAF Bomber Offensive	9
Normandy	7
Arnhem	1
Germany	3
Hong Kong	1
Singapore	2
India	2
Home Front	11
Unidentified	5
Supreme Sacrifice	**67**

Bibliography and Sources

Each entry for the service personnel commemorated on Portadown War Memorial has been made up from a wide variety of sources. Notes to be borne in mind are as follows:

1) Approximately two-thirds of British Army Service Records for personnel who served in the Great War were destroyed by enemy action during World War Two (courtesy of a Luftwaffe bombing raid on London in 1940).

Service Records for Guards regiments, the Royal Navy and Royal Flying Corps/Royal Air Force personnel were deposited elsewhere and survived the bombing. These records are available.

Service Records for Empire personnel were deposited in the archives of their respective countries and survived the bombing. These records are available.

Service Records for personnel who served in World War Two are available to next of kin only.

2) The Officers/Soldiers Died Register contains information relating to service personnel who were killed in action, died of wounds or died while serving in the Crown forces during and shortly after the Great War. Personnel who died after they were discharged the service are not normally included in the Register.

3) The Commonwealth War Graves Commission (CWGC) Debt of Honour Register contains information relating to service personnel who were killed in action, died of wounds or died while serving in the Crown forces during and shortly after the Great War and World War Two. Personnel who died after they were discharged the service are not normally included in the Register.

4) Some entries in the Officers/Soldiers Died Register contain spelling mistakes for example Portadown appears as Portadam under the entry for Driver William Thompson, Army Service Corps and Drumcree appears as Dronkee under the entry for Private William J. Magee, Irish Guards. There are other similar discrepancies.

5) Entries for the CWGC Register were compiled after the end of the Great War and World War Two. Next of kin and relatives were invited to forward details of servicemen who had made the supreme sacrifice. Many entries do not contain details of the serviceman's next of kin,

spouse, hometown or age. If the place of residence is given it may not correspond to that on Portadown War Memorial. There are also discrepancies relating to the ages of servicemen.

6) The spelling of many surnames varies from source to source and is indicative of a period of poorer literacy standards than today added to the fact that English people were recording numerous Irish sounding names. As an example the surname of the author's grandfather, Signalman Henry Kane, a relatively straightforward name, appears variously as Cain, Kain, Keane, McKeane and Kane.

7) A number of service personnel are commemorated on Portadown War Memorial with incorrect regimental and rank details.

8) Each entry contains verifiable information. Where that information is not verifiable or does not appear in documentation it has not been included. For example servicemen are only noted as having been members of the Ulster Volunteer Force/Orange Institution/Ancient Order of Hibernians/Rechabites etc if there is documented evidence to prove this. For example four members of Prince of Wales LOL 56 fell in the Great War but so far the author has been able to identify only one of them. The Ancient Order of Hibernians laid a wreath at Portadown War Memorial on 13 November 1925; so far the author has been unable to identify any members commemorated.

9) A number of entries contain extracts from letters of sympathy sent to next of kin by the deceased serviceman's comrades or commanding officer. Invariably these letters contain phrases such as "he died instantly" or "he suffered no pain". The reality would have been quite different as war is a bloody business and soldiers suffer horrific injuries, pain and death. The letter writers' main concern was to indicate to anxious relatives that their loved one did not suffer and that this would somehow put their minds at rest. Those on the Home Front who had no experience of war had no idea what the soldiers were going through and what conditions were like at the front.

10) A number of entries contain extracts from local newspaper reports. The two newspapers were the Portadown News and Portadown Express. The length of newspaper reports depended on each individual serviceman's circumstances.

It was rare in the extreme for photographs of servicemen killed

during the Great War to appear in the local newspapers. When the war ended the Portadown News published the casualty lists for Portadown, which was accompanied by photographs of officers only who had lost their lives. Newspapers of the period (as now!) sometimes got their facts wrong.

11) The Soldiers Died in the Great War Register lists approximately 75 servicemen born in Portadown and District (including six born and also resident in Portadown) who are not commemorated on Portadown War Memorial. The Soldiers Died Register lists an additional 11 servicemen listed as resident (although not born) in Portadown who are not commemorated on Portadown War Memorial.

12) The Commonwealth War Graves Commission Debt of Honour Register for the Great War lists a further 23 service personnel naming the town of Portadown in their, their parents' or in their spouses' addresses who are not commemorated on Portadown War Memorial.

13) The Commonwealth War Graves Commission Debt of Honour Register for World War Two lists a further 25 service personnel naming the town of Portadown in their, their parents' or in their spouses' addresses who are not commemorated on Portadown War Memorial.

14) The true number of service personnel from or having a connection with the town of Portadown who made the supreme sacrifice in the two world wars is in the region of 522. Further research is necessary on these 135 servicemen and women who have some connection with Portadown.

The Great War Casualties

Commemorated on Portadown War Memorial	321
Not commemorated on Portadown War Memorial	109
Supreme Sacrifice	430

The Second World War Casualties

Commemorated on Portadown War Memorial	67
Not commemorated on Portadown War Memorial	25
Supreme Sacrifice	92

Supreme Sacrifice in two world wars at least	522

The author had four articles requesting information, which appeared in the Portadown Times on 17 December 1999, 18 February 2000, 16 May 2003 and 23 April 2004.

Relatives, Friends and Historians

I am extremely indebted to the following relatives, friends and historians who supplied information, documents, gave interviews and loaned photographs for inclusion in the book. Trevor Bonis, Very Brady, Shirley Branyan, Steve Brew, Gordon Caldecot, Brian Courtney, Billy England, Norman Harrison, Hazel Jeffers, Prof. Keith Jeffery, Phyllis Kerr, Thelma Irwin, John Larder, Hugh Liggett, Andrew Lutton, Jim Lyttle, Errol Martin, George McGuire, Doris McMullen, Ross McNeill, Emma Montgomery, Dan Murphy, Diane Murphy, Albert Nicholl, Audrey Nolan, Robert Pike, Chris Pointon, Matt Poole, Judy Porter, Sam Preston, Ross Raymond, Derek Sadler, Eva Sherman, Thelma Simpson, Blacker Smart, Sammy Smith, Henry Thompson, Robert Todd, Henk Welting, Jack Whitla and Spiers Wilson.

Books

Banks, Arthur *A Military Atlas of the First World War* Heineman Educational Books Ltd 1975

Bridgland, Tony *Waves of Hate - Naval Atrocities of the Second World War* Leo Cooper 2002

Chorley, WR *Royal Air Force Bomber Command Losses of the Second World War Vol.2 1941* Midland Counties Publications 1993

Chorley, WR *Royal Air Force Bomber Command Losses of the Second World War Vol. 4 1943* Midland Counties Publications 1996

Chorley, WR *Royal Air Force Bomber Command Losses of the Second World War Vol. 5 1944* Midland Counties Publications 1997

Cunliffe, Marcus *The Royal Irish Fusiliers 1793-1950* OUP 1952

Doherty, Richard *Clear The Way - A History of the 38th (Irish Brigade), 1941-47* Irish Academic Press 1993

England, Robert *Living, Learning, Remembering* Centre for Continuing Education University of British Columbia 1980

Errington, F.H.L. Lt-Col. (Editor) *Inns of Court Officers Training Corps During the Great War* Naval and Military Press Reprint 2000

Grand Lodge of Free and Accepted Masons of Ireland *Roll of Honour The Great War 1914-1919* Naval & Military Press Reprint No Date

Jarvis, SD & DB *The Cross of Sacrifice Vol 1* Roberts Medals Ltd 1993

Jeffery, Keith *Ireland in the Great War* Cambridge University Press 2000

Johnstone, Tom *Orange, Green and Khaki The Story of the Irish Regiments in the Great War 1914-18* Gill and Macmillan 1992

Kipling, Rudyard *The Irish Guards in the Great War - The First Battalion* Spellmount Ltd 1997 Liverpool,

London Irish at War, No Date

Middlebrook, Martin *The First Day on the Somme 1 July 1916* Penguin 1988

North Irish Horse *Battle Report North Africa and Italy* W & G Baird Ltd 1946

Officers Died in the Great War

Orr, Phillip *The Road to the Somme* Blackstaff Press 1987

Soldiers Died in the Great War

Stokes, Roy *Death in the Irish Sea - The Sinking of the RMS Leinster* Collins Press 1998

Westlake, Ray *British Battalions in France and Belgium* Leo Cooper 1997

Westlake, Ray *British Battalions on the Somme* Leo Cooper 1998

Westlake, Ray *British Regiments at Gallipoli* Leo Cooper 1996

Royal Irish Fusiliers Museum, Sovereign's House, Armagh

1st, 5th, 6th, 7th, 8th, 7/8th and 9th Battalion, Royal Irish Fusiliers, War Diaries

Royal Irish Fusiliers, Great War Newspaper Cuttings Albums Vols I-III

1st Battalion, Royal Irish Fusiliers, Casualty Return Forms 1914-1918

9th Battalion, Royal Irish Fusiliers, Muster Roles for 'C' Company, 1st July 1916

9th Battalion, Royal Irish Fusiliers, Casualty Returns compiled by Rev Samuel Mayes 17 August 1917

Archives, Commissions, Museums, etc

Airborne Forces Museum, Aldershot

Argyll and Sutherland Highlanders Museum, Stirling

Australian War Memorial, Canberra

Commonwealth War Graves Commission, Maidstone

Durham Light Infantry Museum, Durham

Imperial War Museum, London

Irish Guards Museum, London

Irish History Library, Armagh

Kings Own Scottish Borderers Museum, Berwick-Upon-Tweed

Naval Historical Branch, London

National Archives of Australia, Canberra

National Archives of Canada, Ottawa

Royal Air Force Museum, Hendon

Royal Regiment of Fusiliers Museum, Bury

Newspapers, Journals, Magazines and Minute Books
Armagh Guardian
Lieutenant-Colonel Stewart Blacker DSO daily letters to his wife 1915-1917
Portadown Express
Portadown News
Portadown Times
Review - Journal of the Craigavon Historical Society Vol. 7 No. 3 (Article on Lurgan College War Memorial by Ian Wilson)
Seagoe Parish Magazine